Shadow

ALSO BY NEIL HUNTER RAIFORD

*The 4th North Carolina Cavalry in the Civil War:
A History and Roster* (McFarland 2003; paperback 2006)

Shadow

A Cottontail Bomber Crew in World War II

NEIL HUNTER RAIFORD

McFarland & Company, Inc., Publishers
Jefferson, North Carolina, and London

For Karen and Benjamin

> The present work is a reprint of the illustrated case bound edition of Shadow: A Cottontail Bomber Crew in World War II, first published in 2004 by McFarland.

LIBRARY OF CONGRESS CATALOGUING-IN-PUBLICATION DATA

Raiford, Neil Hunter, 1969–
    Shadow : a Cottontail bomber crew in World War II / Neil Hunter Raiford.
       p.   cm.
    Includes bibliographical references and index.

    ISBN 978-0-7864-6622-1
    softcover : 50# alkaline paper

    1. United States. Army Air Forces. Bomb Group, 450th—Biography. 2. Shadow (Airplane) 3. World War, 1939–1945—Aerial operations, American. 4. World War, 1939–1945—Campaigns—Europe. 5. Flight crews—United States—Biography. I. Title.
D790.R24   2011
940.54'4973'0922—dc22   2004017521

British Library cataloguing data are available

©2004 Neil Hunter Raiford. All rights reserved

No part of this book may be reproduced or transmitted in any form or by any means, electronic or mechanical, including photocopying or recording, or by any information storage and retrieval system, without permission in writing from the publisher.

On the cover: View of Manduria, Italy (Ted Morris); inset: Shadow crew (Grant D. Caywood)

Manufactured in the United States of America

McFarland & Company, Inc., Publishers
  Box 611, Jefferson, North Carolina 28640
    www.mcfarlandpub.com

Acknowledgments

A project of this scale is not possible without the help of others. Along the way I met some true heroes, though they would never admit it. First and foremost, I will be forever indebted to my wife's grandfather, Maurice Holt Gilliam. His willingness to share the painful memory of war and his excellent recall of those events led me on the journey of a lifetime.

Interviews with veterans provided the backbone of this work. I was extremely fortunate to find eight of *Shadow*'s original ten crew members still alive. All of them were most generous with their time and memories. Each freely shared his photos, letters, diaries, etc. They are, in alphabetical order: nose gunner Stan Butynski; pilot Grant Caywood; co-pilot Maurice Erickson; tail gunner Maurice Gilliam; navigator Herb Gouldon; engineer and top turret gunner Richard Jacobson; ball turret gunner Ted Morris; and left waist gunner Norman Woodward. *Shadow*'s bombardier, Robert Stricklin was the only member to die during the war. Manuel Esquivel, the crew's radio operator and right waist gunner, died of Alzheimer's disease in 1980.

I could not have completed the book without the help of *Shadow*'s pilot, Grant Caywood. He graciously shared all of his documents, photos, and memories. He called me "bird dog" throughout the project for all of the information that I was trying to "tree." The truth is, at the top of most of those trees Grant was there answering my endless barrage of questions. Grant was also instrumental in editing every chapter and putting me back on the right path more than once. He is truly one of the most fascinating and wonderful people that I will ever know. Thanks, Captain.

Manuel Esquivel's sons, Jim and Rick, shared information about their father and provided a copy of their mother's reminiscences.

Jim Wheat, a fellow genealogist, and Sammie T. Lee of the Dallas Public Library provided the first solid leads on locating Robert Stricklin's family. Cheryl Howerton, another genealogist, provided copies of some Stricklin obituaries, which ultimately helped me find Robert Stricklin's sister, Irene Stricklin Frazier. Once located, Irene Frazier provided me with a wealth of information about her older brother.

In the course of my research, I discovered two of *Shadow*'s replacement pilots, Vincent Olney and Floyd Robinson. Sadly, Vince passed away in 1978, but his sister, Susan Rhynalds, and his second wife, Marilyn Siebels, helped me get to know this wonderful man. Fortunately, I found Floyd alive and well. I am grateful for all of the information he shared, including his two wartime diaries.

I am indebted to Harold McCraw, the brother of Reaford C. McCraw. Harold helped me get know his heroic brother and freely shared family documents. I am also appreciative to Carol J. McCraw, who answered an Internet query and put me in touch with Harold.

Suzanne Snaith Levy, the daughter of Lt. Col. William G. Snaith, was most helpful in sharing information about her father.

I must also thank Carol Ritter, the daughter of John Barnacle, who provided invaluable information about her father and the crew of *True Love*.

Samuel Stein, the 450th Bomb Group Association's membership chairman, freely shared his treasure trove of period newspaper articles. He also provided key information about the ground crew's key role during missions. The story is more complete thanks to his input. I am also indebted to several other members of the 450th Bomb Group Association who helped at various stages in the project. They include Floyd Perkins, Harold Saperstein, Robert Davis, and James Strickland. Ben Franklin, the executive director of the Fifteenth Air Force Association, was most gracious with his group's time and resources.

The staff at the Air Force Historical Research Agency at Maxwell Air Force Base in Alabama was very helpful in providing microfilm copies of the 450th BG's intelligence reports and other useful documents. The National Archives and Records Administration in College Park, Maryland, provided key information related to the 450th BG from their Records of the Quartermaster General (Record Group 92). The Department of the Army, U.S. Total Army Personnel Command in Alexandria, Virginia, furnished copies of Robert Stricklin's deceased personnel file. I must also thank the staff at the National Personnel Records Center in St. Louis, which answered every one of my queries and provided what information they could from their fire damaged military records.

My family has been very supportive throughout the writing of this book. My parents, Hunter and Arlene Raiford, offered encouragement when needed. Special thanks go to Larry Gilliam, my father-in-law, who rescued the manuscript after my laptop crashed. His patience and knowledge of computers saved countless hours of rewriting. My son, Benjamin Hunter Raiford, was a daily inspiration. I know that one day he will appreciate the sacrifices made by his Papa Gilliam and the veterans of World War II. Last but not least, I would like to thank my wife Karen. Her unfailing encouragement and belief in what I was doing gave me the confidence to finish this important project.

Contents

Acknowledgments	v
450th Bomb Group Airmen	viii
Introduction: Unconditional Bond	1
1. Dutiful Sons	9
2. Training	35
3. A Liberator Crew	53
4. "Cottontails" in the Heel of the Boot	71
5. A Typical Mission: Enemy Above and Below	89
6. March 1944: Baptism by Fire	110
7. April 1944: "Goodbye *Shadow*"	125
8. May 1944: Ploesti—Again!	156
9. June 1944: Fifty and Home	173
Epilogue: Legacy	198
Appendix A: Organization of the 15th Army Air Force, May 1944	205
Appendix B: Combat Missions	207
Chapter Notes	211
Bibliography	225
Index	231

450th Bomb Group Airmen

Shadow's Original Crew (720th Squadron)

Grant Caywood—Pilot
Maurice Erickson—Co-Pilot
Herb Gouldon—Navigator
Robert Stricklin—Bombardier (KIA 1944)
Maurice Gilliam—Tail Gunner
Stan Butynski—Nose Gunner
Richard Jacobson—Top Turret
Ted Morris—Ball Turret
Manuel Esquivel—Waist Gunner (died 1980)
Norman Woodward—Waist Gunner

Shadow's Replacement Pilots (720th Squadron)

Vincent Olney (died 1978)
Floyd Robinson

450th BG Ground Crew (721st Squadron):

Samuel Stein

Shoo Shoo Baby (720th Squadron)

Marshall Samms—Navigator

True Love (720th Squadron)

Reaford C. McCraw—Pilot (KIA 1944)
John Barnacle—Ball Turret Gunner

Introduction: Unconditional Bond

Maurice Gilliam, in Whiteville, North Carolina, was not expecting the call he got one Tuesday afternoon in October 2001. "Hello," he answered with his usual cheerful greeting.

"Hello," said an unfamiliar voice. "This is Stan Butynski and I am in Whiteville."

A rush of memories came over Maurice. He had not seen or spoken to Stan in fifty-seven years. They flew together on a B-24 named *Shadow* during World War II. During missions, they were at opposite ends of the bomber; Maurice was the tail gunner and Stan was the nose gunner.

Stan told Maurice that he had come for a visit. It was about 5 P.M. and Stan and his wife Marge had already checked into the local Holiday Inn Express and had had supper. Maurice quickly gave Stan directions to his house, and for the next five hours they and their wives caught up on the past sixty years—jobs, children, grandchildren, great-grandchildren, and, of course, the war. After several rounds of laughs, tears, and hugs, Stan and Marge said their goodbyes to Maurice and Stella. They returned to the hotel and the next morning drove back home to Michigan.

What would compel Stan, at age seventy-seven, to drive over nine hundred miles, unannounced, to visit someone that he knew for only eight months and with whom he had no contact for nearly sixty years? The answer, on the surface, appears simple: they served together during the war. But a deeper look into their shared experience reveals a much more complex answer. It is not merely that they were in the same unit or airplane. They, along with the other members of *Shadow*'s ten-man crew, worked toward a common goal during the first half of 1944. To return home each one had to successfully complete fifty combat missions as he helped to defeat Hitler's war machine. In the process they forged an unconditional bond in the skies above Europe. It is an unspoken bond that endures for life; it cannot be broken.

Although some did it, crews that completed a fifty-mission tour of duty are statistical anomalies. The average life span of an AAF combat airman in 1943 was about fifteen missions. This number dramatically decreases if those who were wounded, taken prisoner, or listed as missing in action are also factored into the equation. Therefore, it did not take long for an airman to calculate his odds of survival. Each mission he flew brought him closer to completing his goal. But in the back of his mind he knew that after a certain number of missions, he was defying the odds.

At the start of the war, the combat tour goal for crews flying with the 8th AAF out of England was twenty-five missions. The crew of the much-celebrated and publicized *Memphis Belle* was the first to accomplish the feat. Heavy losses (of bombers and men), however, forced the AAF to raise the goal as the war progressed—first to thirty, then to thirty-five. When Italy capitulated in the second half of 1943, the 15th AAF was created. It was formed to fly missions out of bases in southern Italy and to strike strategic targets against the "soft underbelly" of Hitler's Third Reich, which were out of the reach of the 8th AAF bases in England. Because many of the 15th AAF's targets were closer than those of their counterparts in the 8th AAF, a decision was made to make the combat tour for these airmen fifty missions. As a concession, crews in the 15th AAF received double credit for long missions, especially to heavily defended cities like Ploesti and Vienna. In the end this was a fair compromise—most airmen with a fifty-mission goal flew fewer than forty actual missions.

Maurice and Stan, along with the rest of *Shadow's* crew, served in the 450th Bombardment Group (15th AAF), which was based in Manduria, Italy. Their B-24 held a ten-man crew. Capt. Grant Caywood of Omaha, Nebraska, was their pilot. Joining him in the cockpit was co-pilot 2nd Lt. Maurice Erickson of Kane, Pennsylvania. The other two officers were bombardier 2nd Lt. Robert Stricklin of Dallas, Texas, and navigator 2nd Lt. Herbert Gouldon of Brooklyn, New York. In addition to Gilliam and Butynski, the remaining enlisted men consisted of engineer and top turret gunner Sgt.

Stan and Margie Butynski

Richard Jacobson of Roxbury, Massachusetts; waist gunner Sgt. Norman Woodward of Lisle, New York; radio operator and waist gunner Sgt. Manuel Esquivel of New Orleans; and ball turret gunner Ted Morris of St. Louis.

The crew first met in Clovis, New Mexico, in November 1943. After ninety days of crew training, they flew *Shadow* to Italy—and into combat. Within another ninety days, most of the crew would complete fifty combat missions.

Unless one has experienced combat first hand in the military, one cannot comprehend the enormous truth in the statement that "war is chaos." Rarely, if ever, do things go exactly as planned. To manage the chaos effectively, soldiers faced with these ever-changing scenarios must react accordingly. They must apply courage, ingenuity, and creativity in order to persevere.

Maurice and Stella Gilliam.

This was especially true of a bomber crew. Their lives were in each other's hands. They had to have faith in each other's ability and training. A miscue by one could get the entire crew killed. But, due to enemy countermeasures (flak and fighters) and the conditions at 25,000 feet (cold temperatures and poor visibility), even the proper execution of their duties did not always ensure a safe return. Some of it was beyond their control. The chaos and intensity of what they experienced together in such a short period of time is what forged the bond.

The events leading up to the October 9, 2001, reunion between Maurice Gilliam and Stan Butynski began about four years earlier. It started simply enough when I asked Maurice (Papa Gilliam), my wife's grandfather, in what unit he had served in World War II. My wife, Karen, had always told me that he did not like to discuss the war. But as an avid genealogist and history buff, I really wanted to know.

I will never forget the Sunday in 1997 that I asked him. We were living in Greenville, North Carolina. My wife Karen was in her third year of medical school at East Carolina University and we were visiting her parents in Whiteville for the weekend. After church and a big Sunday dinner with her family, I mustered up the courage to ask Papa Gilliam about World War II. For the next hour or so he told me of his training and his time in Manduria, Italy. He told me about his B-24 named *Shadow* and how it was named for the pilot's black cocker spaniel, and that she actually flew on training missions with the crew. I hung on every word and frantically took notes so that I could make some attempt to preserve the information for future generations of our family. After he finished, I realized it wasn't that he did not want to talk about the war and the wonderful friends he had made. He did not want to bore people with it; he did not think anyone would be interested. To him, it was just one of many chapters in his life—one he had completed a long time ago.

When Karen and I got home that night, I searched the Internet to find out all I could about the 450th Bomb Group. At that time, there was no website devoted to the group.* Most search engine queries came back with message board postings, in which veterans of the 450th or their family members were trying to contact other veterans who had served in the group. One posting mentioned the 450th Bomb Group Association. I searched a little more and found the contact and address information. I immediately wrote a letter to the group's secretary, Floyd Perkins, and asked how to join.

Later that same week, I received an envelope full of information from Papa Gilliam. In it were copies of his discharge papers, photocopies of pictures, and a typescript copy of his mission diary. It was a treasure trove of information, and to this day it is one of the most memorable packages that I have ever received. I updated my genealogy files, made additional copies of all that he sent, and carefully filed it all away. In the coming weeks, I found a few books about the group. I read them with interest and shared them with Papa Gilliam. I also heard back from Floyd Perkins with the 450th BG Association. He sent an application and information about the group. I joined and signed up Papa Gilliam as well. Another leaf had been added to the tree.

About a year later, I read Tom Brokaw's *The Greatest Generation*, which renewed my interest in Papa Gilliam's war experience. But I did not do anything at the time. In the fall of 1999, Karen and I learned that she was pregnant with our first child. That prompted me to start interviewing our older relatives on both sides of the family. Through genealogy, I had been chasing the names and dates of dead ancestors for over ten years. With the pending birth of our son, I realized how important it was to document the lives of our family while they are still alive. I wanted to write brief biographical sketches on all of them that I could, so that my son would know something tangible about his ancestors—something more than names and dates. This new project gave me a wonderful opportunity to ask Papa Gilliam more about his war experience.

Among the dozens of standard questions that I asked all of the family, I asked Papa Gilliam about the war. In one of the questions I asked him to list the members of his crew and their hometowns. In the answers to other questions, the names of childhood friends and even some relatives escaped him. But he remembered all the

---

Now there is a wonderful website devoted to the group at www.450thbg.com.

names his B-24 crew and most of their hometowns nearly sixty years later. This recall is even more amazing when one realizes that the last time he had any contact with any of them was in the summer of 1944 in Italy, just before he returned back to the United States.

Armed with this list of the crew, I thought it would be an interesting addition to Papa Gilliam's biographical sketch to contact some of them and ask what he was like during the war. I carefully reviewed the list and decided to start with Stan Butynski. Before the war he was living in Hamtramck, Michigan. An Internet phone search revealed a Stan Butynski in Gaines, Michigan, about 70 miles from Hamtramck. I wrote down the address and number and then gave him a call.

"Hello, my name is Neil Raiford from Glen Allen, Virginia [we lived there during Karen's residency at the Medical College of Virginia in Richmond]. I am not trying to sell you anything. Did you serve with the 450th Bomb Group during World War II?"

"Yes I did," he said, surprised.

"My wife's grandfather, Maurice Gilliam, was the tail gunner on *Shadow*."

Stan immediately opened up and we had a wonderful conversation for the next half hour. I took notes as fast as I could. He said that the crew's ball turret gunner, Ted Morris, was still alive and still in St. Louis; their pilot, Grant Caywood, was somewhere in California; and their radio operator, Manny Esquivel, had died sometime back. Stan agreed to answer more questions and to share some photos. I told him I would be in touch again soon.

I looked up Ted Morris' number next; he was in St. Louis just as Stan had said. He and I also had a wonderful conversation. Again, I frantically took notes. Ted had been in contact with Esquivel after the war and he confirmed that Manny had died about twenty years back. To the best of his knowledge, Caywood was in Sacramento. Like Stan, he agreed to answer more questions later and to share some of his photos and papers.

A few days later I found Caywood's number and contacted him. His wife hung up on me the first two times; she thought I was a telemarketer. Grant answered the phone the third time, and we have been friends ever since. As the crew's pilot, he was in the best position to give me the "big picture" view. He had saved everything, including orders transferring the crew to different bases. Grant agreed to answer any and all questions I had. We exchanged e-mail addresses and immediately began corresponding. Over the next few months, Grant answered my questions. He also generously shared his wonderful collection of photos from the war and the personal memoirs he wrote for his family.

It had been a wonderful string of luck. After I found Caywood, things became a little more difficult, but the paperwork he sent to me was instrumental in my search. Finding the other crew members, or their family members, would require countless more phone calls, letters, and Internet queries. But within a few months I had located all but two of the original crew or their family members — Richard Jacobson and the family of Robert Stricklin (the only member of the crew to die during the war).

As I located each new crew member, or his family, I asked a standard set of questions that invariably led to more. I began circulating a contact list, with home addresses, e-mail addresses, and phone numbers. For the first time in nearly sixty years the crew of *Shadow* were able to contact each other. Stan used this list to plan his trip to see Maurice.

It became apparent early in the interviewing stage that I had stumbled on to a wonderful story. What started out as a simple biographical sketch of Papa Gilliam was turning into something more, much to my excitement. As my researched progressed, I discovered that each of *Shadow*'s crew had a story to tell. Gradually the scope of the project came into focus. I could not tell Papa Gilliam's story without telling the stories of others as well; the bond could not be broken. In the spring of 2002, I decided that the best way to put the puzzle together was to write a book.

The puzzle, however, was not an easy one. Most, if not all, of the military personnel records that I needed had been destroyed in the July 1973 fire at the National Personnel Records Center in St. Louis. Additionally, according to 450th BG historian Robert Davis, a good number of the 450th's records, which were shipped home in three footlockers after the war, were lost in transit and have never been located. What I did have were the 450th Bomb Group's S-2 (Intelligence) Narratives for each combat mission from the Air Force Historical Research Agency at Maxwell Air Force Base, Papa Gilliam's combat diary, Caywood's papers, and the extensive interview notes. It was enough to start, and I was sure that I would uncover more as I dug deeper and I did. But to make the story complete, I still had to find Richard Jacobson and the family of Robert Stricklin.

Locating Jacobson and Stricklin would require patience and persistence. The only lead I had for Richard Jacobson was that before the war he lived in Roxbury, Massachusetts. My first course of action was to send a letter to all of the Richard Jacobsons in Massachusetts—no luck. I posted queries on genealogical websites and sought help from the 450th Bomb Group Association and from the 15th Air Force Association—again with no success. A new lead, which turned out to be false, placed Jacobson in Chicago. More calls, letters, and queries yielded nothing; it was another dead end. Months later I still had not made any progress. On a whim, I decided to look in Florida. An Internet phone search listed several Richard Jacobsons in the state. So after 16 months and a few more phone calls, I finally located him. Richard (Jake) was as surprised and excited as I was. We had a great talk and he agreed to share more information and to do a more extensive interview.

After finding Jacobson, that left only the family of Robert Stricklin. The only leads I had to go on were the fact that he was from Texas and that he was the only one to die during the war. I did not know if he was married and if so, if he had any children. Even his name posed a problem. On some records his name appeared as Stricklin and on others it appeared as Strickland. Dozens of letters and phone calls to Robert Stricklins—and Stricklands—in Texas produced no leads. (I started with the Stricklins named Robert on the assumption that a son, nephew, or grandson might bear his name.) In addition, numerous genealogical queries yielded no results.

My first break came with the National Personnel Records Center in St. Louis; they answered my second request for information on him. Although they did not have his military record, their letter stated that Robert B. Stricklin died on July 15, 1944, and that he was buried in the Ardennes American Cemetery (Plot C Row 39 Grave 13) in Neupre, Belgium. From my research on the 450th Bomb Group I knew that the July 15 mission was to Ploesti. With this information I was able to make a specific request from the National Archives and Records Administration (NARA) in College Park, Maryland.

Within a month the NARA replied with a copy of Robert Stricklin's Missing Aircrew Report (MACR), which listed him as the bombardier on Capt. William G. Snaith's B-24. The bomber had exploded in a fireball over Ploesti. Snaith, the only survivor, was blown clear in the blast and ended up in a prisoner of war camp. The MACR contained a next of kin listing for each crew member. Stricklin's mother, Irene, was listed as his. She lived at 2624 Birmingham Avenue, Dallas, Texas. Now I had a city to begin my search. With his mother's name and address, I could search period phone directories and census records. I contacted the Dallas Genealogical Society and the Dallas Public Library for assistance. Both provided more information and leads. The directory and census information provided the names of Stricklin's father and siblings. More genealogical research utilizing the social security death index provided death dates for two of his brothers. I then ordered copies of their obituaries from local papers, which gave me the names of surviving family members. My persistence paid off after eighteen months when I contacted Mrs. Irene Stricklin Frazier, Robert's baby sister and only surviving sibling. She was able to fill in most of the gaps in his portion of the story.

In the course of interviewing and locating the original crew, I also found two of *Shadow*'s replacement pilots: Vincent Olney and Floyd Robinson. *Shadow*'s copilot, Maurice Erickson, was the only one to remember Olney and Robinson at first, because he had flown with them. Another exhaustive search (letters, phone calls and Internet queries) and an advertisement in the *Oxford* (Nebraska) *Standard* put me in contact with Vince's second wife, Marilyn Siebels. Unfortunately, I learned that he died in 1978, but Marilyn provided some key information. I then located Vince's sister, Susan Rhynalds. She provided the information that Marilyn could not. Robinson was easy to locate once I had his name. His biographical profile was listed in the 450th Bomb Group's history published by Turner Publishing. A quick phone search and call put me in touch with him. I also had the good fortune to locate Sam Stein, a member of the 721st Squadron ground crew, who provided invaluable insight into that aspect of the war.

History is written by the participants; historians merely report the story to the best of their ability. The purpose of this book is not to deify or put *Shadow*'s crew on an unearned or unwanted pedestal. Their humbleness and humility, rooted in childhoods during the Depression, will not allow that. Rather, it explores the bond that made Stan drive to see Maurice after fifty-seven years. It records for history the lives of these remarkable men, these dutiful sons, and the legacy they leave behind.

1

Dutiful Sons

To appreciate and understand fully the men who flew the important missions over Europe, one must first examine their boyhoods. An exploration of their formative years sheds light on how these boys, these dutiful sons, became patriotic soldiers and extraordinary men. There are as many differences in them as there are similarities, but they were all children of the Depression. They came from cities and farms, some of them were poor, but none were rich. They grew up in self-sufficient homes where nothing was wasted. Each of them had a strong work ethic with no sense of entitlement. They were all responsible boys, with an intense loyalty to family. They had been taught right from wrong and their moral compasses were properly aligned. The war, in a wonderful, strange, and horrible way, would offer them opportunities that they would not otherwise have had; it forever changed them in profound ways.

Maurice Holt Gilliam, Tail Gunner: Reidsville, North Carolina

The boy who would spend his combat missions staring from his turret in the aft end of the B-24, manning two .50-caliber machine guns, looking for enemy fighters, was Maurice Holt Gilliam. He came into the world on December 28, 1922, the oldest of four children born to Lawrence Holt Gilliam and Stella Boyd Hicks. He was born in Axton, Virginia, in the home of his maternal grandparents, Thomas and Sallie Lou Hicks. As was common practice in the day, his mother returned to her childhood home for the birth of her first child. Shortly thereafter, Stella and her new son made the forty-mile journey back home to Lawrence and their two-story frame farmhouse in rural Rockingham County, North Carolina. Lawrence built the home himself on a tract that backed up to the Haw River, adjacent to his father's farm. The 180-acre farm was located near the Thompsonville crossroad (modern day Williamsburg Township), about seven miles southeast of Reidsville. The two driving economic forces of the region were tobacco and textiles.[1]

The Gilliams were not recent immigrants to the country. On the contrary, they had been on American soil for nearly three hundred years by the time Maurice was born. His seventh great-grandfather, John Gilliam, arrived in southeastern Virginia in the first half of the seventeenth century. John's grandson, Henshaw Gilliam, was Maurice's 5th great-grandfather and was a prominent member of Surry County, Virginia, society. He owned a vast amount of land. By the year 1800, his second great-grandfather, David Gilliam, moved the family to neighboring Guilford County, North Carolina, in search of better farmland. His mother's family had also been in Virginia since the second half of the eighteenth century. There is no doubt that Maurice came from good pioneer stock.

On the surface, Maurice's parents seemed to be complete opposites. His father, Lawrence, was a strict man of few words. He was a Democrat, but was politically active only by exercising his right to vote. Prior to marriage to Stella, Maurice's father worked as a painter and as a brakeman for the railroad. Lawrence had hopes of one day working his way up to engineer, but he soon realized that the dream was beyond his grasp. Maurice recalls that his father "always got excited at the sight or sound of a steam engine." He would often tell his children stories from the time he worked the rails. After marriage Lawrence continued to take painting jobs in the community to supplement the family income. Although he rarely, if ever, displayed open affection for his children, he loved them intensely. It was seen in subtle ways and seemed all the more meaningful when it came. This was more than likely a by-product of his father's personality and his upbringing in a family of twelve children. Lawrence was industrious and had a strong work ethic. He instilled these traits in all of his children.[2]

Maurice's mother was a plump woman who stood barely five feet tall. She was the loving and caring one. She had a contagious laugh and wonderful sense of humor. Stella was the one who did all the hugging and doting on the children. Maurice's most steadfast memory of her is that "through all the high and low moments of life, Mama was always there to help." From her, he learned love, generosity, and patience. Everyone wanted to be around his mother, while people kept a respectful distance from his father. Both of his parents grew up on farms in large families and knew the importance of self-sufficiency. Maurice inherited the best from each of them. "They gave me the freedom to learn … but always by the right rules."[3]

Lawrence was about 5 feet 9 inches tall and was a commanding figure in the family; he was always up before sunrise. After building a fire in the kitchen stove, he went out to feed the cows and mules. With his pre-dawn routine complete, he would come inside and tell the family, "Hey, time to get up!"; thus their days began. Each morning, Stella prepared a breakfast of eggs, sausage or ham, milk, biscuits and gravy for the family. Many days she would also prepare lunch at this time, because she was often working in the garden or on the farm during the morning and would not otherwise have time to fix it. Supper was frequently warmed up leftovers from lunch. The entire family ate together at each meal except for lunch during the school term. At breakfast Lawrence would coordinate the farm work for the day. While it was Lawrence who directed the farm work, it was Maurice's mother, Stella, who governed the chores around the house. Here she taught Sallie and Gayle how to cook, can (preserve) vegetables from the garden, sew, and do countless other household tasks. The women of the house also did their fair share of the farm work and helped in the tobacco fields or wherever they were needed. The family was a true "work force"; all of them did their share.[4]

Characteristic of most farms during this time, Lawrence had almost everything to ensure his family's self-sufficiency. In addition to the crops they harvested and the garden vegetables they grew, they had mules, cows, pigs, and hens. These provided ample food, plow power, milk, sausage, ham, eggs, and chicken for the family. In the 1920s Lawrence jointly purchased a Fordson tractor with his father. This allowed the Gilliams to do more harvesting on their own and saved paying someone else to do it for them. Lawrence took his own wheat and corn to the mill to be ground into flour. Gas, oil and similar items were purchased at Faucette's, a general store about a mile from the house at Thompsonville. Certain staples, such as sugar, molasses, honey, and Karo syrup, among others things, were procured at Mitchell's store in Reidsville. Often butter and eggs were traded for the needed items. Maurice's father owned a two-seat Ford Model-T, which he drove to church, to visit more distant relatives, and to make special trips to town. While working on the farm "you either walked or rode the cart and mule." Although the Depression left them no money for frills, the family always had food on the table and love in the home.[5]

The two-story frame farmhouse that Lawrence built for the family was the nucleus of their lives. It still stands today and is occupied by Maurice's sister, Sallie; it is situated about a quarter mile off of the road that now bears the family's name. Meals were the setting for all sorts of family discussions about the day's work, the happenings at school, church, or within the community; it included the local gossip, of course. It was only at mealtime that the busy family could see each other, because most of the day they were off working or at school. Stella reveled in having the family all together at each meal. The home was modest, without electricity or indoor plumbing. At first only one room was finished upstairs, and for a short time they boarded a local teacher for extra income. During that time Maurice slept downstairs in a small room that would later become the family bathroom. As the family expanded and the boarded teacher left, two more bedrooms were finished upstairs. Maurice and his two sisters will never forget how cold the upstairs was in the winter. "We would warm up by the fire downstairs and run upstairs quickly to get under our [homemade] quilts," he recalled. On cold winter mornings they would reverse the process. The long work days and lack of electricity curtailed many activities, but on a typical evening one would find Lawrence reading the paper, Stella sewing, and the children sewing, playing, or reading. Due to the scarcity of nearby houses, no electricity served the home until the early 1950s, long after Maurice returned from war.[6]

Lawrence and Stella were blessed with three other children. Their first daughter, Sallie, was born in 1924. A second son, Volney, was born in 1930. He would later serve his country in Korea and would die in a prisoner of war camp in 1951. Another daughter, Gayle, was born in 1933 and completed the family. Due to the age differences in the children, Maurice was closest to his sister Sallie as they grew up. He and Sallie were more caregivers than playmates to Volney and Gayle.[7]

Since Maurice was the oldest, it was his lot to help his father with most of the farm tasks. For Maurice, a typical day started with milking the cows, which he did seven days a week. He often needed a kerosene lantern to light his way in the early hours of the morning and the late hours of the evening. Other morning chores included the gathering of eggs. The myriad farming duties included plowing behind the family's two mules (Lula John and Kate), cutting wood, clearing land, and harvesting the crops. The crops were tobacco, corn, wheat, and barley. "Putting up tobacco" was another seemingly endless chore. By the time he was eleven or twelve, Maurice was able to drive the family's Fordson tractor. This allowed his father to work the reaper while Maurice pulled it. The types of work were determined by the season and by who would be available to help. During the winter months, when Maurice was in school, he could not work until the afternoon. However, he was expected home promptly after school so that he could help his father with whatever needed to be done. As always, those instructions came at breakfast. During the summer months when he was out of school, Maurice and the rest of the family worked from dawn to dusk.[8]

For his first six years of school, Maurice attended the two-room school at Thompsonville. He walked there each morning along a well-worn path in his grandfather's fields, at first by himself and then later with his sister Sallie. It was just over a mile, and it took him no more than fifteen minutes to traverse (if he didn't stop at his Grandpa's house). "I usually left for school in a trot. I ran almost all the time back then." Grades 1 through 4 were taught in one room, and grades 5 through 7 were taught in the other. The building had no electricity, running water, nor toilets. The older boys in the school were responsible for getting water from a nearby house; they put it in a large bucket on the school's front porch. From here the students could get a drink of water, dipped and poured into cups made of notebook paper. Two privies (outhouses) were located about fifty yards behind the school. Two wood stoves provided the school's heat during the winter. When needed, the 5th and 6th grade boys were excused from afternoon classes to cut wood for the next day's heat. Almost every day on the trip home, Maurice and Sallie would stop at their grandparents' home. Grandma Gilliam would put out cookies or apple fritters on her dining room table for them, and they would read the comic page from the newspaper. Maurice still remembers the odor of the carbide gas that was used to light their home and the smell of his grandmother's cooking on their wood stove. Of course, he and Sallie were brief with their visits, so they could return home quickly to help wherever their parents needed them.[9]

1. Dutiful Sons 13

Typical of most boys growing up on farms in the 1920s and 1930s, Maurice found ways to entertain himself when he had finished his work. As he grew up, his best friends were schoolmates Whitt Garrison, Paul Robertson, and Lindsay Burton. There were also two first cousins, Julian and Donald Gilliam. Together they played ball, went fishing, held foot races, and had distance jumps. One popular diversion called for them to cut down grape vines, which they then used to swing across ditches and streams. Swimming in the nearby Haw River was also a favorite. Maurice recalls that he loved to play in the water and that he could make a few strokes, but he tried never to get into water over his head. That changed one day when his father came down to where the kids were playing. "Daddy caught me on the bank and threw me into the river over my head. When I came to the top, I swam out and have been

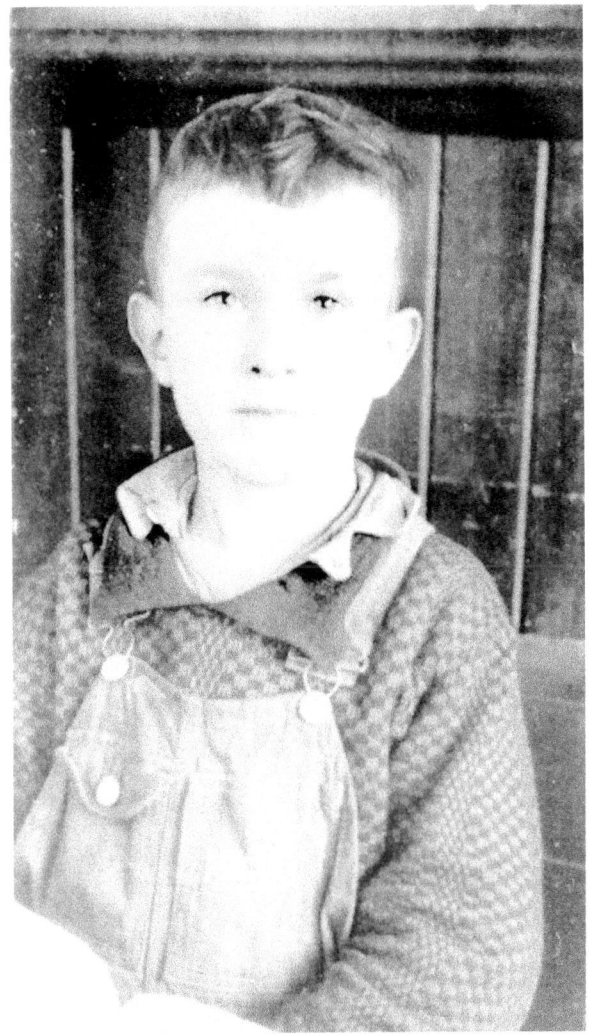

Maurice H. Gilliam, 8 years old. (Maurice H. Gilliam)

swimming ever since." Lawrence felt strongly that you learn by doing, whether at work or play—sink or swim. Maurice's family did not have a radio, but their neighbors, the Pritchetts, did. They lived on a large adjoining farm about a mile from the Gilliams. Maurice remembers walking to the Pritchetts' house to listen to their radio. On Saturday nights they could pick up *The Grand Ole Opry* from Nashville, Tennessee.[10]

In 1936, when Maurice was thirteen, several of the local schools were consolidated and a new school was built at Williamsburg. It had all the "modern facilities schools had in those days"—electricity, bathrooms, and an auditorium-gymnasium. In this new school he attended seventh grade. The next year all of the students in his class were transferred to Reidsville High School. At this time Maurice began to ride the bus, but he still had to walk the mile to Thompsonville to catch it. Because his only way home from school was the bus, and he was expected home promptly each afternoon to work, Maurice was unable to play sports in high school. His only extracurricular school activity was as a member of the agriculture club, Future Farmers of America. Their motto: "Learning to do, doing to learn; earning to live, and living to serve," concisely describes the work ethic that was instilled in him at home and at school. One of his ninth-grade classmates, Louise Stanfield, had a German pen pal. She convinced Maurice to write to one as well. Louise made the necessary arrangements, and he began writing to his own German pen pal, Lalessia Ansin. Over several months and into his 10th grade year, Maurice wrote a letter to his new friend about every six or eight weeks. It was a novelty, and he enjoyed getting a letter from overseas. During this time, "Hitler was beginning to make waves in Germany," he recalled, and he asked his German pen pal what she thought of Hitler. "After my Hitler question, the letters from Germany stopped."[11]

Maurice did not realize it at the time, but the next year, 1940, would prove to be one of the most important years of his life. This was attributable to two events. The first one began simply enough when the handsome, polite, eleventh-grade farm boy began dating a local girl two years his junior, Stella Leath McKinney. She was from the area, and they had known each other since grade school; Maurice would never date another girl. The other event was his baptism. The events leading up to the saving of Maurice's soul began oddly enough a year earlier when his grandfather bought a brand-new 1939 Chevrolet. The purchase of a new car is always a big event in a small community, and this was no exception. Maurice was excited, because he had recently obtained his driver's license, and he had great hopes of driving his grandfather's new car. Unfortunately that was a privilege reserved only for his father and grandfather. Maurice's aunt, Vera Gilliam, was a fervent Christian. She was something of an "old maid"—unmarried and living with her parents—but everyone liked her. On several occasions she had tried to "witness" to her brother's son and to have Maurice commit his life to Christ. Although

Maurice Gilliam school photograph, Reidsville High School circa 1937. (Maurice Gilliam)

religion played a large role in the family's home life, the distance to church, poor rural roads, and lack of transportation prevented Maurice's family from attending church regularly. All of this did not deter the shrewd and persistent Aunt Vera. She knew how much Maurice wanted to drive her father's new car and tried a new angle at converting her nephew. In July 1940,

Orange Julius, in Charlotte, N.C., owned by Maurica Gilliam's uncle, Ramey Hicks. Maurice worked here prior to registering for the draft. (Maurice Gilliam)

nearby Lowes Methodist Church was having a summer revival. Vera asked Maurice to drive her. She told him if he would do so, she would arrange for him to take her in her father's new car. It was an opportunity that Maurice could not pass up. "Aunt Vera worked her magic on me and before I knew it I was making my profession of faith one Thursday evening," he recalled.[12]

Upon graduation from Reidsville High School in 1941, Maurice continued to help his father on the farm. It was typical of most boys in the area to continue in the family farming tradition. After the harvest from the fall crop that year, Maurice wanted to purchase his first car with his share of the proceeds. "The cost of the car I found was beyond my means, but the salesman knew my dad." It was a used 1939 Ford at Lucky City Motors in Reidsville, and it cost $525. One evening the salesman brought the car out to the farm for them to see. With hardly a word, Lawrence paid the difference between the money Maurice had and the cost of the car. This was the subtle way Lawrence showed his love. This was his hug.[13]

That winter, after the crops were in, Maurice took a job at McCollum's Market, a small grocery store in Reidsville. Work this far from home was now possible thanks to his new car. He was also able to attend church at Lowes Methodist on a regular basis. After a few months at McCollum's, he took a more lucrative job in a silk mill in Burlington. He continued to live at home and to date Stella during this time.[14]

His maternal uncle, R.W. Hicks, ran an Orange Julius store in Charlotte, North Carolina, about 120 miles south of Reidsville. The restaurant was a small, one-story building located on a triangular lot at 2238 Wilkinson Boulevard. In early 1942 Uncle Ramey recruited his nephew to come down to work for him there. His offer included room and board. Back home good jobs were getting hard to come by at the time. Maurice promptly acccptcd, partly out of an obligation to family and partly for the job opportunity in a larger city. By April of that year, Maurice had moved to Charlotte to live with his Uncle Ramey and Aunt Helen. At the Orange Julius his primary job was sandwich maker, but he served in all capacities as needed, including soda jerk, curb catcher, table waiter, and bus boy. Life would forever change for him in Charlotte. There on June 30, 1942, Maurice registered for the draft. Realizing he could choose the branch of service he wanted if he volunteered—he did not want to be drafted into the Navy—he chose to volunteer for the Army Air Force, because he had "always had a fascination with flight and airplanes."[15]

Grant Dodd Caywood, Pilot: Omaha, Nebraska

The father figure and natural born leader of the crew (and later of the squadron) who always had a yearning to fly was Grant Dodd Caywood. He was born on April 3, 1918, in Des Moines, Iowa, the only child of Grant Cecil Caywood and Gladys Venus Dodd. Grant's father was called "Pat" and his mother was affectionately called "Bud," which was short for rosebud. After the birth of their son, Pat moved his family to St. Louis, Missouri, where he worked as an engineer, making 155-millimeter artillery shells for the war effort. A few years later, Grant's father moved the family again, to Omaha, Nebraska, where he had obtained a better engineering position. Later Pat would work not only as a professional engineer, but would also serve as president of Travelers Health Insurance. It was in Omaha that Grant would spend his formative years.[16]

Grant's upper middle-class family lived in Dundee, "the best part of Omaha," first at 310 South 55th Street and later at 510 South 57th Street. Pat designed the second house, borrowed the money from the local savings and loan, and contracted it out to a local builder. Grant attended the nearby Dundee School. It was about a mile from their house; Grant usually rode his bike or ran to school, but Bud drove him in inclement weather. Bud taught her son to read before he entered kindergarten; this allowed him to skip a grade in school. Always intelligent, Grant "was generally bored with elementary school." Like most "city boys" his chores consisted of mowing the lawn, washing the car, and doing the dishes.[17]

Religion played a large role in Grant's childhood. The Caywoods attended the First Baptist Church of Omaha, located four or five miles from their home. They were in attendance every time the church doors were open—Sunday school and worship services on Sundays and prayer meetings on Wednesday nights. Grant's father, a "teetotaler," was a deacon in the church, as well as chairman of the Intermediate Department, which consisted "mostly of high school kids." Each morning, Grant remembers, "We had a 'family worship' before breakfast." It consisted of Pat reading passages from the Bible and each member of the family taking "turns at the invocation." Almost nightly Pat read to the family from "the Bible or from the *Book of Life*, a set of books aimed at young people." Although he has a strong Christian faith to this day, he freely admits that the excess of religion during his youth made him "all churched out."[18]

Airplanes and the magic of flight have long held a fascination for young boys;

Grant was no exception. At a very early age he became enthralled with aviation. This interest was further fueled when he accompanied his father to the Omaha Municipal Airport when Pat flew on business trips. Grant began building airplane models and looking forward to his next visit to the airport. He continually scanned the sky for passing planes.

Grant earned an aviation merit badge in Boy Scouts. He was a member of Troop 17 of the Covered Wagon Area Council in Omaha. He joined as a "tenderfoot" at the age of twelve and became enthralled with all of the adventure that scouting offered him. "I remember sitting on the pot and reading the [Boy Scout] *Handbook for Boys* until my folks kicked me out of the bathroom." As with all his endeavors, Grant excelled in scouting and earned the prestigious rank of Eagle Scout. He served in various leadership roles within the troop, including patrol leader and senior patrol leader. As an adult, Grant continued to play an active role in scouting. He assisted as a "neighborhood commissioner, scout master, merit badge examiner," and participated in special local events.[19]

Aside from his parents, as Grant grew up, his favorite person was his uncle, Dwight Campbell. Campbell, who had married Pat's sister, was a justice on the South Dakota State Supreme Court. He lived in Pierre, South Dakota. Campbell had an American Eagle open-cockpit biplane, which he flew to Omaha when he visited family. When he came he took Grant for rides. Grant would sit in the front seat, don helmet and goggles and enjoy every second of the experience. It was a great thrill and privilege for a boy his age. These adventures with his uncle only increased Grant's desire to fly.[20]

Grant will always remember his fourteenth birthday, April 3, 1932. His Uncle Dwight was in town and had promised him a flight. That morning, after breakfast, Grant bounded up the stairs to wake up his uncle. "Uncle Dwight, Uncle Dwight, time for an airplane ride." Unfortunately, his uncle was a little under the weather that day and did not feel much like flying. He moaned and rolled over to face Grant, "Oh hell, Grant, you take it; you take it." That was all the permission he needed. In a flash, he was back downstairs relaying to his mom what had just transpired. Bud "was a real good sport" and "without much comment" drove him to the airport—he was too young to drive a car.[21]

Once at the airport, Grant found an obliging mechanic to assist him. He had seen Uncle Dwight perform all of the necessary procedures before. Grant knew that he could do it. The mechanic helped him start the engine and he was on his own. Grant vividly remembers this first solo flight. "I pushed the go lever all the way to the front. The airplane started to roll and the tail came up. It wanted to turn to the left; so I gave it a little right stick. I pulled the stick back. I was flying. The thrill, the exhilaration, the delightful excitement were indescribable. I flew around Omaha for about a half hour, leaving the throttle wide open. How I found the airport, I will never know, but I did. I pointed the nose at the field and pulled the go handle all the way back. I made about four landings on that approach, and the airplane rolled quite close to the hangar. A little throttle got it to a parking place. I turned off the switch." Bud, his generous and understanding mom, was waiting there for him. There is no doubt she was proud. She had let her little bird fly—figuratively and literally. And thus a pilot was born.[22]

Grant was now hooked. He spent all of his spare time at the airport. "I washed airplanes, put air in the tires and oil in the engines," he recalled. Before long he was also helping with mechanical work. He did all of this for more flying time, mostly in Piper Cubs. At the time, Grant flew with no certification or licenses, something inconceivable today.[23]

He attended Omaha Central High School. Because it was a land grant school, the male students were required to take military training. This fact, along with his ability to fly, would have a tremendous impact on Grant when the war started. The school produced a military regiment of two full battalions. Three days a week the boys wore West Point uniforms and drilled constantly. Grant enjoyed the military aspect of school, and he excelled in it. He became the number three cadet at Omaha Central. Jokingly, he recalls, "I might have been no. one if I had studied Latin. The Latin teacher told my mother that she would pass me if I promised not to take any more Latin."[24]

Despite his attempts to hide it, Grant was very intelligent. Academics came easy to him when he wanted to apply himself. Technical classes and English held the most scholastic interest for him, and it was in these he was most proficient.

Grant was also quite athletic in high school. He participated in football, track and swimming. He was inducted into the National Athletic Honor Society. On the gridiron he earned all-state honors as an end; on the track he ran the 440. As good as he was at football and track, he was even better at his favorite sport, swimming. His prowess in the pool earned him a four-year scholarship to Iowa State College in Ames.[25]

Popularity among the students came easily for Grant. This can be attributed to his wonderful sense of humor, his good looks and manners, his military achievements, his athletic ability, and the leadership quality he has always seemed to possess. All of these traits were tempered with modesty. He was the type of person everyone wanted to be around. He and his best friends, Dick MacDuff and Ed Clark, were known as the "3 Stupes"—short for stupid. When Grant was not busy with work, sports or flying, he hung out with them. They hunted, fished, and attended the usual social gatherings. He did not reveal his aviation interest and talent to his friends until later in college.[26]

After graduating from Omaha Central in 1936, it was off to Iowa State. Ames was just north of his birthplace, Des Moines. Grant's father, Pat, had also attended and graduated from Iowa State. Aviation was still his passion, and shortly after his arrival in Ames, Grant made it out to the local airfield, Wearth Airport. There he struck up a friendship with Marion Wearth, the fixed base operator. Grant became a part-time mechanic and instructor for Wearth and was able to keep his flying skills honed. While working there he also "finally got real licenses." It was Marion Wearth who would be responsible for one of Grant's most incredible experiences.[27]

When the air races came to Des Moines, Wearth offered his young protégé a chance to fly in the Piper Cub race. Grant jumped at this thrilling opportunity, but coyly admits, "I had never flown in an air race. So he [Marion] took me up and showed me how to round a pylon. He neglected to tell me how close to the other airplanes I would be. He signed me up and paid the entrance fee." Despite his lack of racing experience—and the close proximity of the other planes—Grant won the race. This was much to the consternation of one of the other participants, one of the most famous flyers and aerial acrobats of the time, John G. "Tex" Rankin. Tex made a name for himself as a barnstormer in the 1920s and formed the Rankin Air Circus, in which he performed amazing stunts that thrilled his audiences.[28]

Tex was skeptical that a college student could be beat his pilots and "rightly assumed there was something different about the airplane," Grant recalled. Marion had shortened the wings and tinkered with the engine. Tex approached Grant about it, but he was ignorant of Marion's changes. Tex then confronted Marion. Ostensibly Tex wanted to purchase the plane. Tex offered Marion a fabulous sum for it and after some prompting from Grant, Marion accepted. But that was just the beginning of Grant's adventures with Tex Rankin.[29]

After purchasing the Piper Cub from Wearth, Tex asked Grant if he would fly the plane for him. He, of course, accepted. Grant proudly writes, "I won all the Cub races until the sponsors began taking better looks at the birds. By that time, the engine was shot anyway, and we retired the cub." Grant also participated in some of Tex's aerobatic antics, including his "drunk act." On Memorial Day 1937, Grant was with Tex when he won the International Aerobatic Championship Trophy in St. Louis—"the 'Oscar' of aerobatics." It was all a great adventure for a young college student.[30]

But adventure is not the legacy and lasting memory Grant has of Tex. "Tex was the greatest instructor I ever had. He taught me truly precision aerobatics. His technical knowledge as well as his aeronautical skills were fantastic," he said. Grant's legacy would be 56 years and 30,000 hours of flying, after which he recalled, "I never had so much as scratched an airplane, except for battle damage."[31]

The Depression still had its grip on the country. "Flying was not steady enough to feed me very well" during college, Grant recalls. To supplement his meager flying income, he took jobs with "contractors and subcontractors in the construction industry." Because of his strong work ethic, physical strength and willingness to work, he never wanted for a job. Remembering the different roles, he said: "I was a plumber's helper, an electrician's helper, a draftsman, a laborer, a carpenter. I tied concrete reinforcing; I caught red hot rivets standing stories high on a beam." Grant recalls the comical rules of life he learned as a plumber's helper, as the plumber advised him while replacing a sewer line, "You only have to know three things: one, shit don't run up hill; two, pay day is Friday; three, don't lick your fingers." Earlier that same year, Grant's father got him a job as an intern draftsman for a steel contractor. Under the contractor's guidance, he made some drawings for the main gates of the Boulder Dam. "They were just simple, rectangular boxes that had stainless steel rollers and were moved with a cable." The design was accepted and he got to make the trip there to see the installation. "My stay at the site was short, but it was a fantastic experience," he said.[32]

As was his high school, Iowa State was also a land grant institution. Grant enlisted in the Reserve Officers Training Corps (ROTC) in the horse drawn field artillery. This was a new experience for him, and he jokes, "I had difficulty telling a gelding from a mare." As in high school, Grant excelled in his university military duties, where he obtained the rank of cadet captain on April 8, 1940. In June of that year, he graduated from ROTC with the reserve rank of second lieutenant. He served as "executive at the guns" in the 341st Field Artillery, U.S. Army Reserves. The 341st was a horse-drawn unit with 75-millimeter French guns.[33]

His popularity also carried over into college. He was a two-term president of the ATO fraternity and lived in their house near campus. Following in his father's footsteps, Grant signed up for the five-year course in architectural engineering. One of the prerequisites for architectural studies was a lot of drawing, which included "life class," which required anatomy. "Anatomy fascinated me; I filled my schedule with medical courses when I could," he said. Grant was able to "challenge" or exempt out of several classes, including physics, chemistry and a few math classes after passing the required tests for each. By the end of his fourth year, he had used this extra class time to complete all of the pre-med requirements—this in addition to his architectural engineering classes. His fifth and final year he completed all of the design classes and continued to take medical classes whenever possible. Grants recalls, "I thought I wanted to be a surgeon and would have happily forgotten architecture, but I had gone too far not to finish." He graduated from Iowa State with a bachelor of science degree in architectural engineering in December 1940. He then planned to go on to medical school at Iowa University.[34]

The drums of war altered these plans; reserve units were being called to active duty. Grant was in medical school, but "the war department would have none of it," he recalls. "They would have no perpetual students. I had a degree and a reserve commission; if I didn't have a deferred job I would have to go to active duty." Grant applied to be a pilot with United Air Lines—a deferred job. United was constantly losing pilots to the Army Air Corps and welcomed someone of his background. After some brief introductory courses, he soon found himself in the right seat as co-pilot of a DC-3. He was happy to be out of the field artillery and flying on a regular basis—after all, it was his passion. He did have one regret though; he would never finish medical school.[35]

Shortly after joining United, as did many of his predecessors, he applied to be a flying cadet (later known as an aviation cadet) in the Army Air Corps. He passed the physical exam and waited his turn to be called, which only took a few months. Grant related that it was customary for the Air Corps to send cadets far from home. Serendipitously, he was sent to Tulare, California, to the Rankin Aeronautical Academy. He was to be in the first contract flight class of his old buddy Tex Rankin.[36]

Maurice A. Erickson, Co-Pilot: Kane, Pennsylvania

The Pennsylvania farm boy who manned the co-pilot's (and later the pilot's) seat was Maurice A. Erickson. He was born on July 2, 1919, at Kane General Hospital in East Kane, Pennsylvania, the youngest child of Maurice Erickson and Eva May Neupert. Maurice had an older sister, Gerry, born in 1916. Maurice's father was of Swedish descent and his mother's family was German. His parents divorced in 1927, when Maurice was only eight years old. After the divorce, Eva moved with her children to live with her parents on their small farm in East Kane.[37]

During the Depression, the family had a series of aunts, uncles, and cousins living with them on the farm. Maurice's mother worked at a local brush handle and toy factory to support the family. Maurice and Gerry helped their grandfather with the farm chores. He recalls, "Things weren't easy in those days, but thanks to Mom, we never missed a meal." The family attended the nearby Methodist church in East Kane. It was the center of all social activities in the community.[38]

Maurice attended 1st and 2nd grades at Central in Kane. After moving to his grandparents' farm, he was enrolled at the three-room East Kane Grade School for grades three through eight; he then attended Kane High School. He walked to school for ten years and in the 11th grade he began riding the bus. Maurice was athletic; he participated in baseball and basketball. As with most farm boys, he enjoyed hunting and fishing with his friends. He also liked to sled and ski during the cold Pennsylvania winters.[39]

Upon graduation from high school in 1937, Maurice went to work at the same factory as his mother. Maurice was still dating his childhood sweetheart, Lillian Geraldine Rolfe. They met in the third grade and they always knew that they would end up together. By 1939, Maurice was trying his hand at carpentry. Meanwhile, Lillian was studying to become a nurse at Deaconess Hospital in Buffalo, New York. Upon graduation she remained in Buffalo. She became an industrial nurse for the Crosby Metal Stamping Company, which "made army helmets among other things." As required, Maurice registered for the draft. However, while visiting Lillian in Buffalo in January 1942, he decided to volunteer for the Army Air Corps. Despite the fact that he had never flown, he wanted to be a pilot. It was his chance to fulfill a boyhood dream.[40]

Theodore H. Morris, Ball Turret Gunner: St. Louis, Missouri

The young aviation mechanic who would spend most of his combat missions suspended beneath the B-24 in a ball turret was Theodore H. Morris. He was born on September 5, 1922, in St. Louis, Missouri, the youngest child of Arthur Holden Morris and Ethel Briell. Arthur and Ethel grew up across the street from each other in St. Louis and were childhood sweethearts. Ted had two older siblings, a brother, Ralph, born in 1914, and a sister, Ethel, born in 1916. Arthur was an attorney, but Ted never really got to know him very well. He passed away, after a prolonged illness, when Ted was a child. After Arthur's death, it fell to Ethel, who had been a housewife, to raise the children and provide for the family. She lived in her mother's house and sold some stocks to make ends meet. The entire family worked together to get through those tough times. After Ted's brother and sister graduated from high school, they both got jobs to help out with the household expenses. They worked in their uncle's clothing business, which made nursing uniforms.[41]

Ted grew up in a middle-class neighborhood, called Arlington Heights at 1923 Burd Avenue, in a nice two-story frame house. There was plenty of love and good food in the Morris household, as both of Ted's grandmothers lived with the family. He had a normal childhood with the usual friends and school activities. As the baby of the family he always had a very close relationship with his mother, which deepened with the passing of his father. Ted's role model and hero growing up was his brother Ralph, who served as a father figure as well.[42]

Ted attended grammar school at Gundlach Elementary, which was only a block from his home. He then attended and graduated from Ben Blewett High School. Ben Blewett was a few miles away, so Ted rode his bike to school everyday. He was quiet but popular in school. The quotation about Ted in his high school yearbook accurately and succinctly describes his personality: "He who has lived obscurely and quietly has lived well." Ted did not like to be in the spotlight; he preferred the shadows. He did not play sports but he was the snapshot editor for the school yearbook. Ted was always fascinated with photography. After graduation he bought a Speedgraphic press camera.[43]

Upon graduation from high school in June 1941, Ted attended a local trade school to learn aircraft riveting. He then obtained a position with Curtis Wright, working as a small parts riveter. Ted was drafted and called up to Jefferson Barracks in St. Louis on December 18, 1942. Because he already had experience in the aircraft industry, he was placed in the Army Air Corps.[44]

Stanley Samuel Butynski, Nose Gunner: Hamtramck, Michigan

The "city boy" who manned the two guns in the nose of the plane was Stanley Samuel Butynski. He was born on June 7, 1924, at home in Hamtramck, Michigan, a suburb of Detroit. He was the oldest son of Samuel Butynski and Bernice Banash. Stan had seven siblings—four sisters and three brothers. When Stan was very young, the large Butynski brood rented a small house in Hamtramck. Samuel and Bernice later purchased a five-bedroom house, which gave their family some much-needed space. Hamtramck was known as "little Europe," Stan recalled. "There were people of all nationalities and all got along with each other." Stan's parents were part of this "melting pot," as they were recent immigrants from Poland. His father worked in a local factory while his mother stayed home to raise the children. The automobile industry was the driving economic force of the area.[45]

Family and friends were the guiding influences in Stan's life. When his family attended church, they went to nearby Saint Francis. However, religion did not play a large role in his childhood. His best friends from adolescence included Tom Wilhem, Stella Bush, and Bill Septika. "We played cards and kid games … [attended] school functions … no one owned a car," Stan fondly remembers. Growing up Stan greatly admired the strong women in his life—his mother and Mrs. Wilhelm. As a boy, Stan performed the normal household chores. He also helped work in the family's garden—planting, picking and weeding. The plot was located in their back yard and it produced all of the vegetables for the household.[46]

Stan attended nearby Holbrook Elementary, Copernicus Junior High and Hamtramck High School. Each was close enough; so he walked to school every morning. In high school, Stan was on the swim team. There he also took four years of aviation classes. In them he learned about aircraft engines, fuselage construction, fabric covering, arc and gas welding, as well as the history of flight. Upon graduation in June 1942, Stan became an apprentice tool and die maker with the Chrysler Corporation. He still lived at home with his parents.[47]

By all accounts, Stan was an honest, hard-working, blue-collar boy. Like all of his contemporaries, he dutifully registered for the draft. He further exercised his allegiance on December 1, 1942, by forgoing the draft and volunteering for the Army Air Corps. The classes in high school sparked his interest in aviation. He wanted to fly.[48]

Manuel F. Esquivel, Jr., Radio Operator and Gunner: New Orleans, Louisiana

The comic of the crew, who would change his citizenship to join the U.S. Army, was Manuel Fernando Esquivel, Jr. He was born in Merida, British Honduras (modern day Belize), on May 14, 1922. His father, who owned a large plantation in Merida, was in the import-export business. Manuel had three brothers, Carlos, Raul, and Renan, but Carlos died as a small child in Merida. Sometime in the early 1930s the family was sent to New Orleans—the details are sketchy. Manuel's father apparently abandoned his wife and children in Louisiana. He remained on his plantation in British Honduras.[49]

Manuel grew up in poverty in New Orleans. "We struggled to live ... they were very tough times," recalled his brother Raul. Raul quit school at the age of fourteen to work at Postal Telegraph (Western Union). In his ninth-grade year, Manuel was also forced to quit school to help support the family.[50]

Things were not all bad for Manuel in New Orleans. In the early 1940s, he met Rita Burtcheall at a neighborhood party. He had found the love of his life. After a courtship, the young couple married in New Orleans on August 30, 1942.[51]

Since British Honduras was a British territory, Manuel was first drafted by England. He wanted to serve in an American unit, so he changed his name from Fernando, his middle name by which he had always been called, to Manuel, his first name. He then applied for U.S. citizenship and registered for the U.S. draft. He received his "greeting" letter from Uncle Sam and was drafted into the Army on October 8, 1942, just five weeks after his marriage to Rita.[52]

Richard Morton Jacobson, Top Turret Gunner: Roxbury, Massachusetts

The crew's engineer and top turret gunner, a star athlete who played semi-pro baseball and the saxophone, was Richard Morton Jacobson. He was born on May 9,

Richard Jacobson held by his mother, Etta, in Roxbury, Massachusetts. (Richard Jacobson)

1923, in Massachusetts Homeopathic Hospital in Boston to Zismund Jacobson and Etta Heyman. "Dick," as he was called, was the Jacobsons' only child. His parents divorced before Dick was born and he never knew his father or any of his father's family. Etta was very hurt by the divorce; she rarely spoke of her husband. For the most part, Dick knew nothing of his father until "he became a man" at the age of thirteen and then his mother told him very little. He grew up in Roxbury, a suburb of Boston. Dick and his mother lived in an apartment at 575 Blue Hill Avenue with her brother, Harry Heyman, and his family. Their modest, comfortable home was located across from the Franklin Park Zoo, in a mixed middle-class neighborhood consisting of Blacks, Irish, and Jews.[53]

Dick's mother, Etta, was an attractive and intelligent career woman. She was a banker who later entered the insurance industry. She worked for Mass Mutual and became one of the first women in the country to make the industry's Million Dollar Round Table. Dick learned courage and independence from his mother's example.[54]

Dick attended religious school (beginning around age 9) and synagogue at the nearby temple, which was only a ten-minute walk from his house. He was confirmed there at the age of 13. Despite having the measles, he fondly remembers his bar mitzvah: "The synagogue was quite large and beautiful. Standing in the pulpit and delivering my service and speech in front of the large gathering was something that I had never done before. I was surprised that I felt comfortable. The feeling was good and while I do not consider myself highly ritualistic, the spirit and the quality of my religion is embedded in my character."[55]

Characteristic of most suburban kids, he performed the typical chores at home—vacuuming and washing the dishes. Dick also had several jobs while growing up in Roxbury. One of his first was at Billy Shane's cleaners, where he wrapped the wire hangers with tissue paper "to make a quarter." He had a newspaper route and also worked in a grocery store owned by the father of his friend Marty Leshner. "What a mess I made out of wrapping up cream cheese and lox for the Jewish ladies who came to the store. I still can't wrap a bundle right!" After he turned sixteen and obtained his driver's license, Dick drove the store's delivery truck. "What a relief!" he jokingly remembers.[56]

Dick spent most of his summers in boarding houses at Nantasket Beach, where he lived with various friends and relatives. These days held some of his fondest memories of youth. The kids there played "box ball." It was a game played at low tide and was similar to baseball. A diamond was drawn in the smooth, firm sand. "There was no pitcher; you would just stand at home plate and try to smack a dimpled rubber ball through the infielders. You were not allowed to hit [the ball] in the air, just on the ground. Boy, were there some spectacular plays!" he fondly reflected. He also played in the adult softball games at Nantasket on Sunday afternoons. Even though he was only eleven or twelve years old, he felt he was the best third baseman on the field. He humbly recalls that Uncle Harry "would sometimes bawl me out for being 'so cocky' and that would take the wind out of my sails pretty fast."[57]

It was not all play for him. Dick was also industrious during his summers at

Nantasket Beach. He and his friend Morty Blumenthal ran a small bicycle repair business. They also had an ice cream and soda wagon, which they would roll down the beach to earn some extra spending money. "We were too young to get a license and eventually had to give it up or go to jail. The men who did it for a living complained that they had to park their ice cream trucks on the street while we could roll our wagon right down on the beach and get all the business." Dick did not see his mother much in the summer, because she had to work. However, she did manage to come down on weekends to spend time with him.[58]

Baseball was always one of Dick's passions and he displayed a natural talent for the sport—a talent that he honed during his summers at Nantasket Beach. When Dick was about 14 years old he was offered a wonderful opportunity. His uncle, Fred Heyman, owned the Log Cabin restaurant near Braves Field in Boston. It was a "large, casual restaurant [with] a very popular bar." Fred knew most of the Braves' management and players and introduced his nephew to them. He was allowed to join the "Knot Hole Gang," a group of kids who were given special passes to attend the games for free. "Of course we had to sit in the bleachers, but it was fun," he said. Dick soon became involved with the Boston Braves junior program, called the "Boston Bee Juniors." One summer he was sent out to Milwaukee (the Milwaukee Brewers were a farm team of the Braves) "for fun and training." With this expanded focus on baseball, Dick became very good. He continued to play each summer with the Braves organization throughout high school.[59]

Dick attended Theodore Roosevelt Junior High and Roxbury Memorial High School. He was very athletic. In the winter he ran indoor track and managed the team. He was also quarterback on the school's football team. Unfortunately, a broken nose while playing during his junior year and the subsequent plastic surgery prevented a senior pigskin season. He painfully remembers the experience: "I was a mess. There was no whites to my eyes, just black, blue, and red. Plastic surgery had a long way to go in those days." The spring brought outdoor track and his favorite sport, baseball; Dick played second base. He also boxed a little bit at the local YMCA. He recalls, "Willy Pep, the boxing champ, lived near me for a while and he used to fool around in the ring at the Y with me."[60]

Dick was also musically talented. He played the saxophone and clarinet. He was in the school band and orchestra; he often played in school plays and shows. Dick was a big fan of Glenn Miller, Artie Shaw, and Coleman Hawkins and played their latest tunes.[61]

Dick was admittedly shy in high school. He did not date a lot, but through sports and music, he was a popular kid. At Roxbury Memorial High "they had a boys' side and a girls' side of the same building with a wall in between." In the 11th grade, seventeen-year-old Dick overcame his shyness—and that wall—and began dating Phyllis Harriet Elias, two years his junior. They "went steady" from the time they met until they married.[62]

Friends played a large role in Dick's adolescence. Among them were his cousins George and Paul Heyman. George, who was two years older than Dick, was a fabulous piano player. Dick remembers his cousin's talent in his knockout version of

Benny Goodman's "Little Rock Get Away." Mel Cohen was another friend. He attended Boston Latin School and "was into his books." Mel later went to cadet school and become a navigator-bombardier. Sadly, he was killed on his second mission when his plane was shot down over Munich. Far and away Dick's best friend growing up was Marty Leshner, whose father ran the grocery store where Dick worked for a time. "He was about five foot ten and just as wide. Marty was all muscle. The only time I got hurt playing football [his broken nose] was when Marty got the flu" and could not block for him. For fun they hung out at the local drug store with other friends from the neighborhood. Dick grew up in a tough neighborhood and street brawls occurred with some frequency. It was good to have Marty on your side. He "was not at all pugnacious." He would stay out of things until they got out of hand; then he would step in and break up the fights. Marty was a gentle giant.[63]

After graduating from Roxbury Memorial High in 1940, Dick attended Boston University (BU) during the day and Boston Technical Institute (BTI) at night. At BU he took business classes. At BTI he studied plastic engineering—he thought it would be wise to know more about the relatively new plastics industry. Dick did not receive a degree from either, because in the fall of 1942 he enlisted in the Army Air Force.[64]

Norman LaVergn Woodward, Waist Gunner: Lisle, New York

The enigma of the crew, the waist gunner (and later ball turret gunner), was Norman L. Woodward. Norman was born on October 10, 1922, in Owego, New York, to Charles Clark Woodward and Rozeltha "Rose" Jane Partridge. Charles was a dairy farmer who was constantly on the move in the Broome County, New York, area. About the time Norman was thirteen, his father purchased a farm in Nanticoke, New York, which finally settled the family down in one place. Norman worked hard on the farm with his father. In the fall of 1942 he volunteered for the Army Air Corps.[65]

Herbert Gouldon, Navigator: Jackson Heights (Queens), New York

The youngest officer of the crew, who navigated the crew successfully not only across the Atlantic to Manduria, but also to and from the target on each mission, was Herbert Gouldon. He was born on May 24, 1923, in Detroit, Michigan. Herb was the third of four children born to Alfred Gouldon and Hilda Rejan Litke. Alfred was in the diamond business. Hilda's parents immigrated from Poland. After settling in New York, her parents opened a wedding gown store in Manhattan and later a hat shop. The diamond business brought Alfred to Brooklyn shortly after Herb's birth. By the time Herb was three, the family finally settled in Jackson Heights. Hilda followed her parents' entrepreneurial lead and opened three beauty salons.[66]

The Gouldons rented the upstairs in a two-family house in Jackson Heights. Herb had two older sisters, Ruth and Hazel, and a younger brother, Stephen. The family was Jewish and attended the nearby synagogue. The Gouldons lived next to the firehouse; so Herb spent many afternoons hanging out with the firemen. Next to the fire station was a candy store that sold flavored, shaved iced for two cents. Herb and his friends would suck out the flavor first and then eat the ice. Afterwards they would chew on the paper cup to get their money's worth. After a few years, Alfred bought a house not far from where they had rented. Jackson Heights was still very rural in the 1920s. Herb remembers that a working farm was only two blocks from the family's house. Typical of most boys, Herb was a Boy Scout and played sports in the neighborhood. On his block, they played everything: baseball, basketball, football, stickball, etc. Usually the teams would play for 10 cents a man. Herb was a gifted student; this allowed him to skip a grade in school.[67]

On weekends Herb and his best friend worked together as theater ushers for twenty-five cents an hour. During holidays, they worked at Macy's; Herb folded ties. They were fired and blacklisted from Macy's when they were caught sleeping on the job. During the 1939 World's Fair in New York, Herb worked "pushing cars," in which he pushed tourists in carriages similar to rickshaws.[68]

During his senior year in high school, a local congressman held an open exam for appointments to the Naval Academy. Herb was one of two hundred or so seniors from the area who took the exam. He placed second in the testing and was granted one of the congressman's appointments. Unfortunately, when he went for his physical exam he was found to have an overbite; this was grounds for disqualification. Although he could not prove it, Herb suspected the denial might have been because he was Jewish. He did not dwell on the disappointment. After he graduated from Newtown High School in 1940, Herb began classes at New York University.[69]

On December 7, 1941, Herb attended a football game with some of his friends. During the game several names were called out over the loudspeaker. They were asked to report to various places. "Col. Donovan, please report to so and so." At the time, nobody thought anything of it. When Herb and his friends left the game, the myriad papers all had special editions with the headline, "Japs Bomb Pearl Harbor." That night, Herb and his friends ended up at the El Dorado bar, where they drank and discussed war. His friends were eager to enlist as aviation cadets; Herb was not. Herb did not think that they had any intention of following through with the talk. They were drunk and caught up in the moment. But, they all made a pact to enlist. Herb was surprised when they beat on his door the next morning at 7:30 a.m. Herb followed his friends' zealous lead and went to 44 Whitehall Street on Monday, December 8, 1941, to enlist in the Army Air Corps. College would have to wait. There was a lack of training facilities, and the overwhelming number of enlistments precluded a place for them in the Air Corps at that time. Therefore, they were placed on furlough to wait for a space to open up. On March 23, 1942, Herb was called up and told to report to Maxwell Field in Montgomery, Alabama, for pre-flight training. By this time he really did want to fly.[70]

Robert Bryant Stricklin, Bombardier: Dallas, Texas

The oldest member of the crew, whose steady hands delivered the bombs over the target, was Robert Bryant Stricklin. He was born on June 4, 1916, in Amarillo, Texas, the youngest son of William Edward Stricklin and Irene Wilson. Prior to Robert's birth the family was living in nearby Swisher County, also in the panhandle. "R.B.," as friends and family called him, was named for his mother's father. He was not actually named at the time his birth certificate was completed—that would come later.[71] His father, called Ed by all who knew him, was born in Illinois. A subsequent move to the Brownwood, Texas, area introduced him to his future wife, Irene Wilson. Ed was a butcher by trade; he worked in a local meat market. In more ways than one Brownwood was Irene's hometown. Her grandfather, Greenleaf Fisk, who fought in the Battle of San Jacinto, founded Brownwood. R.B. was the second youngest of the couple's six children. He had two older brothers, Wilson Edward (called Strick) and Charles Fisk. R.B. had two older sisters, Bessie Merle (called Merle) and Mattie Bell (called Sweetie). His younger sister, the baby of the family, was Irene Gertrude (called Little Irene). Since R.B. and Little Irene were the youngest, while growing up they were very close.[72]

By 1920 the family had moved to Dallas, where Ed was able to find a better job, still as a butcher. Ed was tall, thin and affectionate with the children. Irene, a homemaker, was the ideal mother, warm, loving, jovial and patient. The house was always "full of activity," sister Irene recalled. At the center of their lives was the Baptist church; the family attended Sunday school as well as the noon and evening services. The children never really knew Ed's parents; they lived in Illinois and were dead by time Irene was born in 1922. However, they did spend time each summer with their mother's parents in Brownwood.[73]

The Depression had a great effect on the family, as it forced them to become quite transient in the late 1920s and early 1930s. Dallas city directories for the period list several different addresses for them, including 2717 Pennsylvania Avenue, 3122 Peabody, and 2725 Peabody Avenue. Ed was working in "Piggly Wiggly Store No. 41," first as a marker manager, then later as a meat cutter; Irene is listed as a homemaker. Despite all of the moving around, the Stricklins fared better than some during the Depression.[74]

Throughout childhood, R.B. was a typical boy; he played ball and rode his bicycle. With his piercing hazel eyes, brown hair, and tall, thin frame, he resembled his brother Charles. He walked to nearby John Henry Brown Elementary School. Maintaining the yard was principal among his many chores; he also had a paper route. His childhood hero was his brother Wilson—"Strick." He enjoyed reading about adventure. He especially liked Mark Twain—*The Adventures of Tom Sawyer* in particular. R.B.'s sister Irene remembers that he was a typical big brother, "always into something. [He] loved to tease and torment me." He was very loving, but he also had a very "quick temper."[75]

Sometime in the mid–1930s, Ed and Irene began to grow apart; they subsequently divorced. The true details are not known, but the times were tough all around and apparently that had some effect on the marriage. The four oldest children were married and living on their own by this time. R.B. and Little Irene stayed with their mother. She moved the family yet again, this time to 3519 Oakland Avenue. In 1936

R.B. graduated from Forest Avenue High School. Afterwards he began working in the grocery store that his brother "Strick" had opened just down the street from their home, Stricklin's Food Store at 3638 Oakland Avenue. To make ends meet, Irene took in sewing and did some baking. The older kids also helped out with money when they could. Irene was strong, from good Fisk stock, and was able to hold the family together during these trying times.[76]

His parents' problems may have had some untold effects on R.B. He never really dated much; there was no steady girlfriend. Work and family always came first. He worked with his brother until February 1942, when he was drafted into the Army. At nearly twenty-six years old, he was the exception rather than the rule when he entered the service at Camp Wolters in Mineral Wells, Texas.[77]

Vincent Henry Olney, Replacement Pilot: Stamford, Nebraska

One of the replacement pilots who flew a few missions with the original crew was Vincent Henry Olney. He was born on September 18, 1920, at home on a farm about three miles south of Hollinger, Nebraska, the first child of Henry Weed Olney and Sophia Marie Petitjean. Henry, born in Colorado, was of German descent; Sophie, born in nearby Stamford, Nebraska, had French ancestry. Henry was a World War I veteran who had been discharged in February 1919. Shortly afterwards he met Sophia Petitjean at a neighborhood barn dance; she had attended the dance with her brother Charles. Henry and Sophia hit it off immediately and their whirlwind romance culminated in a wedding that same year in November. The couple quickly set up house and began a family. In addition to Vince, the couple had two other children; another son, Leonard, later called "Curly," was born in June 1922, and a daughter, Cornelia Susan, was born in 1933. The family lived about eight miles southwest of Stamford. As were most people in rural Furnas County, Vince's father was a farmer.[78]

Vince most resembled his mother's youngest brother, George Petitjean, in appearance and personality. He also shared physical similarities with his grandfathers, who were both short and stocky. Within the family, Vince was his dad's favorite; they were always close and Henry depended on him a great deal. He was a good big brother, Susan affectionately recalls, "I can remember him combing and brushing my hair." A glimpse into Vince's loyalty and sense of right and wrong is best observed in a story told by a very good family friend, Dr. Bently: "If I said black was white, Vince would swear to it. But he would sure let me know about it when we were alone." Leonard (Curly) was his mom's favorite, and everybody loved Cornelia Sue (later called Susan). Because of her difference in age, many people did not know that Vince and Leonard had a sister—it became quite a family joke.[79]

Vince and his family lived in a very active and friendly community, where everyone knew each other and had everything in common. They would often have dinners and dances at each other's homes. Vince's father, Henry, entertained guests with his violin. Both sets of grandparents lived near enough to be very involved in Vince's formative years. He spent a lot of time with them. Religion also played a central role in the Olneys' lives. The family regularly attended mass at the Holy Family Catholic Church in Stamford, where Vince was baptized as an infant. His mother's family was Catholic; his father was a convert. However, Henry still had a sense of obligation to his boyhood church, Bethel Evangelical Church. Susan was told a story about her father after he passed away. On the way to mass during the 1920s, Henry would stop by Bethel to start the fire in the fireplace so that the church would be warm when the congregation arrived—Henry was also a dutiful son.[80]

Vince's father was very strict with the children, but they respected him. When Vince was a child his father got a pony for the boys to ride to school, which was about a mile away. The pony was very ornery and bucked them off each day, about a quarter mile from the house. Henry advised them that if they fell off they were not supposed to cry; if they did "the pony would disappear." The warning obviously toughened up Vince and Leonard, because the pony stayed—much to their dismay some days.[81]

Susan recounted that the family had a "dry land farm, with no electricity." They did have running water in the house—"it was pumped up to a storage tank in the house by windmill power." Initially all of the plowing and harvesting was done with horses and mules. In addition to a few hogs, the family raised chickens and had several milk cows; they sold the extra eggs and cream to supplement the family income. Every summer the Olneys had a large garden which filled their cellar with canned items for the winter months. Henry had worked in a butcher shop when he was in high school and was able to butcher all of the family's meat, Susan said, and he also did "a lot of butchering for the neighbors." Nothing was wasted. The family cleaned the intestines and used them to make sausage. Sophia took the "head and other bones, boiled them until the meat could [be easily] cleaned off the bone. The meat was cooked with apples, raisins and various seasonings [and] put into jars as mincemeat for pies. The fat of [the] hogs was rendered to make lard," which in turn was boiled with cracklings and lye to make laundry soap.[82]

The Olneys' chief crop was wheat, and its harvest began each year in late June or early July. Starting at a very young age, Vince helped his father with the "binding and threshing"—in the days "before the monster combines," Susan explained. "The binder was a machine pulled by a team of horses or a tractor. The wheat was cut, fell on a canvas conveyer belt, then was rolled up and [manually] tied in a bundle with twine. The bundles were then set upright in groups of five or six [and were] called shocks of wheat. Then came the threshing crew. All of the neighbors worked together." Teams in the field put the bundles on hayracks. From there, others threw the bundles into the threshing machine "to complete the harvest job." Trucks then took the wheat to a grain elevator in Stamford.[83]

During the harvesting, "the ladies would prepare the noon meal for the crew; [it] usually consisted of fried chicken, fresh ear corn, green beans, potatoes and gravy [and] was finished off with pie or cake for dessert." The heat in July could be unbearable, so a number of water containers were placed in the fields. Around 4 P.M. the ladies would usually take some iced tea out to the fields. Each day, one of the last trucks returning from the elevator would bring a case of cold beer back, so that everyone could have some before they went home for the evening. In the fall and winter the corn was picked and shucked by hand before it was placed in the corn-crib. Susan recalled, "In January or February the corn sheller would come in with a truck or two, shell the corn off of the cob, and haul it to market. Vince would sometimes stay home from school to help with the corn picking."[84]

Things went well for the Olneys throughout most of the 1920s. Unfortunately, in the late '20s Vince's father, Henry, developed some health problems. He initially had trouble with his lungs as a result of exposure to nerve gas in France during World War I. He was later diagnosed with "shell shock"—known today as post-traumatic stress syndrome. Henry got progressively worse and in 1932 he was put in the veteran's hospital in Lincoln, Nebraska, for nearly a year. There he was diagnosed as having a nervous breakdown. The stress of the Depression did not help matters. Nor did the drought, which hit about the same time. The family was not even able to raise enough grain and hay to feed the cows, which had to be "sold at distress prices." Susan recalls one day when she was about four years old, "The wind had been blowing all day and the air was full of dust. We came home to find the floor and all the furniture covered with a heavy coat of dust. I remember my mother standing in the dining room just sobbing. Life was not easy for anyone on farms in the Great Plains."[85]

Henry had always leaned heavily on Vince and depended on his help on the farm. After his illness and other troubles, this was even more the case. In addition to helping with the crops, Vince's daily chores included milking the cows and feeding the hogs. "After the cows were milked, the milk was run through a separator. The cream ran into the cream can. The skim milk was fed to any baby calves [and whatever] was left was fed to the hogs over ground grain," Susan said. Because he was the oldest, Vince also often had to look after his brother and sister.[86]

For grade school, Vince and his siblings attended a one-room county school about a mile from their farmhouse. Although he was very smart (skipping a grade and graduating at 16), Vince was the class clown. He always had a great sense of humor. He could also take a joke, as evidenced in a favorite family story. Vince, like all his friends, loved to hunt. After school and after he had finished his work he would grab his shotgun and a few shells and go hunting—most often for pheasant or rabbit to provide some meat for the family. One night he and his friends went coon hunting with some of the older men. Vince was with the dogs when they picked up a scent and began to follow it. The oldest coonhound quickly returned to his owner; the younger hounds had treed a billy goat. The incident became a legend in the area, but Vince took all the teasing in stride. Duties on the farm limited his extracurricular activities at school, but he was still very popular. He began driving the family car to school at age twelve—before he could do so legally—because the family could not afford the gas the extra round trip would require. Vince graduated in a class of twenty-two from Stamford High School in May 1937. Their class motto, from Julius Caesar, was "Veni, vidi, vici" (I came, I saw, I conquered). Vince would later take the motto to heart to follow a dream.[87]

After graduation, Vince went to work for his "Uncle George Petitjean, as a traveling magazine salesman." They traveled extensively throughout the Great Plains and Midwest in a "wood-sided station wagon." In 1939, his aunt and uncle decided to move to California, so Vince returned home to the farm. That summer, Henry bought a Huron threshing machine and an International Harvester tractor. Vince, Leonard and Henry did wheat threshing in the community in the summers of 1939, 1940, and 1941. Vince stayed at home the rest of the year to help his father and brother farm—Vince always felt an obligation to family. The bombing of Pearl Harbor had a tremendous impact on Vince, who was still living at home. He was so moved with patriotism that he left three weeks later for Omaha (Sunday afternoon, December 28) to enlist. He requested the Army Air Corps when he volunteered on December 29, 1941. Secretly, Vince had always wanted to fly—he just thought he would never get the opportunity to do so.[88]

Vincent Olney, Stamford High School photograph. (Marilyn Siebels)

Floyd Irvin Robinson, Replacement Pilot: Indianapolis, Indiana

Another replacement pilot who flew with the several missions with the crew was Floyd Irvin Robinson. He was born on February 13, 1918, at home in Indianapolis, Indiana, to Alva Mason Robinson and Bethel Mae Cobb. Floyd's parents and grandparents were from Kentucky, but Alva moved to Indianapolis to seek better employment opportunities. Floyd's father was a cake salesman for Ward's Fine Cakes, whose bakery was headquartered in Chicago. His mother, Bethel Mae, was a housewife and looked after Floyd and his two siblings, Earl and Anne.[89]

Floyd grew up in a "friendly Hoosier neighborhood" at 614 Oakland Avenue in Indianapolis, near the park areas of Brookside and Riverside. He walked to nearby Riverside Elementary for the first eight years of school. His family regularly attended

Centenary Christian Church. Growing up, Floyd had the usual neighborhood friends. In the summer, they played baseball and golf, and went swimming. It the winter they sledded and played basketball in the church league. They also played in the nearby parks.[90]

Floyd initially attended high school at Short Ridge; he then transferred to Arsenal Technical School for his junior and senior years. Upon graduation in 1936, he wanted to attend college; however, his family could not afford to send him. He had dreams of attending the United States Military Academy at West Point (USMA), but that too seemed out of reach. Not giving up, Floyd learned of an incentive program that the U.S. Army offered to one-year recruits at nearby Fort Benjamin Harrison, Indiana. In it the recruits were allowed to attend the West Point Preparatory School (WPPS). "At that time the U.S. Army was allotted 60 cadet appointments per year to the Academy," he recalled, of which roughly 15 became vacant each June. Recruits at the WPPS scoring high enough were awarded an appointment to the USMA.[91]

Floyd really wanted to attend so he enlisted in the 11th Infantry Regiment of the Indiana National Guard at Fort Benjamin Harrison and attended the WPPS there. Unfortunately, he did not score high enough to receive one of the vacant appointments. Still determined, he decided to re-enlist for three years and attend the WPPS for a second time. Meanwhile, he began "networking his Indiana congressman in Washington, D.C." Floyd recalls, "Fortunately, U.S. Representative Larrabee from my Marion County congressional district awarded me a 2nd alternate spot." His luck continued. When the first alternate failed a math exam, Floyd received his hard earned appointment to West Point; he entered on July 1, 1938. Four years later, in 1942, Floyd graduated from the Academy as a second lieutenant and was assigned to the Army Air Corps for pilot training.[92]

2

Training

The young men who comprised the ranks of the AAF in World War II were quite remarkable. They were an entirely volunteer force. All of these young trainees were children of the Depression. Most had rarely, if ever, been far from home. They did not go on vacations to far away places. Their biggest excursions probably took them no more than a few hours from home. And those were more than likely to visit relatives. The training that they were about to undergo would be the first great adventure for most of these boys. They would soon be participating in events that, up until this point, they had only seen in Movietone reels with their friends and sweethearts at the local theater. Their worlds were about to expand beyond that of their farms and neighborhoods.

Instinct. That is what the Army Air Force was trying to develop in their soldiers during training. Every man in the AAF had to learn to be a soldier, so after induction a five-week "basic training" was required. This training paralleled that of their infantry counterparts. The regimen consisted, according to an Army Air Force guide, of "73 hours of drills and marches; 15 hours of physical training; 54 hours of marksmanship; 13 hours of military procedure; 8 hours of first aid; 12 hours of sanitation; 3 hours of personal adjustment; 5 hours of care of clothing and equipment; 5 hours of defense of chemical attack; 5 hours of individual security and camouflage; 4 hours of map and photo-interpretation; and 4 hours of defense against air attack."[1] After this initial instruction, the AAF soldier began more specialized training in one of two major categories: flying training or technical, administrative and service training.[2] The average AAF soldier would spend nearly a year in training before he saw combat action.

Maurice Gilliam was greeted with no fanfare on February 19, 1943, when he entered the service of his country. He did so in the company of strangers when he boarded a bus in Charlotte, North Carolina—two hours from his home. He was a little uneasy to leave his friends and family, but he knew that he was duty bound to undertake this trip. The bus took him to his induction point, at Camp Croft, Fort Jackson, South Carolina. After a week or so of processing in South Carolina, Maurice was sent to Keesler Field in Biloxi, Mississippi, for basic training. Basic training was pretty much the same for all Army and AAF inductees during World War II. It was an intensive five-week indoctrination to military life. Maurice's first week at Keesler was spent on KP (kitchen police), where he learned the fine art of washing dishes. He recalls, "I began with the breakfast meal and ended after the evening meal. Once it was after midnight before I got back to the barracks." The remainder of his time in Biloxi was spent actually training. He learned military discipline, marching and drilling—seemingly all day long. Physical training, the rifle range, physical exams, shots, and paperwork filled the rest of his days there. It was at Keesler that Maurice felt his first calling to the ministry.[3]

In late March 1943, Maurice boarded a troop train for Buckley Field in Denver, Colorado. After the processing of more paperwork and testing, he was sent to Lowry Field, also in Denver. At Lowry, he was trained in turret maintenance. While in Denver, Maurice mailed home a ring to his girlfriend, Stella McKinney. As did many other servicemen during World War II, he proposed through the mail. Stella accepted and anxiously waited for his safe return. Maurice remained at Lowry until July, when he was sent to gunnery school at Tyndall Field in Panama City, Florida.[4]

An assignment in Florida meant yet another cross-country train trip for Maurice. The hours spent in the Pullman cars could have been drudgery, but he was getting to see the country. On the ride he could relax a little, and think about Stella and when he would see her again. It was still great adventure for a farm boy from North Carolina. However, a six-week school in Florida during July and August was far from fun. It was hot. Maurice recalled that the "intense heat and humidity made it feel like a steam kitchen. By 0900 one's fatigues would be drenched in perspiration."[5]

Tyndall was located a few miles east of Panama City on a peninsula that jutted out into the Gulf of Mexico. Activated in June 1941, it comprised approximately 27,000 acres and was one of the largest gunnery schools in the world. The base had an ingenious design that was ideally suited to the training of aerial gunners. The rules at Tyndall were stricter than at the other bases to which Maurice had been assigned. It was "a no nonsense military command designed for the survival of the fittest." In addition to rigorous physical training, Maurice and his classmates had classroom and field training. Classes consisted of learning everything from the dynamics of bullets to the identification of all types of aircraft. The latter required the student to recognize, identify and name (friend or foe and type) the aircraft after it was flashed on a screen for only a fraction of a second. They also learned how to assemble and disassemble their .50-caliber machine guns. They became so practiced in this maneuver that they could (and were required to) do it blindfolded.[6]

The field training taught the student how to shoot. They began by shooting .22-caliber rifles at moving targets. They then shot at skeet with a 12-gauge shotgun from the back of a jeep traveling at 25 to 35 miles per hour. This was great fun for Maurice, who had grown up hunting on the farm. Once they were proficient at that, the shotgun was mounted on a turret in the back of a truck. These jeeps and trucks drove along a path around the perimeter of the base—a part of the base's ingenious design. Next in progression was learning to fire the .50-caliber machine gun. Once they were adept with the machine gun on the ground, they fired the gun from a plane. This time their target was a banner, which was pulled by a target plane. Each student's bullets were color coded so that the instructors knew who hit the target. In the final phase of gunnery training at Tyndall, the students, in the back seat of a North American AT-6 (Army Trainer), performed strafing exercises in the Gulf of Mexico. Throughout the six weeks, the students hoped to pass and earn their silver wings. Maurice did so in early September 1943.[7]

From Tyndall, Maurice was sent back across the country to Salt Lake City, Utah, for reassignment. Salt Lake served merely as another processing point in the seemingly endless line of training and bureaucracy of the Army. Shortly after arriving there he was granted his first furlough, a ten-day leave. Reidsville was a three-day train ride from Salt Lake so Maurice wasted no time in heading home to see Stella. Once back home, he and Stella drove down to York, South Carolina. There, on October 10, they were "married on the spot." There was no waiting period in South Carolina, as there was in North Carolina. The four days at home passed quickly for Maurice and Stella. All too soon he had to leave his new bride and make the three-day journey back to Salt Lake City. In early November, Maurice received orders to report to Clovis, New Mexico. He was being assigned to a replacement combat crew.[8]

Grant Caywood began his AAF training in primary flying school at Rankin Aeronautical Academy in Tulare, California. At the time he started, potential pilots were sent directly to primary; later in the war, they were screened in a pre-flight school. Primary flying school also lasted 10 weeks. Each class had about 600 students. The curriculum consisted of 70 hours flying in 125 to 225 horsepower "open cockpit biplanes

Stella and Maurice Gilliam, wedding photograph, October 1943. (Maurice H. Gilliam)

Firing a .50-caliber machine mounted on these swivels was the first stage of machine gun training. Once proficient here, the student then advanced to fire a gun on the back of a moving jeep. (Neil H. Raiford)

(PT-13/17 or PT-21/22) or low-wing monoplanes (PT-19/23/26); 94 hours of academic work in ground school; and 54 hours of (general) military training."[9] "Each cadet was to make at least 175 landings" in their 70 hours of flying.[10] The 94 hours of ground school were divided into five major topics. "Aircraft and equipment" gave the cadet an understanding of the aircraft and how it worked. "Navigation" prepared them for cross-country flights. "Aircraft recognition" allowed the pilot to determine whether approaching aircraft was a friend or foe. "Principles of flight" and "radio communication" completed the study in ground school.[11]

The potential pilots who "washed out" of pilot training could attempt to become navigators or bombardiers, whose pre-flight training mirrored that of pilots. A student could wash out for a variety of reasons, but the ability to solo on schedule was the most often cited one. At times the wash out rate for pilots was over fifty percent. This should have come as no surprise. Most flying cadets had never driven a car, much less flown a plane, and they were expected to fly solo after just six hours of instruction.[12]

Grant and his fellow classmates—all college graduates—were in Tex Rankin's first contract primary flying school class. The school's commandant, Captain Daly, was a West Point man. Grant told them nothing about his flying experience or his prior relationship with Tex. However, they knew about his military training and he was soon made "cadet captain"—the number one student slot. This meant it would be Grant's responsibility to "get the unit in shape and drill the cadets in the basics."[13]

2. Training

In the second phase of machine gun training, .50-caliber machine guns are mounted on turrets in the back of jeeps. Gunners had to become proficient at hitting a moving target while they themselves were moving. This was part of the ingenious training developed by the Army Air Corps. (Neil H. Raiford)

They soon learned of his flying ability. The training planes at Rankin "were PT-17 Stearman, open cockpit, biplanes with Lycoming R670 (220 horsepower) engines." Grant recalls, "I knew and had even taught all the maneuvers. I don't think I fooled anyone about my previous flying, but it was easy to become the number one pilot." He graduated from Rankin in Class 41-H.[14]

Next Grant was sent to Moffett Field in Sunnyvale, California for basic flying school. It was yet another 10-week course for the aviation cadet. According to the AAF guide, it consisted of "70 hours in a 450 horsepower trainer; 94 hours in ground school; [and] 47 hours in military training." By the end of basic flying school training, instructors classified students "for single-engine training (fighter pilot) or 2-engine training (bomber, transport or 2-engine fighter pilot)."[15]

Prior to the war Moffett had been a permanent Navy base, and was converted to accommodate AAF pilot training. It was typical of bases all over the country which were being constructed or modified to accommodate the ever-growing need for training space. In addition to "some very advanced NACA wind tunnels," the base boasted the largest dirigible hangar in the world. The basic training planes were "Vultee BT-13s with 450 horsepower Pratt and Whitney R985 engines." The cadets nicknamed the planes the "Vultee Vibrators." Grant explained that the training "was mostly to become accustomed to a larger airplane. We did the same maneuvers we had learned in primary and began instrument flying, night flying and formation."[16]

After graduating from Moffett, Grant was off to Mather Field in Sacramento, California, for advanced flying school. Advanced school, like the previous pilot training, was a 10-week course (for both those classified as single-engine or 2-engine). It consisted of "70 hours of flying; 60 hours of ground school; [and] 19 hours of military training." Those classified for single-engine instruction flew AT-6s and took a gunnery course. Those designated for two-engine training flew AT-9/10/17 or 24s. At the end of advanced, the graduating students received their silver pilot's wings and were either appointed flight officers or commissioned 2nd lieutenants.[17]

Unlike most AAF trainees, Grant remained in one state for all of his pilot training. When he arrived at Mather, the field was still in the midst of some major renovations. It was being converted from a World War I base to an advanced pilot training school. His was only the second cadet class at Mather. Grant remembers, "It was hot and dusty." This time around the planes were the North American AT-6s, with 550 horsepower Pratt and Whitney R1350 engines. The "flying was about the same [as in basic flying school], but more intense."[18]

Grant had made a decision not to get romantically involved at this time. He reasoned, "I may or may not get home when this thing is over; so I was afraid to tie up with any female." However, an unexpected order from Mather's commandant changed his resolution—and his life. The men were ordered to report in their Class A uniforms and board a bus. "We asked him, 'What's up?' 'You'll find out,' he replied." Grant writes of the event, "The Junior League was giving us a tea dance at the Senator Hotel. We said, 'What the hell is a tea dance?'"

"You'll find out," the commandant replied.

Each cadet was given a card with a number on it. The commandant "then explained that the Junior League had rounded up a group of beautiful girls from Sacramento who would also have numbered cards." They were to match numbers and dance with that girl for the evening.[19]

"One charming young thing, tastefully dressed, not a hair out of place, peaches and cream complexion, came taxiing over to me," he fondly remembers. "My number was 7. Hers was 43. She turned her card over and wrote 7 on the back of it. 'Well, our numbers match. Shall we dance?'" she said. Her name was Jeanne Nicolaus, and from that moment forward Grant spent every free moment he had off base with her.[20]

By the fall of 1941 Grant had completed all of his pilot training and graduated with wings. "Now that I was an officer, Jeanne decided that it would be O.K. for me to marry her. My former thoughts of maybe not coming home from this mess had disappeared in a puff." By the time that Japan bombed Pearl Harbor on December 7, 1941, Grant had been "assigned as a tactical officer and flight instructor to the cadets at Mather." He also piloted flights for the navigation school there. As the war intensified the need for pilots increased. To help fill this need, a program was initiated whereby civilian pilots with at least 200 flight hours (in aircraft over 200 horsepower) could be considered for the AAF. Grant explained, "All they had to do was apply to the Civilian Pilot Examining Board at Mather, present their log books, take a physical examination, and a very cursory flight test." Grant was assigned to be the chief pilot of the board at Mather, with Jack West as the administrative officer. During this stint Grant met many Hollywood stars trying to become AAF pilots through the board. He writes, "I was ordered to accept them if at all possible. All I did was take them up and have them recover from a spin—a maneuver in which all you have to do is to let go of the controls, and the airplane recovers itself. The word got around. I remember Jimmy Stewart, Richard Arlen, Bob Stephenson (Bing Crosby's manager), Clark Gable, and a bunch of others." Stephenson repaid the base by arranging for Bing Crosby and Bob Hope to perform at Mather twice. "These Hollywood types really did a good job overall. They were used to hard work and tried very hard.... Clark Gable was sent to gunnery school ... and put in Public Relations. Richard Arlen did well. I accepted Jimmy Stewart [as a pilot] and later became his twin engine instructor."[21]

On April 11, 1942, "with half the population of Sacramento looking on," Grant Dodd Caywood married Jeanne Nicolaus. Grant wore his dress uniform and after the beautiful Episcopalian ceremony, the newlyweds "marched out under an arch of sabers." While at Mather, Grant and Jeanne had an addition to the family. She was a black cocker spaniel they named Shadow Lashes Caywood, because of her black coat and long eyelashes. Shadow loved to fly with Grant and he often took on her training missions. Shadow's first flight was on November 24, 1942, at Mather in an AT-7.[22]

Shadow was small for a cocker spaniel. Grant and Jeanne got her from a local breeder in Sacramento when she was about eight weeks old. Grant recalled that she was very loving and "housebroken the first day." She would not bite, but "she might lick you to death." As a puppy, he carried her in the pocket of his fanny duster coat. Like her eyelashes, her ears were also long; so long that they would drag in her water dish when she drank. Jeanne would sometimes clip Shadow's ears back behind her head with a clothespin so they would not get wet. She did not like baths, "but would submit." Shadow loved to lie on her back in Grant's lap and get her belly rubbed. She never had need of a leash. Grant remembered, "She would heel, sit, stay, bring the newspaper, slippers, etc. She was the easiest dog to train that I ever had. Shadow had an obvious smile when she was pleased." She loved to fly and when she heard an airplane fly overhead, she would run to the window stool to watch it. While flying with Grant she would sit attentively in the co-pilot seat, often with her front paws on the wheel.[23]

While piloting for the navigation school, Grant often had to fly from Mather to Salt Lake. "Those were the days of not very good radios and some equally not very good pilots. We cracked up airplanes like mad, either on the Sierra Nevada or the Wasatch Mountain ranges. So they set up a required checkpoint at Beowawe (Bay-oh-wah-way) in the middle of Nevada." Grant was curious what Beowawe meant. He soon discovered that it was Indian for "pretty girl." He started calling his wife Beowawe, *Beo* for short. "The name stuck."[24]

In late February 1943, the navigation school relocated from Mather to San Marcos, Texas. Grant, Beo and Shadow moved with the school; he was assigned as training executive. He arranged to go through navigation training, so he now had both pilot and navigator wings. On April 27, 1943, the Caywoods had another addition to the family—a fine son they named Grant Nicolaus Caywood. They called him George.[25]

The training of navigators at San Marcos was fairly routine work for Grant. A crew consisted of three navigation cadets, a navigation instructor, and a pilot—and sometimes a dog. The planes were Lockheed Hudsons, with two Pratt and Whitney 1200 horsepower engines. "The gasoline tanks were integral with the wings; so when the airplanes cracked up there were fireworks and a lot of black smoke. We called them the 'Burbank Bonfires,'" Grant remembers. One day he saw up close just how they got that nickname. He was the airdrome officer for the day, sitting in a jeep reading a comic book, when a Hudson came in and flipped on its back. Grant immediately rushed out to the scene in his jeep. He was the first there; there was no fire. "I opened the door, walked in on the overhead, and saw a Major [Strother] immobile and hanging by his safety belt. I undid his belt, and, naturally, he fell on me. I scrambled out with him as a dead weight on my back." He placed the major on the hood of the jeep. He then heard a sizzle. Instinctively, Grant immediately backed up the jeep. They reached a safe point just as the "Burbank Bonfire" exploded. Major Strother never forgot the incident—and he would later play a major role in Grant's life.[26]

He often flew 100 hours a month at San Marcos, which in addition to his administrative duties left him little time with Beo. However, Grant did get to see Shadow "at the office," as she often flew on the training missions with him. A hilarious inci-

Shadow, Grant Caywood's black cocker spaniel. (Grant D. Caywood)

dent occurred on one such mission. A navigation cadet got lost outside of San Marcos. "They were always lost," Grant remembers. So Grant put the plane on autopilot and placed Shadow in the pilot seat so he could get over to the right side to help the cadet. When the cadet saw Grant leaving the cockpit, he looked up to see what he thought to be Shadow flying the plane. The cadet grabbed his parachute and ran for the door to jump. They caught him just in time and sat him down. He was bewildered. He had washed out of pilot training and now he had washed out as a navigator. Shadow just looked at him and smiled, as the autopilot moved her front paws.[27]

In September 1943 the Caywoods moved again, this time to Fort Worth. There, Grant made the transition to four-engine planes. Transition flying training was the final stage in pilot training; it was where they learned to fly the planes they would take into combat. As with the other flight courses, it lasted 10 weeks. It consisted of 105 hours of flying and additional ground school.[28] In his transition training, Grant flew and instructed in B-24s and B-17s. Grant wondered when (and if) he would be assigned a combat crew. They remained in Fort Worth for only about two months before that question was answered. In November 1943 he was assigned to a B-24 crew at Clovis Air Base in Clovis, New Mexico.[29]

Maurice Erickson, the farm boy from Pennsylvania, nearly missed the train he was to board to begin his military service. He and his fiancée, Lillian, took a bus up from Pennsylvania to Buffalo, New York. Since he volunteered in Buffalo, where she was working, that is where he was inducted. "We were cooing and missed the bus stop at the train station," he recalled. After a last minute scramble and a quick goodbye, Maurice made the train. His destination was Maxwell Field in Montgomery, Alabama, where he began his pre-flight training. Maxwell was one of only four such classification and pre-flight centers in the country—the others were at Nashville, Tennessee, San Antonio, Texas, and Santa Ana, California. Pre-flight training was a 10-week school (as short as seven weeks during some stages of the war), which consisted of 30 hours of sea and air recognition; 48 hours of code; 24 hours of physics; 20 hours of math; 18 hours of maps and charts; in addition to "daily physical and military training." Potential pilots were tested and those whom the AAF deemed qualified were sent then to primary flying school.[30]

After being classified as pilot-worthy in pre-flight, Erickson was sent to Carlstrom Field in Arcadia, Florida, in June 1942 for primary flying school. Carlstrom was a contract flying school operated by the Embry-Riddle Company, which later became famous for its aeronautical university. Although taken at different locations, his pilot training mirrored that of Grant Caywood. For basic flying school he was sent back to Montgomery, Alabama, this time to Gunter Field. After successfully completing that 10-week course in late summer, he was off to George Field in Lawrenceville, Illinois, for advanced flying school for another 10 weeks. In early 1943, after Advanced, Maurice was assigned to Otis Field, eight miles northeast of Falmouth, Massachusetts, where he flew B-25s on anti-submarine patrol. Afterwards he graduated to the B-24; he trained and instructed at different bases while waiting for a permanent assignment to a bomb crew. Special Order Number 335, dated

December 1, 1943, from the 471st Combat Crew Training School in Pueblo, Colorado, placed him in Grant Caywood's newly formed crew.[31]

Because he already lived in a large city, Theodore Morris was inducted into service in his hometown of St. Louis, Missouri. There at Jefferson Barracks, on December 18, 1942, he began military life. At Jefferson Barracks, Ted shuffled through paperwork and shots. By January 4 he was in St. Petersburg, Florida, still being processed into the AAF. Shortly afterwards he was sent to Clearwater, Florida, for his five-weeks of basic training indoctrination.[32]

After basic, Ted was sent via train to Keesler Field in Biloxi, Mississippi. There he was enrolled in an aircraft mechanics course and worked on B-24s. His background with Curtis Wright made him a good fit in a mechanic's role. However, the AAF was desperately short of aerial gunners and Ted's military career took a turn that would have a tremendous impact on the rest of his life. In late July 1943 he was sent to Harlingen, Texas, for flexible gunnery school.[33]

Hot and dusty are the first words that come to mind when one tries to describe what summer is like in the Texas Rio Grande Valley. Ted sweated the entire time he was there. Everyone's clothes were soaked with perspiration by the end of breakfast. His training there was similar to that of the thousands of other gunnery students in the country at the time. Ted proudly earned his sliver gunner wings in late September 1943. Upon graduation he was sent to Salt Lake City, Utah, which was just a processing point for gunners prior to crew assignment. Shortly after his arrival, Ted, like countless other recent gunnery school graduates assembled in Salt Lake, was granted a ten-day furlough. The leave passed quickly and by early November he was in Clovis, New Mexico, ready to meet his newly formed crew.[34]

In early 1943, eighteen-year-old auto factory worker Stan Butynski entered military service when he boarded a Greyhound bus in Detroit, Michigan. As with Maurice Gilliam, no family or friends were there to see him off on his journey. The bus took him to Fort Sheridan in Highwood, Illinois—north of Chicago. Fort Sheridan was one of several recruit reception centers that received masses of new soldiers; later it also served as a prisoner of war camp. Due to the volume of new soldiers processed, Stan's induction point had been nicknamed "Boomtown." From Sheridan, he was promptly sent to Biloxi, Mississippi, for five weeks of basic training. After basic, Stan was sent to Willow Run, Michigan. Located just northwest of Ypsilanti (which in turn was just southeast of Ann Arbor), it was less than forty miles from his home. Willow Run was best known during this time for Henry Ford's enormous factory, which produced many B-24s for the AAF.[35]

While stationed at Willow Run, he could sometimes go home on the weekends. One weekend, instead of going home, he attended a U.S.O. dance in Ypsilanti. At this dance in May 1943, Stan met Marge O'Key. He "never went home again." Stan had found the love of his life. He soon proposed to Marge and she immediately accepted. All too soon, he was sent to Wendover, Utah, for six weeks in flexible gunnery school. After gunnery school, Stan went through a series of other short training and processing assignments. By November 1943 he was in Clovis, New Mexico, assigned to a replacement bomber crew.[36]

2. Training 45

The main gate at Harlingen Army Air Field, Texas. (Neil H. Raiford)

The newlywed Manuel Esquivel entered the service on October 8, 1942. He was inducted into the Army at Fort Beauregard in Alexandria, Louisiana. After a brief processing period, he was sent to Keesler Field in Biloxi for basic training. Manuel injured his back and "spent most of his training in the base hospital," his wife Rita recalled years later. "I often kidded him by saying that he should have received the Purple Heart for being injured [during] basic training. He didn't think that was very funny."[37]

From Keesler, Manuel was sent to Fresno, California. Always a quick study, he learned how to play blackjack on the train. By the time he reached California he had won enough money to send Rita train fare to join him. In Fresno he was given a battery of tests, on which "he broke all records." Despite his lack of formal education, Manuel had an "innate ability to learn." It was decided that he would be best utilized in the Army Air Force. Rita soon joined him in Fresno, taking the five-day train ride from New Orleans. They were able to get an apartment near the base. Rita describes their small abode as consisting of "a living room with a Murphy bed [in the wall to pull down], and a kitchen. The bathroom was across the hall with no hot water." Rita got a job with a local finance company making $25 a week, which along with Manuel's income was enough to pay the rent. Luckily, Manuel was able to come home every night to the apartment. Although it was small, it was home and they could be together. It was there that they spent their first Christmas together.[38]

Truax Field in Madison, Wisconsin, was the next stop for Manuel. The aptitude tests at Fresno indicated that he should be a radio operator. At Truax he learned Morse code and radio operation. Once again, Rita followed him. This time, she recalled, "The only place that I could find to live [in Madison] was one bedroom in a private home," with a bathroom across the hall. However, space was not the issue. Unlike in Fresno, Manuel was confined to base, except for a once a week pass. Rita described for her sons how their resourceful dad tried to get around this issue. "One day Dad got a pass from another soldier who was not using it because he said he needed some sleep. He used Dad's cot so anyone who saw the bed with someone in it would think it was Dad. During the day, a medic came to awaken Dad because he needed a certain injection. The other soldier had already had his injection, so he had to explain the circumstances. Needless to say, Dad had a welcoming party for him that night when he returned to the base." Despite the cold weather of winter, Madison was a beautiful town. Rita enjoyed window-shopping or seeing a movie with Manuel on his day off, but the rest of the week was miserable for her. She was happy when his three months of training was over in Madison.[39]

Because most radio operators on heavy bombers served dual roles, radio operator and gunner, Manuel was next sent to gunnery school. Because she did not get to see him much in Madison, Rita decided not to accompany him to Buckingham Field in Fort Myers, Florida, for this training. His training followed that of Maurice Gilliam and the tens of thousands of other gunners. Manuel shot skeet from the back of a truck, learned how to identify enemy aircraft and learned to shoot a machine gun from an airplane.[40]

In late September 1943, after earning his silver gunner wings, Manuel was sent to Salt Lake City, Utah. Rita joined him there shortly after his arrival. This was yet

Roosevelt Field, New York. Located in Mineola on Long Island, Roosevelt Field was home to one of the Army Air Force's technical training centers, which trained airplane mechanics. (Richard M. Jacobson)

2. Training   47

Richard Jacobson holds his saxophone at Rome Air Depot, New York. While there he formed a band and helped arrange a show for the men of the base. (Richard M. Jacobson)

another period of processing for him. Like Maurice Gilliam, Manuel was issued a ten-day furlough. He and Rita took advantage of the time by taking a train back to New Orleans to see friends and family. Shortly after his return he was sent to Clovis, New Mexico, to meet his assigned combat crew.[41]

The Rome Air Depot in upstate New York was the induction place for Dick Jacobson on November 4, 1942.[42] It was just a staging area for him, but he remained there a month or two. Dick remembers that it "was as cold as all get out … I mean 20 below zero." One of his duties was "to tend the coal furnace for the barracks during the night shift" from 6 p.m. to 6 a.m. He finally got out of the assignment by forming a band and helping to arrange a show for the base. The "Madman's Minstrel Menagerie" went off without a hitch for two nights in late December.[43]

By early 1943, Dick's flurry of training began. He was sent to Atlantic City, New Jersey, for basic training. He excelled in the training and was placed in charge of his barracks, leading the men in formation and other various duties. After basic he was sent to La Guardia Field, Long Island, New York, to learn general aviation at the Academy of Aeronautics. "The work was almost all classroom stuff, learning weather and cloud formations, as well as technical info about the lift of aircraft," he remembered. Once he completed that training he was sent to Roosevelt Field, Mineola, New York (also on Long Island), to the AAF Technical Training Center. There, on June 19, 1943, he received a diploma for successfully completing a course in airplane mechanics. Then he was sent to the Casey Jones School of Aeronautics in New Jersey, where he learned everything from "climbing obstacle courses to reading instruments and weather maps." This myriad training was confusing for Dick, who was unsure what his role would be in the AAF.[44]

That question was answered with his next assignment, which was Tyndall Field in Panama City, Florida. Dick was going to be a gunner. Like Maurice Gilliam, Dick attended the AAF Flexible Gunnery School at Tyndall. Dick was there at the same time as Clark Gable but did not get to see much of him. His training experience mirrored that of Gilliam's. He remembers "standing in a metal ring in the back of a Jeep and trying to hit a flying skeet that would come flying out of a tree or a clump of bushes all the while trying not to get thrown out of this Jeep as it sped around the course." Tyndall was the first palce that Dick had ever flown in an airplane. It was an open-cockpit AT-6 and it was quite a thrill for him. Dick recounted his most enduring memory of the training: "My right shoulder was black and blue for weeks from all the practice on the skeet range with a shotgun that bucked like a damn mule." By October 1943, Dick had completed his gunnery and other training and was awaiting assignment to a bomb crew. Those orders came in early November when he was told to report to Clovis, New Mexico, to join his new crew.[45]

Norman Woodward entered service on October 19, 1942, nine days after his twentieth birthday. After basic training, he followed the same training path as *Shadow*'s other gunners. By early November 1943 he was in Clovis, New Mexico, waiting to meet his new crew.[46]

In late March 1942, Herb Gouldon boarded a troop train in New York. From there, he made the journey to Maxwell Field in Montgomery, Alabama, to attend pre-flight training. Herb's Boy Scout training came in handy in pre-flight, and he easily completed the 10-week course in August 1942. He was then sent to Taylor Field in Ocala, Florida, for primary flying school. In his eighth of ten weeks there, Herb was making a routine landing in some gusty winds. By mistake he hit the brake and did a ground loop. It was grounds for dismissal; Herb had washed out of pilot training. On his Army records the incident is listed as a "flying deficiency." Unfortunately, the Army Air Corps did not have time to nurture potentially good pilots, and Gouldon was certainly that. Those with previous flight experience or an innate ability were usually those who made the cut. But Herb had shown great officer potential, and he was offered the opportunity to become a navigator.[47]

In late 1942, Gouldon was sent to Selman Field, two miles northwest of Monroe, Louisiana, for pre-flight navigation. Navigators and bombardiers attended the same pre-flight school. The 10-week curriculum consisted of "48 hours of code; 28 hours of mathematics; 24 hours of maps and charts; 30 hours of aircraft recognition; 12 hours of naval recognition; 12 hours of [the] principles of flight; 20 hours of aero-physics; [and] 9 hours of altitude equipment." Herb was elected group commander for his class. He excelled in the classes and successfully completed the course in March 1943.[48]

Each member of a bomber crew needed to be an expert gunner. For this reason, after pre-flight, navigators and bombardiers were sent to six weeks in gunnery school—the same training as their enlisted counterparts. Navigators were then sent to a 20-week navigator school. Gouldon was sent to the Pan American contract school in Coral Gables, Florida, located on the campus of Miami University, for his advanced training. There he lived in one of the university's dormitories. As did all future navigators, he spent "104 hours in the air on practical navigation problems and 782 hours in ground school. The latter included: pilotage, 8 hours; instruments, 83 hours; dead reckoning, 54 hours; radio, 8 hours; celestial navigation, 53 hours; meteorology, 47 hours; code and recognition, 9 hours each." The Pan American school was filled with instructors who were ex–merchant seamen and excellent celestial navigators. Therefore, students learned naval expressions and terminology at Coral Gables. The students there had an advantage over their counterparts trained in Texas; they flew most of their training over water. This would come in handy for Gouldon several months later when he navigated *Shadow's* crew across the Atlantic to Dakar, Africa. Herb vividly remembers one incident during his advanced training. To take some celestial navigation readings, the students were forced to stand on their tables, stick their heads out of the plane, hold their octants, and take observations. On one mission, while Gouldon had his head out of the top of the airplane, it took a dip. A fellow student grabbed his legs and saved his life. Graduates of this intense training were awarded silver navigator's wings, appointed flight officers or commissioned 2nd lieutenants, and then sent to unit training. Herb finished at the top of his class and earned his wings on August 6, 1943.[49]

Because he hand finished first in his class, Herb had his choice of assignments. He chose to fly anti-submarine patrols out of Jacksonville, Florida. His group flew B-25s and patrolled the southeast Atlantic coast. The Navy originally flew the routes, but gave the assignment to the Army Air Corps; the Navy's slower airplanes were easy targets for the German subs. While in Jacksonville, Herb was on a three-day schedule. He flew one day, had one day off, and on the third day was on a two-hour standby. He completed 75 hours in that role before the Navy took back the assignment in late 1943. A new assignment soon followed; Herb was sent to Clovis, New Mexico, to join a B-24 combat crew.[50]

Robert Stricklin, the grocery store clerk from Dallas, was first drafted into the Army. He did his initial training somewhere in the state of Washington (exact location unknown). Perhaps it was his age or the daring sense of adventure that had burned in him since reading Mark Twain, but whatever the reason, R.B. did not want to be a foot soldier. He requested and was granted a transfer to the Army Air Corps. He wanted to be a pilot.[51]

R.B. did not initially qualify for pilot training. He was underweight and had to gain several pounds before he was accepted into pre-flight school at Lackland Field in San Antonio, Texas. For unknown reasons he washed out of pilot training, but he was given a chance to become a bombardier. As previously mentioned, bombardiers attended the same pre-flight school and gunnery training as navigators. R.B. passed all the initial requirements and was sent to bombardier school at Goodfellow Field, three miles southeast of San Angelo, Texas.[52]

In the 20-week school, trainees like R.B. spent "120 hours in AT-11 training planes on practice bombing runs and 718 hours in ground school. The latter consists of: navigation, 96 hours; bombing, 388 hours;" and 234 hours of related training in areas such as meteorology, code and air and sea recognition. Graduates proudly earned silver bombardier's wings, and like their navigator counterparts, were appointed flight officers or commissioned second lieutenants, then sent to unit training.[53] R.B. excelled as a bombardier. He had found his true calling in the war. When he joined the crew for unit training at Clovis, New Mexico, in November 1943 he was 27½ years old—the oldest member of the crew by nearly two years.

Vincent Henry Olney, the farm boy from Nebraska, wanted to be a pilot. When he volunteered in Omaha after Pearl Harbor, he chose the Army Air Corps. His sister Susan recalls that becoming a pilot was not an easy task for him. "Vince had two obstacles to overcome before entering flight training," she said. First of all, at over 200 pounds, he was 30 pounds overweight. Secondly, the Army Air Corps preferred college graduates and Vince had only a high school diploma. "He was really determined to become a pilot." He lost the weight and took a college equivalency test. At Kelly Field in San Antonio, Texas, Vince attended pre-flight school and qualified to take pilot training. From Kelly he was sent briefly to Lowry Field in Denver. His family drove from Nebraska one weekend to see him while he was there. Vince was then transferred to Pampa Army Air Field in Pampa, Texas, to begin his pilot training. His sister Susan recalls that he was always a practical joker: "I remember Vince telling many stories of the practical jokes that he and the cadets played on one another." One story involved a cadet nicknamed "Red." Red was the alert cadet for their barracks—he was to let the others know when an officer was entering the barracks. One Saturday morning before inspection, Red yelled, "Here comes the colonel!" As he ran by Vince to his bunk, he grabbed Vince's bedding and pulled it off. For this infraction, Vince received laps on the runway in full gear. He repaid Red a few weeks later by dumping out the contents of his footlocker before another inspection. It was all in good fun. Vince always laughed when he told both stories. After successfully completing the ten-week primary flying school there, he was sent to Coffeyville Army Air Field in Kansas for basic flying school training.[54]

Robert Stricklin as an aviation cadet. (Irene Stricklin Frazier)

Fate would play a part in his life while at Coffeyville. The Jungs, a local family who owned a bakery, often entertained a few cadets on weekends. The cadets stayed in their home, were fed home-cooked meals, and taken to a local club for entertainment. Their gesture of appreciation and patriotism was similar to ones that were occurring all over the country. Vince was invited on one such occasion. The Jungs had a handicapped child who required the care of a nurse. Their nurse was Alice Lucinda Hansen of Coffeyville. The first time that Vince met Alice he told her, "I am going to marry you." She told Justine Jung, "That cadet Olney is the craziest person I've ever met." But, the feeling of affection was mutual. Vince returned to the Jungs' every weekend possible during the remainder of his time in basic. He successfully graduated from Coffeyville in Class 43-G.[55]

Vince was then sent back to Pampa for advanced flying school. There he learned to fly by instruments in the AAF's "Link" trainer, which allowed the cadets to train "without ever leaving the ground."[56] He also learned how to fly at night at Pampa. On one of his night landings, Vince had a minor accident in one of the twin-engine trainers (a UC-78B). The July 5 accident occurred at approximately 2235. The report states that "the left [landing] gear collapsed as a result of a moderately hard landing" due to a "material failure." Charles J. Olson was the co-pilot; neither he nor Vince was injured. At the time of the incident Vince had logged a total of 205.2 flying hours—35.9 of those on instruments.[57] The summer heat in Texas was nearly unbearable, but Vince survived his ten weeks in Pampa and proudly earned his pilot wings on July 29, 1943. He invited Alice to attend the graduation ceremony there and pin the wings on him. A few days later, Alice and Vince were married. Vince wrote his parents after the ceremony to tell them about their new daughter-in-law; needless to say, they were a little shocked. He was then sent to Roswell Army Air Field in New Mexico for four-engine training—Alice accompanied him.[58]

Upon graduation from West Point on May 29, 1942, Floyd Robinson was assigned to the Army Air Corps for pilot training. He was to immediately report to a contract school in Corsicana, Texas, for primary flying training. He drove with some classmates who had the same assignment. "God was our copilot," he said years later. Floyd passed with no trouble and was then sent to Randolph Field in San Anto-

Basic flying training class 43-G at Coffeyville Army Air Field. Left to right are Lt. T. Alton, Robert H. Phenis, Ray E. Pierce, Vincent H. Olney and John E. Orr. (Marilyn Siebels)

nio, Texas, for basic flying school. From there, he attended advanced flying school at Brooks Field, also in San Antonio. While at Brooks in September 1942, a fellow USMA classmate who lived in San Antonio set Floyd up on a blind date. She was a local girl named Charlotte More Hill. He was head over heels in love. Floyd received his coveted silver pilot wings in December 1942, graduating in Class 42K.[59]

Afterwards, luckily for the smitten Floyd, he remained at Brooks Field for aircraft observer training. He took advantage of his luck and in January 1943 he asked Charlotte (with her father's blessing) to marry him. She said yes and they were married in San Antonio on March 8, 1943. That April he began his final pilot training, transition flying, at Davis-Monthan Field, four miles southeast of Tucson, Arizona. Floyd was going to be a bomber pilot, so he made the transition to four-engine planes. He trained with his initial crew at Biggs Field in El Paso, Texas. In late January 1944 he boarded the Liberty ship USS *A.P. Hill* in Hampton, Virginia, for a month long voyage to Naples, Italy. From Naples he was sent to Bari, Italy, to await further orders. It was there in Bari that he was assigned to the 450th Bomb Group in nearby Manduria.[60]

3

A Liberator Crew

Clovis, New Mexico, boasted a population of about a hundred people in December 1943. Just seven miles west of the little town, thousands of Army Air Force personnel were being trained at a recently constructed air base. It was there that Grant Caywood met his newly formed crew for the first time. As pilot, he was in charge. He would make all of the important decisions regarding the crew. He arrived there via private automobile about November 10—his preferred method of travel between permanent assignments. Beo and Shadow accompanied him.

Time has faded the exact details of the crew's first meeting at Clovis. AAF training had placed them with so many new airmen and groups over the past year that this first meeting seemed routine and uneventful. The crew could not realize the bond they were about to form. The first official order listing them as a crew came on November 13, 1943. The initial lineup of "Crew #4-N-33" consisted of Capt. Grant D. Caywood, Pilot; 2nd Lt. William C. Donaldson, co-pilot; 2nd Lt. Robert B. Stricklin, bombardier; Sgt. Richard M. Jacobson, engineer and gunner; Sgt. Manuel F. Esquivel, radio operator and gunner; Sgt. Stanley S. Butynski, aerial engineer and gunner; Sgt. Theodore H. Morris, aerial engineer and gunner; Sgt. Maurice H. Gilliam, aerial gunner.

Just prior to assignment, most of the crew had been stationed in Salt Lake City, Utah, getting their final vaccinations and awaiting orders. In late October, they were briefly sent to Pueblo, Colorado. From there, the crew was to leave for Clovis on or about November 15.[1]

They would be flying a B-24, which required a combat crew of ten, so this original listing of eight was missing two crew members, a navigator and another gunner. By December 1, the final crew roster was complete. Herbert Gouldon was added

Photographs of officers *(clockwise from top left)*: Grand D. Caywood, Maurice A. Erickson, Robert B. Stricklin and Herb Gouldon. (Ted Morris)

as navigator and Norman Woodward came in as an aerial engineer and gunner. Maurice Erickson replaced Donaldson as co-pilot. An eleventh crew member joined them on several training exercises at Clovis. It was Caywood's black cocker spaniel, Shadow. She became their unofficial mascot.[2]

An assignment for training in Clovis and B-24s meant that Caywood's crew had been designated for heavy bombardment. At this point in the war, only two types of heavy bombers were being utilized in combat, the B-17 and the B-24—the B-29 would not see combat action until June 1944. Heavy bombers carried a larger bomb load and had a higher service ceiling than medium bombers. But, they were less maneuverable and more vulnerable at lower altitudes than the mediums. Medium bombers, like the North American B-25 Mitchell and the Martin B-26 Marauder, were more effective in tactical operations, the air support of ground troops from an altitude up to 15,000 feet. The heavy bombers' chief role came with strategic operations: to bomb specific targets from altitudes up to about 30,000 feet. Although very different in functionality, both types played a much needed and important role in the war.[3]

The B-24 can trace its origin back to 1937 when an inventor, David R. Davis, drew up plans for a new airfoil (wing) that in cross section resembled a "falling teardrop." The Davis wing, as it was called, was sold to Consolidated Aircraft Corporation in 1938 for use on its proposed Model 31 "flying boat," which was later produced as the PBY-1 for the U.S. Navy. Consolidated's president, Reuben Fleet, "was one of the few believers" in the new and "unbelievable" wing; without his backing, it probably would have never been used. The new wing was a high-lift airfoil that had tremendous advantages over its predecessors. Although longer than the wing of Boeing's B-17, it was narrower, had a smaller surface area, and a greater flight range. It was the Davis wing that allowed Consolidated to be in a good position to respond to the Army Air Corps' December 1938 request for a new bomber.[4]

The request, officially known as Specification C-212, called for an aircraft that could out-perform the B-17. It solicited a bomber with a top speed of 300 miles per hour, a 3,000-mile range, a 35,000-foot service ceiling, and an 8,000-pound payload capacity. The chief of the Army Air Corps, Henry H. "Hap" Arnold, also saw the need to have another source to produce the B-17, which at the time was the only four-engine heavy bomber. By late January 1939, Consolidated Aircraft had a proposal together that answered the AAC's request. Potentially, the proposal could also solve Arnold's dilemma, to have another source for making heavy bombers.[5]

The proposal, wooden mock-up, and preliminary tests were promising and a contract was signed with Consolidated in February. In addition to the Davis wing, the new bomber would have a tricycle landing gear with a steerable nose wheel. At first considered a gimmick, this new wheel under the aircraft's nose allowed greater handling and visibility for the pilots. It would also allow new pilots, not trained to the same standards as their "prewar predecessors, to handle the new generation of fast, powerful warplanes." Several prototype or experimental models were produced under the name XB 24 (the X before an aircraft number stands for experimental). By May 1941, after several enhancements to weight and design, twenty B-24A's had been built for the USAAC. However, because of need, these were sent to England for use in the Royal Air Force.[6]

The B-24 was nicknamed the "Liberator." A common misconception is that the British gave the bomber the name, because it "was their custom to give nicknames to aircraft rather than the numerical designations applied by the Americans. However, the aircraft was christened *Liberator* as a result of a contest held at the Consolidated plant in San Diego." The wife of Consolidated's founder, Dorothy Fleet, anonymously submitted the name that was chosen. In early 1942, the company's public relations manager, John W. Thompson, tried to change the name to "Eagle," but the attempt failed.[7]

From the beginning, the B-24 Liberator was utilitarian in design. There were no doors, only hatches. There was simply no wasted space. To most it lacked any glamour. For many, at first sight, it seemed a clunky and awkward aircraft. With its billboard-like fuselage and twin tails, it was much less sleek and alluring than its legendary predecessor, the B-17 "Flying Fortress." This was due in large part to the proactive public relations work done by Boeing, and the locations of B-17 bases throughout England with ready access to the Army's media machine. The Flying Fortress overshadowed the "ugly duckling." The bomber was not pressurized, there was no "extra space" to move easily around it, and its aluminum skin could be cut easily with a knife. However, for the crews assigned to B-24s, their first impression changed. Even though some still had a love-hate relationship with the aircraft, the Liberator became a thing of beauty. For those who truly understood its capacity and functionality, there was no other bomber for them.[8]

The B-24 went through an evolution in the design and experimental stages that, in the end, resulted in over fifteen different models. Each successive model brought enhancements to the turrets, bombsight, and auto pilot functionality, as well as less technologically driven cosmetic changes. The B-24D was the first one produced on a large scale. It called for a crew of ten, three more than previous models. The B-24H was the first Liberator with a nose turret. The B-24J had the largest production run; nearly 6,700 of them were made. Most combat-ready Liberators (Models B-24G through M) had four 1200-horsepower Pratt and Whitney R-1830 (43 or 65) Twin Wasp, 14-cylinder engines to power the airplane—each engine's three-bladed propellers weighed 500 pounds. The bomber was 18 feet tall, 67 feet 2 inches in length, and the Davis wing had a span of 110 feet. Empty, the Liberator weighed 38,000 pounds; with a normal load, it weighed 65,000 pounds at takeoff. Its maximum speed was 278 miles per hour, with an average cruising speed of 237 miles per hour.[9] The normal bomb load capacity was 8,000 pounds, with a maximum sustained load of 12,800 pounds. The range, depending on the model, was about 2,100 miles. Although in final production the bomber fell a little short of the specs called for in Specification C-212, the B-24 became the workhorse bomber of the U.S. Army Air Force.[10]

The design of the B-24 is a testament to the fact that, as with most bombers, it would be attacked from all sides. The Liberator was equipped with ten .50-caliber machine guns, two each in the nose, tail, ball, and top turrets, and one mounted at each waist window. Unlike the B-17, the B-24's ball turret was retractable; this

450th Bomb Group B-24 *Toni Gayle*. (Stan S. Butynski)

afforded greater protection to the ball gunner at takeoff and landing. The bomber's turrets were hydraulically and electrically driven, which allowed for more effective use of the airplane's guns. The high velocity of air flowing over its surface in flight made it very "difficult to turn the guns in the airstream by hand."[11]

The B-24 Liberator was produced in greater numbers (all models and variations) than any other aircraft in World War II—archival documents suggest 19,401 as the most accurate figure. Their production is a wonderful testament to the United States' capacity to mass-produce goods quickly when needed. This figure becomes even more staggering when one reads the following analogy written by the AAF in 1944: "One four-engine bomber requires enough aluminum for 55,000 coffee percolators; enough alloy steel to make 6,800 electric irons; enough steel for 160 washing machines; enough rubber to recap 800 automobile tires; and enough copper for 550 radio receivers." It became clear early on that Consolidated would not be able to produce all of the B-24s needed by the Allies.[12]

To help turn out the number needed, the Army sought help for Consolidated from four other manufacturers. In addition to the Consolidated plant in San Diego, which produced 7,645 Liberators, Consolidated and Convair in Fort Worth, Texas, made 3,034; Douglas Company in Tulsa, Oklahoma, completed 964; North American in Dallas, Texas, built 966; and Ford Motor Company in Willow Run, Michigan, manufactured 6,792 B-24s. Although Consolidated's San Diego plant assembled the greatest number, it was Henry Ford's Willow Run plant that became the most famous. There in Michigan in 1941, Ford rallied to construct an 80-acre plant. He then applied his mass production techniques to the process. At the height of production, the factory employed 42,000 employees and assembled a new B-24 every fifty-five minutes; at any given time over a hundred Liberators were in various stages of assembly within the plant.[13]

During November 1943 in New Mexico, Caywood's crew was becoming familiar with the B-24, the bomber they would soon fly in combat. However, before any formal crew training could begin, Caywood had to assign the gunners to their respective positions. Esquivel, as a radio operator, was assigned to one of the waist guns (the right). Woodward joined Esquivel in the waist; he would man the left waist gun. Jacobson became the crew's engineer and by custom would operate the top turret just behind Caywood and Erickson. Because the turrets were small, the size of the airman played a role in these assignments along with his qualification and training. As Steinbeck accurately summarized about the turret gunner in his book, *Bombs Away*, "His trade is one of the few in the world where a good little man is a great deal better than a good big man." Gilliam, who was 5 foot, 6½ inches, volunteered for the perilous tail turret position. Caywood assigned the nose guns to Butynski. The claustrophobic ball turret guns were assigned to 5 foot, 7 inch tall Morris, who also served as backup radio operator.[14]

With the assignments determined, crew training could begin. "The second part of AAF Training—unit and crew training—is devoted to making coordinated effective teams out of (airmen) specialists—teams within airplanes, teams of airplanes, teams of airplanes and ground personnel, teams of ground personnel alone, according to the *AAF Guide*"[15] In accordance with AAF standards, crew and unit training were divided into three phases and were to last approximately 90 days. "First, the trainees increase their proficiency in individual skills, learn to work as a team, and become familiar with equipment and techniques. Secondly, formation flying is stressed. Finally, trainees move into a training area which approximates a battle zone, fly long formation [simulated] bombing missions by day and night, learn to live, work, and fight [together as they would] under combat conditions," the guide states.[16] Over the past year, each of the crew had trained in his respective position. Now the crew would learn to function as a team. In combat they would have to act as one.[17]

Clovis Army Air Field was ideally suited for this phase of training. It was located 4,295 feet above sea level in the high desert plains of eastern New Mexico, near the Texas Panhandle—about 100 miles due west of Lubbock, Texas, and 220 miles southeast of Albuquerque. Its near perfect weather allowed flights almost every day. In addition to crew and unit training, flight, gunnery and photo recon training were also practiced. In December 1943, "no fly zones" did not exist, and the crews training at Clovis often flew over places such as Tucumcari and Alamogordo, which some nicknamed "Alamaagoo." As they flew over the desert, crews could see activity below at these bases, but they did not realize the importance of the work. Alamogordo was the home of the White Sands Missile Range where the Trinity tests were conducted.

On one of their first flights at Clovis, the mission called for only the pilot, co-pilot, navigator, flight engineer, and radio operator. Caywood invited his tail gunner, Gilliam, to come along as well. Gilliam sat alone in the waist area in the rear of the plane. He was looking out over the "flat open spaces of New Mexico, when all of a sudden a siren sounded and lights flashed. Someone had pushed the emergency button, calling for all on board to jump out of the plane." Gilliam remembered what occurred next. "I checked all four engines, all were performing well. I was wearing my parachute harness, but seeing no reason to jump, I put on the earphones and waited—holding the chest chute." Soon Caywood called over the interphone and asked Gilliam, "Are you still back there?" Gilliam advised that he

Shadow's ball turret gunner, Ted Morris.

was, and Caywood explained that they had pushed the button by mistake. "We all laughed and continued the mission."[18]

Caywood's crew was soon sent to Langley Field, Virginia, to begin their next phase of training. On or about December 11 his crew, along with dozens of other crews, boarded troop trains and headed east for the week-long trip. For some, it was the third or fourth cross-country jaunt via rail in a year.[19] They spent Christmas 1943 at Langley. Several of the crew received care-packages from home—Gilliam's contained Milky Ways and home-baked treats; it arrived just in time for his twenty-first birthday on December 28.[20]

The weather was cold and dreary that Christmas; they all longed for home and loved ones. However, not all were without family. Maurice Gilliam's wife, Stella, joined him there. They rented a room in a private house on Oak Avenue in Newport News. Mrs. Weeks, the owner, took an immediate liking to Stella, and they spent time together during the day while Maurice was on base. They did not have kitchen privileges, so they ate out every night. Each day for the trip back and forth to base, Maurice took a trolley part of the way and then caught a bus to Langley. The forty-five minute trip, each way, was worth it to him; he was home every night for all three weeks of Stella's stay.[21]

Manuel Esquivel's wife, Rita, also came to Langley. Ever devoted, Rita had followed her husband to yet another base. They rented a bedroom from a lady who lived near the base. There was no heat in the room. As Rita recalled, "The only heat was from the chimney which ran through the closet. We had to leave the closet door open to keep moderately warm." The shared bathroom was down the hall. Since the Army pays at the end of each month, a lot of airmen ran out of money towards the end of the month. That was the case with Manuel Esquivel in December 1943. Fortunately, he was able to borrow some money from the Red Cross so that he could take Rita to dinner and to a movie. Rita remembered the thoughtful and touching gesture that was waiting for them when they arrived back at their room. "The landlady had surprised us with a small Christmas tree with homemade candies beneath it."[22]

Langley Field, located in Hampton, Virginia, is on a small peninsula that splits the Back River into two branches before it empties into the Chesapeake Bay. It was an excellent place to train in a heavy bomber, because it had ready access to the Atlantic Ocean and the entire eastern seaboard. Caywood's crew continued to learn to act as a team and to become more familiar with the B-24. Caywood recalls, "We went to altitude to get used to the oxygen mask and the cold air up there. We practiced navigation to a site and practiced bomb runs thereon. We fired the guns at nothing in particular just to become accustomed to loading and firing the equipment. We practiced formation flying and instrument flying. We also practiced getting the plane out of bed, serviced, and operating, as well as putting it to bed when we were done for the day."[23] They were learning to live, work, and fight under combat conditions. Cooperation among the crew was a primary concern for Caywood. Each of the men had to know his position; each member of the crew also cross-trained so that he could do more than one job—this would prove crucial once in combat. Their location allowed them to fly long-range missions, day and night, up and down the Atlantic coast. They were perfecting their knowledge with practical experience. Erickson recalls that the training at Langley "was at an intense pace."[24]

While at Langley, Caywood wanted to show the crew what the plane would do under various stresses. He already knew; he had learned in transition flying training. To demonstrate how the plane would react with one engine out, one day while flying a test mission over North Carolina, he turned one off and feathered it. The crew was a little shocked, but there seemed to be no ill effects. He then turned off a second one, then a third. After the third, the crew was a little worried. What was their captain doing? With the third engine out, the plane started to descend gradually. Caywood was satisfied with the demonstration and soon fired the engines back up in reverse order. Gilliam, in the tail turret, heard each one kick back in as they were started. Little trails of black smoke came from each engine in turn. Although a little unorthodox, Caywood knew that this was what training was all about, and he was using the time wisely. In combat, his crew would more than likely face one or all of these scenarios he tested. Exercises like this would decrease their anxiety on actual missions. Caywood was earning the trust of his crew. His mannerisms and confidence commanded respect, but he had common sense as well. They were developing an intense loyalty to their pilot.[25]

3. A Liberator Crew   61

B-24s at Langley Field, Virginia. (Maurice A. Erickson)

Radar and night flight training at Langley helped to teach pilots to stay in formation, and it taught navigators to navigate without landmarks. Although they were primarily for pilots and navigators, the rest of the crew also flew night missions. Gilliam remembers one such night training exercise at Langley. Caywood had been instructed to fly from Hampton, Virginia, down to Wilmington, North Carolina, and back. Gilliam was in the waist of the B-24 with the other gunners. He recalls, "To pass the time I would look out the window at the ground below and try to imagine where we might be and what it was like down there." After all, North Carolina was his home state. He remembers the approach to Wilmington, which was well lighted, because of the port there. As they neared the city, searchlights from the ground focused in on their aircraft. The lights lit up the interior of the bomber. It was a magnificent sight.[26]

The crew was able to relax a little at Langley thanks to the dances held by the USO. Esquivel and Gilliam had their wives with them, while others of the crew had some friendly local ladies with which to dance. Stella Gilliam remembers dancing with Stan Butynski, because Maurice did not like to dance. He explains why: "Every time I put my foot down, someone else's foot was there."[27]

In basic training, new recruits lose their identity. In the Army, the farm boy from Rockingham County, North Carolina, who was known as Maurice to all his friends and family was identified by a service number and was called simply "Gilliam." Richard Jacobson, the gregarious ball player from Boston, called "Dick" by everyone,

Caywood's crew at Langley Field, Virginia. Back row (left to right): Esquivel, Jacobson, Caywood, Stricklin, Gouldon, and Erickson. Front row (left to right): Gilliam, Woodward, Butynski with Shadow, and Morris. (Maurice A. Erickson)

was known only as "Jacobson." And so it was with the remaining members. However, a miraculous thing happened in unit and crew training. A new identity for them was created. They would soon be issued their own bomber, which they could name. The *crew* was their new identity. They were now Caywood's crew.

An unconditional bond was beginning to form. Perhaps they were following their instincts, or Army tradition, or just human nature, but they began to give each other nicknames. They respectfully called their pilot "Captain" or "Caywood." The bombardier, R.B. Stricklin, was called "Strick," as was the older brother, Wilson, whom he admired so much—it was perhaps a nickname he gave himself. The copilot, Maurice Erickson, became "Eric." Maurice Gilliam, the tail gunner, was given the nickname "Moe." Manuel Esquivel, the radio operator, took the appellation "Static" or "Manny." The other waist gunner, Norman Woodward, was aptly called "Woody." Richard Jacobson, the top turret gunner and engineer, was dubbed "Jake." The ball turret gunner, Ted Morris, was affectionately called "Teddy." Stanley Butynski, the nose turret gunner, was called simply Stan. There was also some good-natured ribbing among the crew. Herb Gouldon remembers one time when Strick was giving Woody a hard time. "Strick was from Texas and he let you know it," Herb recalls. "Woody," Strick chided, "why are you always wearing cowboy boots? You aren't from Texas. What did you do before the war?" Quick as a whip Woody replied, "Well, I

Shadow's nose gunner Stan Butynski refueling a B-24 at Langley Field. (Maurice A. Erickson)

grew up on a ranch with cows and horses, and that's why I wear boots. What did you do in Texas before the war?" Somewhat embarrassed, but still able to make fun of himself in the situation, Strick replied, "I worked in a grocery store." It was all in good fun.[28]

On Thursday, February 3, 1944, Caywood received the final staging orders for his crew. By Saturday, they were to be at Mitchell Field, located at Hempstead, Long Island, New York.[29] They all knew that they would be overseas within a month; they were a replacement crew. This meant that they were either replacing a crew that had completed its tour of duty or, more than likely, a crew that had been shot down. In preparation, each of them wrote letters home advising family and friends of their pending assignments, their excitement, fears, trepidations, and their new APO address so they could receive letters in return.

The assignment at Mitchell was the first trip to New York City for most of the crew. Because of all of the "temptations" of the city, the enlisted men were restricted to base. However, this did not deter Moe, Jake, Manny, Stan, Woody, and Teddy. They were able to "go over the fence a few times, thumb a ride to the train station, ride into New York City and go to theaters or Times Square," Gilliam recalled. Caywood, who had his car and who was never one for too many rules, gave the guys a ride to the train station a couple of times.[30] The enlisted men of Caywood's crew were becoming close friends.

***Shadow*'s top turret gunner Richard Jacobson at Langley Field. (Maurice A. Erickson)**

Boston was not far by train, so Richard Jacobson's girlfriend, Phyllis Elias, came to see him while he was at Mitchell. There she met the crew and said goodbye to Jake. Maurice Gilliam also had a visitor while at Mitchell. It was an unspoken act of love that he will never forget. Unannounced, his father, Lawrence, took a train up to Long Island from North Carolina to visit him before he went overseas. This was quite an unusual gesture from a man who rarely displayed emotion or affection; it is one of Maurice's fondest memories of his father. It also helps to shed light on the importance and danger of the journey the crew was about to undertake.[31]

About the time Maurice's father arrived, the crew was granted an unexpected week of furlough. Most of the crew went home to visit their loved ones. Maurice took the train back to Reidsville with his father to see his wife and mom.[32]

At Mitchell, the crew was issued combat flight clothing and equipment, which consisted of coats, pants, hats, goggles, helmets, boots, gloves, flak vests, life vests, electrically heated flying suits, and oxygen masks.[33] The combat clothing was intended to keep the airmen warm at temperatures that, at bombing altitude, could reach fifty degrees below zero. All of them were issued the famous A-2 leather jacket, which is synonymous with the Army Air Force in World War II. The pilots wore this jacket on missions, while the rest of the crew wore more heavily insulated sheepskin jackets. Their combat pants were A-3 and A-5 leather flying trousers. Most of the crew sported B-2 leather baseball caps while on the ground, but in the air they donned B-6 leather flying helmets. They also had M-3 steel helmets for further protection. Richard Jacobson recounts that the M-3 saved his life from flak on at least two occasions—his

Manuel "Static" Esquivel, Norman "Woody" Woodward, and Richard "Jake" Jacobson, pictured left to right. (Richard M. Jacobson)

daughter still has the helmet with several dings. Their goggles were the standard issue B-7 (model AN-6530). Their flight footwear consisted of zippered A-6 sheepskin boots. They were difficult to walk in and had the feeling of bedroom shoes. Most pilots did not wear them, "because it was hard to feel the rudders with them on." Many airmen wore their regulation shoes under the A-6s and those that did not often tied their regulation shoes to their gear in case they were shot down. Flak vests and oxygen masks were also issued to all, as were life vests, called "Mae Wests, after the buxom Hollywood star." Once inflated the vest's nickname became obvious. Officers were issued the standard AAF A-11 "Hack" watch, which would be used to synchronize the time for missions. In addition, the crew was also issued an electrically heated flying suit, which was worn under the outer clothing.[34]

All of this flight clothing was "difficult at best," laments Caywood; but it was necessary since the "B-24 was the coldest airplane anyone ever invented."[35] In it, airmen were always too hot on the ground and too cold in flight. The electric flying suits were plugged into a rheostat, one of which was located at each position in the B-24. They were great when they worked, which wasn't often. Jacobson recalls that the heated suits worked "much like a heating blanket, but invariably they would short out and give you a hell of a burn—and then you would really freeze." Movement was also limited. If an airman moved too suddenly or too far, the outfit would "bite" them with a shock. After they were in combat for a while, Caywood's crew gave up on the heated suits and opted for the heaviest fur lined suits. No matter what the type, combat flight clothing was cumbersome to wear. Jacobson jokes that in full gear "if they stuck a propeller in your rear you might be able to run a mile in about two hours."[36]

In addition to clothing, the crew was also issued their bomber while at Mitchell Field—a B-24H, serial number 42-52611. She was made at Ford's Willow Run, Michigan, plant and was painted in the standard olive drab camouflage paint. Starting in December 1943 most AAF planes produced dropped the camouflage paint and retained their original aluminum, metal color. For B-24s this meant a weight reduction of about 80 pounds, with a negligible increase in airspeed. It was due more to rationing than to anything else. Unanimously the crew decided to name their new plane *Shadow*, after Caywood's dog, which had flown with them several times throughout training. Caywood painted the plane's nose art while at Mitchell. In a white cloud, below the name "SHADOW!," he drew a cartoon version of Shadow, standing on a bomb and shooting a pistol.[37]

On February 9, Caywood received orders for his crew to report to Morrison Field, West Palm Beach, Florida, by February 24, en route to an overseas destination.[38] They were to leave Morrison on or about February 25 and to fly *Shadow*. They would not travel via ocean ship, as did some crews. As they left New York, Caywood flew by the Statue of Liberty. This tugged at the heartstrings of each member of the crew as he silently reflected that freedom is not free—there is a price to pay and they were about to pay it. The crew had a special assignment on the way to Morrison Field which caused a little excitement. They were to drop off a Sperry Gyroscope executive at Langley Field. Beginning in the 1930s, Sperry Gyroscope was a key government contractor. They worked to develop the microwave technology necessary for modern radar. For the AAF they developed computer controlled and stabilized bombsights, as well as automatic pilots. The company, founded in 1910 in Brooklyn, outgrew its headquarters during the war, so the government built them a new facility at Lake Success, Long Island.[39] Due to the integral relationship, the AAF frequently provided transportation for Sperry personnel as schedules permitted, and this was one of those occasions.

Shadow's bombardier Robert Stricklin in full flight gear. (Irene Stricklin Frazier)

Shadow's Crew. Back row (left to right): pilot, Grant Caywood; co-pilot, Maurice Erickson; navigator, Herb Gouldon; bombardier, Robert Stricklin. Front row (left to right): ball turret gunner, Ted Morris; tail gunner, Maurice Gilliam; radio operator, Manuel Esquivel; engineer/top turret gunner, Richard Jacobson; nose gunner, Stan Butynski; waist gunner, Norman Woodward. (Grant D. Caywood)

Ironically, somewhere over Virginia, before reaching Langley, a very typical malfunction occurred with the autopilot. A vacuum tube probably burned out. Whatever the cause, *Shadow* suddenly nosed down violently and all aboard were jostled.[40]

Engineer and top turret gunner Richard Jacobson recalled the experience with great clarity after nearly fifty-eight years. "I was in my normal position, just back of and in between Caywood and Erickson. We were at our normal cruising speed and altitude, when suddenly, without warning, we went into a severe nosedive. Everything in *Shadow* left the deck, including me! I remember Caywood with his feet up on the instrument panel tugging on the wheel. There was a shut off switch for the autopilot on the instrument panel and a lever between the pilot and co-pilot. I was desperately trying to reach either, even as I hung partially suspended in the air. To this day I do not know who cut off the autopilot or if any of us got to either switch, but we pulled up only a few hundred feet from disaster." Jake has always suspected that it was Erickson who got to the switch, because he was the "heaviest and strongest of the trio."[41]

Once in Florida, they received orders attaching them to the 15th Army Air Force. They were to fly the South Atlantic Route to Italy. They would be assigned to a specific group upon arrival.[42] This route was also known as the "Southern Route." For Caywood's crew the journey began on February 25, 1944, and it consisted of stops at Waller Field on Trinidad (an island off of Venezuela), and in Belem and Natal, Brazil. In Natal, a series of delays kept them there for nearly a week. Caywood admits that a fraternity brother of his was the engineering officer there. "He *found* a lot of discrepancies that had to be corrected." The crew "had a ball." They went swimming in the ocean, where "the waves were head high." Maurice Gilliam remembers eating bananas right off of the tree. Richard Jacobson recalls "how extraordinarily white the sand was … the water was crystal clear and the beach was studded with beautiful nut trees."[43] The relaxation there was good for the crew; it would be their last for some time. On March 3 they left Natal and flew across the Atlantic to Dakar in Senegal, Africa. From Dakar, they flew to Marrakech, in French Morocco, then to Algiers, Algeria, and Tunis, Tunisia. On March 8 they left Tunis for their final destination, Manduria, Italy.[44] Most stops were quick, overnight, and just long enough to service the plane and get back on the journey. *Shadow's* navigator, Herb Gouldon, plotted each leg of the journey and gave Caywood the appropriate headings and other necessary information.

Jacobson recalls of the nearly eleven-hour flight, "The trip from [Natal] Brazil to Dakar, Africa [on March 3], was all over water and the longest non-stop [flight] of our journey. In order to have enough fuel to complete the trip, as engineer, I would have to transfer fuel from the auxiliary wing tanks—located on the outer edge of the wings—to the main tanks when we were about half way through our journey." Just as Jake was starting the fuel transfer he began to smell smoke. "The fuel transfer pump was on fire." He reacted immediately, grabbed a fire extinguisher and put out the fire. The crew was now faced with a new problem. How were they going to transfer the fuel and get all the way to Africa? Caywood hoped that if he flew in a slip "with the left wing well tilted" downward that the attitude "would flow enough gas to the right in-board tank to get the job done. Jake hoped—and prayed—that in the process of dropping the left wing that the force of gravity would not push gas in the left wing to the left out-board auxiliary tank. Thanks to the flying skills of Caywood and Erickson, the fuel on *Shadow* was transferred, and they made it to Africa. As a conscientious and curious engineer, Jake spoke with the ground crew after *Shadow* landed and asked how much fuel was left in the tanks. The crew chief smiled at him and told him that only about five gallons remained. Gouldon was also instrumental in navigating the crew successfully across the ocean. Their flight to Dakar had been almost all at night. Gouldon used his celestial navigation skills to negotiate the Atlantic. But their approach to the African coast was obscured by haze and sand. Gouldon had to calculate "sunshots" to determine *Shadow's* longitude. As he had, and would continue to do for months, Gouldon got them to their destination.[45]

Caywood had an interesting but harrowing experience as he disembarked *Shadow* at the French base in Dakar on March 3. He was the last of the crew out of the airplane, the others had been shown to their quarters; he was just making sure everything was in order. As Caywood climbed out, a French guard "shouting in French" approached him. "I had no idea what he was saying. He went back into my

3. A Liberator Crew 69

Shadow in flight. (Grant D. Caywood)

airplane, where I had left my .45-caliber pistol—in its holster—in my seat. An Arab in white baggy pants was just getting out of *Shadow*. The French guard roughed up the Arab, took my .45, put a shell in the chamber, applied it directly to the Arab's chest and pulled the trigger. This was the first time I had ever seen anyone killed." Caywood, a little confused and shocked by the incident, was assigned to quarters without comment; he "did not sleep well that night." The excitement continued the next day when Jake went out to inspect *Shadow* after the long and grueling trip. "I came up from underneath as usual and headed for the flight deck. I heard a noise and saw what looked like a man wearing 'local dress' in the waist of the plane. I started back towards him and he came rushing towards the bomb bay opening and took off before I could stop him. I spotted a small piece of cloth in one of the hydraulic lines. This guy had been trying to stuff the lines with soaked pieces of cloth." The events from the previous day now came into focus; it was the second deliberate attempt at sabotage in two days. If the incidents had gone undetected the plane would have been in serious trouble once airborne. (Fuel siphoning was also another major problem with which bomber crews had to contend once in Africa.) Jake sarcastically reflected on their recent journey overseas, "The fun was just beginning!"[46]

The crew was allowed to relax for a day or so after their long flight. A period photograph, dated March 4, 1944, shows Gilliam, Jacobson and Morris in a dugout canoe with a few of the Senegalese "locals." For the next three days they made suc-

Gilliam, Jacobson and Morris (seated) in a canoe off of the coast of Africa with a few Senegalese locals. (Ted Morris)

cessive trips to Marrakech, Algiers, and Tunis; they remained overnight at each. It was in Tunis, on March 7, that Caywood received the official assignment to the 450th Bomb Group, 720th Squadron, 47th Wing, 15th AAF. The next morning they flew to their new home—Manduria, Italy.[47]

4

"Cottontails" in the Heel of the Boot

The circumstances leading up to the assignment of Caywood's crew to the 450th Bomb Group, 15th Army Air Force, started months before, in the summer of 1943. The heavy Allied bombings of Rome and other major Italian cities, the advances by Allied forces in Sicily, and the pending threat of a mainland invasion led to a strong anti-war movement throughout Italy. On July 25, these events forced Italy's monarch, King Victor Emmanuel III, to strip Fascist leader Benito Mussolini of his office and place him under arrest. However, the king knew that Germany would not sit idly by after he displaced Hitler's "faithful, junior partner." Italy immediately began seeking help from the Allies to get out of their union with Germany. Secret talks occurred throughout August in Lisbon, Portugal. It all culminated in a mess tent in Sicily on September 3, when Italy signed a secret armistice with the Allies—General Giuseppe Castellano represented the Italians and General Bedell Smith represented the Allies. The treaty was not made public until September 8. This was to allow a "peaceful" landing of Allied troops on the shores of Salerno. It was thought that some Italian troops might put up a resistance if they knew of the armistice and the pending "invasion" of Allied troops.[1]

Italy's capitulation led directly to the creation of the U.S. 15th Army Air Force. Up until this time, most of the effective bombing missions against European Axis targets came from the Combined Bomber Offensive (CBO), which consisted of the U.S. 8th Army Air Force and Britain's Royal Air Force (RAF), located at bases throughout England. However, many of the strategic targets controlled by Germany (oil fields, factories, marshalling yards, etc.) were located in Europe beyond the reach of the CBO. The winter weather in England was also an obstacle; it sometimes limited daylight missions flown from there to less than five days per month. Although the armistice with Italy and the troops landing at Salerno only gave the Allies a foothold in southern portion of the country, it was a beginning. If bases could be established in southern Italy, in the bottom half of the boot, a vast array of new targets would be within range of Allied bombers.[2]

The AAF worked diligently through the remainder of September and October 1943, and on November 1 they activated the 15th Air Force with headquarters in Tunis, Tunisia. Its creation was accomplished by splitting the 12th AAF, which had been flying missions in North Africa and the Mediterranean, into two air forces. Both of these were to be commanded by Major General James Doolittle. The first of the two would be tactical and would still be called the 12th AAF. The second air force would be strategic and was constituted as the 15th AAF. To clarify terms, *tactical* bombing is "the use of airpower for direct support of ground troops," while *strategic* bombing is the use of airpower in the high-level bombing of strategic targets in order to impede the enemy's ability to wage war. The results of strategic bombing were less immediate than that of tactical bombing. Depending on the target, the lapse of time before the bombing was felt on the front line varied from two weeks up to twenty-five weeks. For example, an attack on an assembly plant may not be perceived for between two and five weeks, while an attack on raw materials may not be felt for up to twenty-five weeks.[3]

Once established the 15th AAF was to fly daylight missions to targets in southern Europe from airbases in Italy, "in the Foggia area." Foggia, which had recently been captured by the Allies, was "a flat, nearly featureless, mosquito infested plateau" in the "spur of the boot." It was well suited for launching air attacks on the Axis' "soft underbelly." In accordance, a month later the new unit's headquarters were moved to nearby Bari—a city on Italy's southeast coast—on the Adriatic Sea. They would stay there for the remainder of the war. In January 1944, Major General Nathan F. Twining succeeded Doolittle as commander of the 15th—a post he held until the end of the war; Doolittle remained as commander of the 12th.[4]

By 1944 the 15th AAF was comprised of the 5th Bombardment Wing, the 47th Bombardment Wing, the 49th Bombardment Wing, the 55th Bombardment Wing, the 304th Bombardment Wing, and the 306th Fighter Wing. To these were added the following miscellaneous squadrons: the 885th Bombardment Squadron, the 37th Photo Reconnaissance Squadron and the 15th Combat Mapping Squadron. Each wing was comprised of between three and six groups, with each group usually containing four squadrons (see Appendix A for chart). For a heavy bombardment group like the 450th, each squadron was supposed to have 12 bombers, 360 enlisted men, and 67 officers—at least on paper. With four squadrons and Group HQ staff, a typical heavy bomb group consisted of 48 combat-ready airplanes and nearly 1,800 airmen. This, of course, varied depending on the theater and did not include replacement or reserve aircraft. The 450th Bomb Group was assigned to the 47th Wing, which during Caywood's tenure in Manduria was commanded by Brig. Gen. Hugo P. Rush.[5]

From the start, the 15th AAF was concerned with four main objectives. In order of priority, they were:

1. To destroy the German Air Force in the air (by making it come up to fight) and on the ground, wherever it might be located within the range of the Fifteenth's planes.
2. To participate in POINTBLANK (the Combined Bomber Offensive), which called for the destruction of German fighter aircraft plants, ball bearing plants, oil refineries, rubber plants, munitions factories, sub pens and bases, etc.
3. To support the battle on the Italian mainland (mainly by attacking communications targets—in Italy, along the Brenner Pass route and also in neighboring Austria).
4. To weaken the German position in the Balkans.[6]

On April 22, 1943, General Order Number 68, from the headquarters of the 2nd AAF, created a new group that was to be called the 450th Bombardment Group (Heavy). The 450th was activated on May 1, 1943, at Gowan Field in Boise, Idaho. Later that month, on the 21st, the 450th was assigned to Clovis, New Mexico. Captain William G. Snaith took initial command of the unit, until Colonel John Stuart Mills arrived in Clovis on June 12. In July the 450th was transferred to nearby Alamogordo, New Mexico, where their training began. Assignees continued to arrive almost daily until the full strength (of air and ground echelons) was reached on August 24, 1943. The 450th was comprised of four squadrons: the 720th, 721st, 722nd, and 723rd.[7]

Training continued for the air echelon at Alamogordo until November 20, when it was transferred to Herington Army Air Field, six miles east of Herington, Kansas. The 450th Bombardment Group had been assigned to the 15th AAF. From Herington they would transfer to Morrison Field in West Palm Beach and fly the southern route to Italy—the same journey that Caywood and his crew would take just a few months later. The ground echelon left Alamogordo on November 26 and was sent via train to Camp Patrick Henry near Hampton, Virginia. There they boarded merchant marine vessels, the S.S. *Bret Harte*, the U.S.S. *Henry Baldwin* and the *Benjamin S. Milam*, and set sail for Italy.[8] The advance party of the 450th's air echelon arrived in Manduria on December 20; the remainder of the group arrived by early January 1944.[9]

Manduria is an ancient city with narrow streets and old buildings, located in the heel of the Italian boot about 22 miles east of Taranto and 64 miles southeast of Bari. All crews flying into Manduria via the southern route flew into Manduria over the Bay of Taranto—the body of water in the arch of the boot. From the air, most first impressions focus on the "collage of dusty roads and poor villages set in the dark green of olive trees." Upon landing the scene becomes even more impoverished. The camp the 450th inherited was a former Italian airfield, located on the outskirts of Manduria "in the middle of an old olive grove." The base, which took its name from the nearby village, was in a dilapidated state. As the group's war diary reports on

William Snaith, 450th BG. (Suzanne Snaith Levy)

December 21 (its second entry), some "Italian officer[s] and soldiers [were] still living on base."[10]

The history of Manduria dates back over two thousand years. The remains of great megalithic walls can still be seen in the northeast section of the city. Built 2,500 years ago under the direction of the Messapians, the defensive walls—and moat—at one point surrounded the entire city. In 338 B.C. Archidamo, the king of Sparta, died at the walls when he tried to conquer it. Hannibal conquered the city in 212 B.C. during the Punic War. For nearly another century, Manduria was sacked and devastated by many invaders including the Romans, Goths, Longobards and Saracens. After the Saracens destroyed the city in 924 A.D., it was renamed "Cassalnuovo," which appears on documents dating back to 1090. The city survived the feudal system of the Middle Ages and became an agricultural center. In 1789 King Ferdinand, "the King of the Two Sicilies," gave back the city its ancient name, Manduria, by royal decree. Umberto of Savoia, King of Italy, officially declared it a city in 1895.[11]

When the 450th arrived in Manduria in late 1943 many of the city's historical

4. "Cottontails" in the Heel of the Boot

Aerial view of the 450th Bomb Group's base in Manduria, Italy. (Grant D. Caywood)

structures were still standing. They included the Palace Dragonetti, Palace Gatti, Palace Giannuzzi, Palace Gigli, and the most famous, the Palace Imperiali, built in 1719 by Prince Michele Imperiali. The Cathedral of Saint Gregory Magnum, whose construction began in the late 1600s and ended in the early 1800s, was also a very impressive sight. Another building of note was the City Hall, which was located in the former convent of Carmel. The piazzas (squares) in the "Old Town" still held some charm. However, for the most part, in late 1943, the war had taken its toll on the locals. They were impoverished, most of them peasants. They had simply been devastated by four years of war and rule under Mussolini.[12]

The first wave of the 450th Bomb Group had its work cut out to convert the base to something usable by the AAF. The 450th's supplies were located on a ship in Bari that was bombed and subsequently sunk by the Germans before it could be unloaded. So to start with, most of the supplies for the group consisted of what each man had in his duffle bag. Since the air echelon had first priority in the barracks, the ground crew initially had to sleep in two-man pup tents. A member of the 721st squadron's ground crew, Sam Stein, recalls that upon his arrival, "There wasn't any lumber or dry ground over which to erect our pup tent. We had to do it in the mud. We went to bed with our clothes on. One blanket was below us in the mud and another blanket over us—a raincoat from each served as the two doors. We also put

Map of Southern Italy. (Samuel Stein)

our overcoat over the top blanket, trying to keep warm. When we got up in the morning, the lower blanket was in the shape of our bodies, like a mold, in the mud below." There was a lack of adequate shelter, food and supplies. Rainy weather and the language barrier prolonged the settling-in period. More crews arrived daily; food was eventually set up in the mess hall; supplies were procured. Most of the combat crews finally took up occupancy in the abandoned wooden barracks. At the beginning of

4. "Cottontails" in the Heel of the Boot

Government building in Manduria. (Grant D. Caywood)

January 1944, the 450th's strength, commissioned and enlisted men, totaled 2,004 soldiers. Although they were still not in an ideal situation, the group was at full strength. Through hard work, perseverance, and a little luck, they were able to send 20 B-24s to bomb the airdrome in Mostar, Yugoslavia, on January 8—less than three weeks after the advance echelon arrived.[13]

Throughout January administrative issues continued to be ironed out at group headquarters. The quartering of personnel was chief among their concerns, since there were not enough "inherited" barracks, and the ones they did have were in various states of disrepair. The four-man tents for the ground echelon finally arrived, but a continued lack of building supplies, constant rains, and cold weather hampered all of their efforts. However, the group's primary job continued without cessation. In January 1944 the 450th flew 20 bombing missions in 24 days to targets in Yugoslavia and northern Italy. At one point they flew missions twelve days in a row. The targets consisted mainly of key rail marshalling yards and transportation centers.[14]

An entry from the 450th's war diary sums up the problems encountered in February: "Bad weather getting worse." The group was only able to fly 11 missions for the month.[15] They were experiencing a sample of what their fellow airmen in England had been dealing with for two years. However, February was an important month for the 450th Bomb Group. Late in the month they participated in "Big Week," a plan that had been postponed since November due to weather, other attacks, and lack of personnel. The plan, devised by Colonel Richard D'Oyly Hughes, called for coordi-

Typical street in Manduria. (Grant D. Caywood)

nated, concentrated strikes on the German aircraft industry by the 8th AAF, 15th AAF, and RAF Bomber Command "to break the back of the Luftwaffe." Principal among the targets were the heavily defended cities of Schweinfurt and Regensburg in Germany and Steyr in Austria. An optimistic weather forecast for late February prompted Hughes to push his plan once again. He took it to Major General Frederick L. Anderson, Jr., the deputy commander for operations, U.S. Strategic Air Forces in Europe, who approved the plan. Anderson then took it to his commanding general, Lieutenant General Carl Spaatz, for approval. Spaatz was a little skeptical of the plan and only gave the "go ahead" for one day of bombing. Big Week began on February 20; moderate success and acceptable loss rates for the day prompted Spaatz to approve the rest of Hughes' plan. The 8th AAF bore the duty on February 21, but the next day the 450th Bomb Group and the 15th AAF were called into action. On that day their target was the Obertrauling Aircraft plant, a Messerschmitt factory in Regensburg, Germany, which had been nearly destroyed back in August. It had been repaired and was producing more fighters than ever. The plan called for the 8th AAF to bomb the plant with approximately 125 aircraft. This attack would be followed an hour later by the 15th AAF, with 84 aircraft—the 450th accounted for half of the 15th's strength that day. The next day, February 23, weather prevented the 8th from flying, but the 450th sent thirty-five B-24s to bomb the Aero Engine Works facility in Steyr, Austria. Bad weather prevented the 450th from bombing Schweinfurt the next day, but

4. "Cottontails" in the Heel of the Boot

450th BG Base in Manduria—tufa barracks and tents. (Marshall Samms)

the 8th AAF was able to send nearly 500 heavy bombers to attack two different plants in the area. The weather cleared on February 25 and the 450th sent 22 B-24s to bomb the Prufering Aircraft Factory in Regensburg.[16]

The last mission of Big Week for the 450th Bomb Group was the February 25 mission to Regensburg. The distinctive "white tails" on their B-24s were noticed by the Luftwaffe and that evening upon their return they received a warning on the radio from propagandist Axis Sally, "better known to the airmen as the *Berlin Bitch.*" She cautioned the "white-tailed Liberators" from Manduria with her sultry, sexy voice that the Luftwaffe would be waiting for them on subsequent missions.[17]

An interesting side note is that Axis Sally was actually an American. Born Mildred Elizabeth Sisk in Portland, Maine, she was known as Mildred Gillars after her mother divorced and remarried. She wanted to pursue a stage career, but that never panned out. In the early 1930s, Mildred moved to Europe, where she worked "as a governess and salesgirl." In 1935, she moved to Germany and taught English at the Berlitz School of Languages in Berlin. Due to the low pay as an English teacher, she accepted a job as an announcer and actress with Radio Berlin. It was not the stage, but for her it was a better job. During World War II she hosted a German propaganda show called "Home Sweet Home," under the name "Midge at the mike," in which she tried to bring down the morale of Allied troops. It usually aired sometime between 1800 and 0200 each night. To gain an audience she alternated her "intelligence reports" with popular American music. After the war, she was eventually arrested and tried for treason. Convicted in 1949, she served 12 years at the Federal Women's Reformatory in Alderson, West Virginia. Afterwards she taught music for a while at a Catholic girls' school and then received a bachelor's degree in speech from Ohio Wesleyan. Mildred died in 1988 at the age of 87. Her chiding, "white-tailed Liberator" comment evolved into the nickname "cottontail." Afterwards the 450th Bomb Group was distinguished from other groups in the area thanks to the nickname. However, this distinction came at a price. Often the Luftwaffe would overlook other groups so that they could focus on the famous Cottontails.[18]

Less than two weeks after the group earned the new nickname, *Shadow* and her crew arrived in Manduria. Almost everyone's first, and lasting, impression of Manduria was the mud, and it was no different for Caywood's crew. It was everywhere. In each of their mission diaries, Gilliam and Jacobson include in their first entries on March 8 a mention of mud. Gilliam wrote, "We landed at our new home, a muddy field outside of Manduria." Jacobson's entry from the same date echoes, almost word for word, the same description. Co-pilot Maurice Erickson recalled that his first impression of the base was quite depressing. "If it wasn't raining, it was going to rain." By the time Caywood and the crew of *Shadow* arrived in March 1944, the base had also earned a nickname: "Lake Manduria."[19]

By March, the inherited base was still being converted to allow military use. Just east of the runways there was a section for each of the four squadrons. The long, narrow, wooden barracks that housed the men were German prefabs. The officers' barracks, like all of the others, were one story and full of rats. They contained four canvas GI folding cots per room. This worked out well; all of the officers from a crew could bunk together. However, it was a tight fit, because the room barely had space for the cots, much less all of their gear. The cots had no sheets. Airmen covered themselves as best they could with ill-fitting wool GI blankets. The barracks did not have running water or heat, but the men managed to create some makeshift accommodations. The enlisted men had less pri-

Samuel Stein, a ground crew member in the 721st Squadron, 450th BG. (Samuel Stein)

4. "Cottontails" in the Heel of the Boot 81

450th BG B-24 #278291. The white-tailed rudders led to the 450th Bomb Group's nickname, the Cottontails. On later models, the distinguishing feature was removed for the airmen's protection. (Grant D. Caywood)

vacy, as they shared a barracks with between 30 and 40 other airmen—approximately six crews of enlisted men. The officer and enlisted barracks were essentially the same except for the room division in the officers' quarters. The barracks where Gilliam and the other enlisted men from Caywood's crew lived was already named the "Cotton Club." Their room had a stove that "was GI crafted, using a 55-gallon drum with a hole cut in the side near the bottom, with a small pipe for a smokestack. Engine oil with a small amount of gasoline added was fed into the barrel through a pipe" from another barrel outside the barracks. "The heat was almost instant." Since there was no indoor plumbing, a long trough was set up for the men to wash and shave. Running water was provided in the communal latrine and there were also some "squat and drop toilets." Gilliam remembered, "Not far from our quarters was an underground air raid shelter. Once in a while there was an air raid siren that awoke us in the night, and we would run to it for cover." Luckily, most of them were false alarms. The barracks were their home away from home—their safe haven. However, the close quarters also served as a painful reminder of the job at hand. As Ted Morris somberly reflected, "Some men were missing from the barracks after each flight."[20]

Between the barracks and squadron areas and the runways were the control tower, the 47th Wing headquarters, and the 450th Bomb Group headquarters. Both of the headquarters buildings were "liberated" farmhouses made of tufa blocks—as was the headquarters of the 720th squadron. Tufa was a sedimentary rock made up of calcium carbonate deposits. It was native to the area, could be sawed to shape, and was used in buildings much like cinderblocks in the U.S.[21]

Aerial view of the 450th BG's base in Manduria, Italy. The front gate, guarded by M.P.s, is in the bottom right corner. The runway spans the top portion of the photograph. The dark section below the runway on the right is an olive grove. The 721st and 722nd Squadron's tents and buildings are on the bottom left. The parachute building is in the right center. To its left with a camouflaged top (above the 721st and 722nd buildings) is the control tower and headquarters. The 720th Squadron buildings are between the olive grove and the parachute building in the top right. The 723rd Squadron (not pictured) was located to the right of the 720th Squadron. (James Strickland)

A British flak crew guarded the field at Manduria. Although they were rarely called into action, they served as a reminder that even at their home base the enemy could attack. Erickson remembered, "The first or second night we were there an enemy aircraft flew over our field." The Brits fired, but no bombs were dropped and no planes were shot down.[22]

Although there was an old hangar on the base, it was not used as such, because of its condition and the number of bombers the group had—60 plus at any given time. Instead, the building was converted for administrative duties. Briefings and debriefings comprised the bulk of its functionality. So for all practical purposes, the base did not have a functioning hangar. The bombers were parked just west of the runway out in the open. It was there that all servicing was completed—rain or shine. The field and runway had no lights so it was important for the birds to be back from their missions by sundown in order to see how to land.[23]

The 7,000-foot runway and parallel taxiway prompted strong feelings among those who traversed them. When the group arrived in December, the base had just the one runway, which was in dreadful condition. The engineers worked to get it in shape. It was soon decided that a taxiway was needed to accommodate the number of planes in the 450th. Construction of the taxiway was nearing completion when Caywood's crew arrived in early March. At the end of the runways were loose collections of large rocks and an olive grove, whose trees had been clipped almost daily since January by Liberator propellers. Most props, in turn, were stained green from the process. *Shadow*'s co-pilot, Maurice Erickson, recalls that the runways were "too short and too narrow." The seemingly constant rains took their toll on the surfaces. They were a matter of extremes; they were either very muddy or very dusty. In either case, with a full load of fuel, a full bomb load, rocks, and an olive grove to negotiate, taking off was not an easy task. Stan Butynski, *Shadow*'s nose gunner, had the best seat in the house to view takeoffs—and the worst if something went wrong. He distinctly remembers, "There were three bumps in the runway. After the third bump you had better be airborne or you crashed into the rocks" and the olive grove. The runways were slightly elevated to permit water to drain. They were fitted with landing mats, also called "Marston mats," which were made out of pierced steel planks and were joined with a locking spring clip. The AAF also used another version made of steel mesh. Although neither was as sturdy as concrete, they were a necessity on the makeshift runways at Manduria. The slight elevation which caused the water to run off is probably the reason that most members of the group remember the mud.

British flak crew at Manduria. These brave men protected the 450th BG's base from sporadic attacks by enemy planes. (Grant D. Caywood)

Aerial view of the 450th Bomb Group's 7,000-foot runway in Manduria, Italy. (Grant D. Caywood)

The area surrounding the runways was always a quagmire. This contempt was compounded by the fact that the airmen had to march in this mud during various parades and exercises. Sam Stein will never forget the problems he and fellow members of the ground crew faced daily in dealing with the mud while servicing the B-24s at Manduria. "Going out to maintain the planes was a job in itself. Each time you put your foot down, the heavy mud stuck to your shoes. As you walked you got taller and taller. After a while the weight of the mud on your shoes was so heavy that to walk you had to scrape it off and start all over again."[24]

The town of Manduria was yet another "part" of the base. One could not help but feel the town's presence, even though it was nearly two miles to the south. Language was always a barrier, since most Americans could not understand Italian and vice versa. The peasants and peddlers from town were a constant fixture outside the base. They were always trying to sell something, usually produce, or beg for something from the airmen. This was especially true of the children, who were poorly clothed and malnourished. Stein reflected, "They wanted candy, gum or anything we could give them. It broke our hearts to see children in that condition." Sadly, their lives seemed more like mere survival rather than living. The Italians loved K rations

4. "Cottontails" in the Heel of the Boot

Shadow parked beside the runway. Note the mud surrounding the runway, which earned the base the nickname "Lake Manduria." (Ted Morris)

Shadow's nose gunner, Stan Butynski. (Grant D. Caywood)

and American cigarettes and would trade most anything for them. Americans bought cigarettes for 5 cents a pack and could sell them for $3.00 a pack to the locals, but most used them to barter. Some of the officers and enlisted men had their clothes laundered by the locals— the going rate was a pack of cigarettes. With all the mud and muck on base, this was steady work for the villagers. "An Italian fellow came down with a push cart and collected

Above: Kids in Manduria. (Grant D. Caywood)

4. "Cottontails" in the Heel of the Boot

Vendors outside the 450th BG's base in Manduria. (Grant D. Caywood)

Ted Morris giving candy to kids in Manduria. (Maurice H. Gilliam)

everyone's laundry. Each piece of laundry bore our Army serial numbers so they could identify and separate the clothing," Stein said. Because there was "little if anything to buy" and "nothing to do" there, the town of Manduria itself held little appeal to most members of the 450th Bomb Group. On non-operational days and days that missions were cancelled due to bad weather, some of the men were given passes to visit nearby towns, such as Taranto and Brindisi. Taranto was a favorite, because it was a larger city and offered the airmen more things to do and purchase. Located just west of Manduria, Taranto was on the water and did not have as much poverty as did the smaller towns in the area. Ted Morris remembers renting bikes and exploring the countryside with the rest of *Shadow*'s enlisted men when they had passes. Some men walked, some hitched rides, but most airmen tried to get off base in some manner whenever they could. Most still considered the Italians as an enemy. Although an unfortunate situation, it was understandable. All soldiers are "brainwashed" to a degree to hate the enemy and this case was no different, because until a few months before, the Italians had been their enemy.[25]

5

A Typical Mission: Enemy Above and Below

Although no two missions were exactly alike, the structural components of most mission days were the same. Easy missions were often called "milk runs." But with all of the interdependent factors, there was no such thing as a milk run. Depending on the theater, it was a twenty-four hour cycle that was repeated almost daily throughout the war. For the 450th Bomb Group a typical mission day started shortly after midnight, usually no later than 0200, when orders were received from the 47th Wing headquarters. Orders usually arrived at the group and wing headquarters around the same time, but not always. They arrived in a sealed envelope via messenger. Upon arrival, the Charge of Quarters, or CQ, accompanied by the messenger, "woke up the commander and the intelligence officer … The bomb loading information had already come in via telephone, and the armament officer and his crew were already loading the bombers," Caywood said. The crews were awakened between 0300 and 0400. The squadron operations officer alerted each crew to their flight status and aircraft assignment the day before via the bulletin board; so many of those anxious men had not slept at all when the early wake up call came. By this time, each squadron's ground crew had been working for hours. Caywood appreciatively remembers their contribution. "The ground crews of the squadron worked as one big machine, dovetailing each of their parts of the work together with that of someone else to get the airplanes ready for the flight crews." The ground crews were responsible for a host of duties that kept the bombers flight ready. They included armament (bombs), armorer (machine guns), communication, maintenance, meteorology, metal works, mechanics, and photography, to name just a few. "The aircraft maintenance crews

450th BG headquarters building at Manduria. (Grant D. Caywood)

were grooming, fussing over, fixing, and worrying about their airplanes most of the night. They always worried; they always worked. They were the most unsung heroes of the squadron. The ground crews were as much a part of the airplanes as the engines or wings. They were always up earlier and later than anyone else in the outfit. The only rest they ever had was when their birds were in the air"—if then.[1]

Sam Stein, a ground crew member in the 721st Squadron, was intensely loyal to his crews. "I was on the field for every takeoff and landing—except for the time I was in Rome at Rest Camp. I used to count the planes as they went up and when they came back." The hard part of counting the planes upon their return came when he saw a red flare from one or more of the planes as they came into sight. This signaled that a B-24 was in trouble or had injured men aboard. Ambulances were on standby. "That's when you started worrying what had happened."[2]

For the flight crews, after their wake up calls, it was a rush to make up their bunks and head for breakfast in the mess hall. Breakfast usually consisted of powdered eggs, toast, jelly, bacon, and coffee. During breakfast the crews sat together, and the conversation, if any, revolved around speculation of the target. Crews ate, slept, and lived the targets. However, many days the crews sat in silence, deep in their own thoughts. The tension always mounted during breakfast. It was then back to the barracks to suit up in flight gear. After breakfast—which was only coffee for some—and suiting up, the officers (pilot, co-pilot, bombardier, and navigator), engineer and radio operator attended the flight briefing in a small room in the hangar build-

5. A Typical Mission

Maintenance on a B-24 in Manduria. The combat airmen considered the ground crews the unsung heroes of the war. They were as much a part of the airplanes as the engines or wings. (Grant D. Caywood)

ing. The briefing time, usually between 0400 and 0500, was set to give the crews as much sleep as possible (if they could sleep) and to get to the target "when the light was sufficient for the bombardier to see the target"—the earlier the better due to enemy intelligence of missions. The room, just large enough to hold all the participants and reminiscent of a lecture room, was guarded by MPs. All windows and openings, including knotholes, were covered. Once all of the crews were in the room the door was locked and the briefing began. At the front of the room was a curtain covering a map of the target. After everyone was securely in the room, the briefing officer pulled the cord to expose the target. Depending on the target, sometimes there were gasps, curses, cheers, or even worse, silence, from the onlookers.[3]

Once the map was revealed, the briefing officer advised the crews of the specific location and route to target. He outlined expected weather en route and over the target, and the Initial Point (IP) where the bomb run was to begin. He told about the expected opposition from flak and enemy fighters, and described the fighter escort (if any), the bomb load, and the radio call signs. He directed which runway the bombers would use for takeoff, each crew's position in the formation, and the exact times to specific positions and rendezvous points. Reconnaissance photos of the targets were also presented so that the navigator and bombardier could have a visual picture of the target in his mind. The briefing ended with a time "hack," which synchronized all watches for the mission.[4]

Immediately after the briefing, attendees met up with the rest of the crew at the squadron's parachute building. The structure, like most other buildings on base, was an inherited, wooden German "prefab." The 720th's was painted a bluish green. Here the crews drew their chutes, flak suits, and escape kits. The escape kits contained a mix of items needed in case of a bail out. For most missions they included local

Enlisted men wait outside during the officers' briefing. Because the combat airmen awoke for each mission between 0300 and 0400, they took every opportunity they could to get a little extra sleep.

maps of the target territory (if available), a compass, chocolate, some food, and "local" money. Also at this time, one or more of the officers picked up first aid kits, which were carefully controlled, because they contained morphine. Trucks and jeeps were waiting at the parachute building to take the crews to their birds. To ensure the mission's secrecy, the pilot waited to brief the rest of the crew once they were at the plane; sometimes, he waited until they were airborne. Each member of the crew loaded his gear and entered his aircraft through the bomb bay. The bombardier installed his bombsight; the navigator got his charts and equipment in place; the waist gunners installed their guns; they all put on the radio headsets at their respective stations for an intercom check-in. They then went through the written pre-flight checklist. After a few missions, crews seldom used these, because the procedure became such a routine they could do it in their sleep. Caywood commented, "Each man knew his position well enough so that it was too much of a nuisance and took too much time to read the words and get a response. We verified it from time to time on practice missions. As a practical matter, we checked each other, and I (as pilot) always called each position to be sure the man was in place. The men would usually respond with their position or nickname and 'OK here'—it was not very formal." Once this check was complete, the pilot gave a signal to the ground crew that he was going to start the engines.[5]

Ideally the B-24s were rolling at daybreak; so next it was time to get into the designated order for takeoff. This was disclosed at the briefing and depended on the crew's position in the squadron's, or group's, formation. Green or red lights from the control tower signaled *go* or *no go* to the pilots. The takeoff interval was between 30 and 60 seconds; however, this often varied. If the runway was dusty, the prop wash would make it impossible to see the end, especially after a few B-24s had lumbered down the runway. Pilots had to be able to see the entire runway in the event of an abort ahead of them. A crosswind was a blessing, because it helped to clear the dust away. The runway itself at Manduria was another problem with which the crews had to contend. *Shadow's* nose gunner, Stan Butynski, remembers tensely counting the bumps in the runway. Crews had to be airborne just after the third bump to avoid crashing into the rocks and olive grove at the end. Due to the full bomb loads and fuel tanks, most of the 450th's propellers were stained green from the leaves of the olive trees, as each struggled to climb just high enough to avoid disaster. However, this was not always the case. Caywood remembers one crew that crashed on the rocks. "The guys inside were screaming, 'Get us out!' They all burned up in the crash." It was horrible. It is no wonder that *Shadow's* co-pilot, Maurice Erickson, recalls that a "safe takeoff was the first triumph of the day."[6]

There were different perspectives to takeoff. The gunners in the rear of the plane could only see out of the rear or sides. With a full bomb and fuel load, B-24 pilots often had the four gunners in the aft of the bomber (ball, tail and two waist gunners) huddle in the middle of the airplane near the bomb bay to shift their weight from the rear of the plane—this sometimes made the difference in clearing the olive trees. In that position, those four could see nothing of the takeoff. They could only listen to the roar of the engines and "feel the thrust of the props" as they labored to lift the ship from the ground. Often they would feel it rise and settle a few times before they were airborne. As mentioned, nose gunners like Butynski had a front row seat. They could see every crack, crevice, rock, and puddle in the runway. However, for

720th Squadron parachute building. (Grant D. Caywood)

most takeoffs and landings, the crew in the nose of the bomber—navigator, bombardier, and nose gunner—stood on the flight deck behind the pilots. This was because the nose compartment was very vulnerable and unprotected in the event of a crash.[7]

Meanwhile, in the "front office," or cockpit, the pilot and co-pilot were doing the real work. Caywood vividly described the procedure in his memoir. Once he got clearance from the control tower, he "smoothly but definitely fed a fistful of throttles to the forward stops. The turbochargers screamed, and with the roar of full take off power, the bomber with its lethal load shuddered and lumbered forward, slowly at first. Then with increasing acceleration that shoved the crewmen into the backs of their seats, the aircraft gained momentum. The nose wheel came off the ground, and the ship raced at the end of the runway. With a maximum load, the wings struggled to get enough lift to raise the huge machine into the air. The great tires were pounding the runway, their wheel struts giving and taking with the bumps." Near the end of the runway, "the pilot gave a little extra tug on the wheel, and the bird staggered into the air."[8]

Once airborne the "rat race to get into formation" began. If they had to meet up with another bomber group—which they did on nearly every mission—that increased the complexity of and the precision with which the formation had to be carried out. The essential component of the bomber formation was called an element or combat box. It usually consisted of six planes in the following sequence:[9]

5. A Typical Mission   95

```
         1
     3       2
         4
     5       6
```

The combat box concentrated each plane's guns to be most effective in the event of fighter opposition, while limiting the risk of shooting one of the aircraft in their own element—or adjacent elements. Flying in this prescribed pattern was key to survival, as it increased both the group's offensive and defensive strength. The number 4 plane, in the middle of the element, had the most protection in the event of such an attack. Depending on the mission, the number of bombers, and condition of the runway, it could take upwards of an hour to get all the group's planes up—most days it took about 35 to 40 minutes. Those airborne circled "the field until everyone was in formation." After the 450th got into its respective combat boxes, it met up with the other groups for the mission en route. Flying in a tight formation was not an easy task. Caywood remembers that the B-24 was, "heavy on the controls and it took a lot of physical strength to fly, especially in a tight formation, but we got used to it." The bombers within each element were often so close that they sometimes clipped each other's wings. His co-pilot, Erickson, recalls that the Liberator "was a muscle airplane. It handled like an old truck—solid, dependable, and faithful." But the physical strain of driving the bomber forced the pilot and co-pilot to take turns at the controls on the long missions.[10]

"Each mission had a flavor all its own. Most of us were optimistic and just did our job," recalled *Shadow*'s engineer, Richard Jacobson. Caywood reflected, "Missions became pretty routine ... there was a desire to get there, hit the target, and bug out for home." Once underway, those not in their respective positions assumed them. The navigator headed to his station in the bomber's nose to

Shadow's pilot, Grant Caywood, at the controls in the "front office." (Maurice A. Erickson)

plot the course to the target. The bombardier also assumed his position in the nose. The engineer made constant checks on the airplane's equipment and fuel, while the pilot and co-pilot drove the bird. The gunners test fired their weapons to ensure that they were working. For the most part, there was radio silence on the way to the target. The life expectancy of a bomber crew was about fifteen missions. It did not take a mathematician to question the odds of returning. Most of the crew was deep in thought. Some wondered if this would be their last mission; all of them thought of loved ones. It could be as many as four hours to some targets; as the engines droned on, the crews fought fear and boredom—some slept. "It was a rough ride, filled with anxiety," recalled Gilliam.[11]

Because the B-24s were not pressurized, after reaching an altitude of about 10,000 feet the airmen put on their oxygen masks. Above that height, oxygen deprivation, or anoxia, became an issue. Frostbite also became a problem. The general rule is that the temperature drops about 3.5 degrees per 1,000 feet of altitude so at altitudes between 20,000 and 25,000 feet—standard for most bomb missions—the temperature could drop to 40 or 50 degrees below zero.[12]

Cold was not the only discomfort. There were no bathrooms on a B-24. If someone had to urinate, he had to use the "relief tube," which had a funnel on one end of a hose, and whose other end was piped to the exterior of the plane. "They smelled bad [if] they were not well cleaned," Gilliam said, and were awkward at best. At certain altitudes they froze. The difficulty was also compounded when one factors in the thick, layered clothing each man had to wear on the mission. There was no facility for defecation. "One just managed," he said. Ted Morris recalls one incident involving Robert Stricklin. Before one mission, Strick drank too much coffee, and once airborne he needed to use the relief tube. Ted was in the ball looking for enemy fighters, when all of a sudden his turret was hit with what appeared to be a "mud storm." Upon takeoff at Manduria *Shadow*'s belly had been covered in mud. When Strick relieved himself, it loosened the mud and hit Ted's turret, which was directly downstream. Before the next mission, Ted took a large can from the mess hall and gave it to his bombardier. He told Strick to use that next time he needed to go at 20,000 feet. The incident became a running joke with the crew.[13]

Noise was another factor. With four props and engines droning and the constant slipstream of air, it was nearly impossible to hear anything else. Not being able to hear the distant flak bursts over the noise provided an eerie comfort, but it also had an isolating effect, especially for the gunners in the turrets.[14]

Training had taught crews to work together as one unit. Each airman in the bomber had a specific interdependent task to perform. The success of the mission was contingent upon the effective execution and coordination of these roles. General Hap Arnold is credited with the quotation, "Nowhere in the world are the lives of men as interdependent as in a bomber on a mission." He could not have been more right.[15]

The pilot was the bomber commander. His job was to manage all of the controls and instruments and drive the aircraft. In addition, he was in charge of his crew twenty-fours hours a day—he was never off-duty for his crew. Their discipline and

5. A Typical Mission 97

Caywood (left) and Erickson on the wing of a downed FW 190. Caywood and Erickson made an excellent team. They had an almost symbiotic relationship in the cockpit. (Grant D. Caywood)

morale were his responsibility. In short, their survival depended on his capable leadership.[16]

The bomber's co-pilot worked very closely with the pilot. They often performed the same duties. *Shadow*'s co-pilot, Maurice Erickson, had an almost symbiotic relationship with Caywood in the cockpit. They worked as one unit, often without verbal communication. "We both knew what to do and did it," Caywood recalls. Sometimes a simple nod or look was enough to let the other know what needed to be done. This could be adjusting the manifold pressure and rpm on each engine, synchronizing the props after take off, or one of the dozens of other things that had to be done to keep them airborne. Both constantly checked the instruments to ensure that everything was working properly.[17]

The navigator's job was to get the bomber to the target and home again; he had to know where the airplane was at all times. He had to plot every course and furnish the pilot with flight directions. He combined various methods to do this, including dead reckoning, radio navigation, pilotage, and celestial navigation. In dead reckoning the navigator uses speed and time to calculate position. Caywood explained, "This has to be corrected because of wind, airspeed, altitude, etc." To accomplish this the navigator either uses celestial navigation, the use of stars and other the heavenly bodies to determine position, or pilotage, the use of visual landmarks as a reference point. Radio navigation is another method employed; in it the navigator guides the aircraft via radio directive devices. Navigation in World War II was an art as well a science. *Shadow*'s navigator, Herb Gouldon, was masterful in the role. The navigator was also trained as a gunner and could perform as such if needed.[18]

As stated, each role was interdependent; without one position properly manned a mission could be in jeopardy. However, there is no argument that the purpose of each mission was to drop bombs on a target. That job fell to the bombardier. He sat below the nose turret gunner, looking out of the Plexiglas window in the front of the bomber. As the bomb run commenced, the bombardier crouched in his seat to look through the bombsight. During this vital time, usually less than five minutes, he controlled and directed the airplane. His steady hands delivered the deadly cargo to the target below. When needed, like the navigator, he could also be used as a gunner.[19]

The B-24's engineer, also called 1st engineer, was the senior enlisted man of the crew; he had to know more about the airplane than any other member of the crew. *Shadow*'s engineer, Richard Jacobson, remembers that the training was "pretty intense, but as in many other things, practical experience was the best teacher." As engineer he was responsible for the operation and equipment on the bomber. Jake always checked over his ship with the ground crew and was always alert to notice problems in the air. The engineer was in charge of the transfer of fuel from auxiliary wing tanks on long trips and for emergency fuel cutoff to disabled engines. Among his duties were the crew's crash procedures and countless other details. The engineer was also a gunner; he manned the two .50-caliber machine guns in the top turret, which was located just behind and

Shadow's navigator Herb Gouldon at his station in the bomber. (Maurice A. Erickson)

above the pilot and co-pilot. "Once in the top turret I had a commanding view of the air space; I could sight enemy aircraft from all directions, and could alert both the pilots and gunners," Jake proudly recalls. While not in the Plexiglas bubble, he sat directly behind the "front office." Jacobson was fortunate in that Caywood was an excellent teacher. He taught his engineer about the flight instruments, so that if either he or Erickson were hurt, Jake could be useful. Because he had the same view at takeoff as the pilots and worked in such close proximity with them, he became very familiar with "the routine of flap positions, air speed, landing gear, etc." This knowledge was crucial, because the engineer had specific and important duties in the event of hydraulic failure.[20]

Shadow's bombardier Robert Stricklin in the nose of a B-24. (Maurice A. Erickson)

The bomber's radio operator operated the airplane's radio, direction finder, radio compass, and related equipment. The pilot had a cockpit ADF (automatic direction finder) or "birddog," which had a needle that pointed to stations for fixing the plane's position. The navigator and radio operator also had an ADF. The radio operator relayed key data to ground personnel, such as informing headquarters of the bombing results of targets. He was responsible for transmitting the navigator's position reports to the formation commander every thirty minutes and he assisted "the navigator in taking fixes." It was also his responsibility to receive weather and other information and to send out distress signals if needed. He maintained the radio log and equipment. When not flying in the lead airplane, or when under attack, he also served as a waist gunner. This was a matter of convenience, since the radio operator's table was located above the bomb bay, just up from the waist gun area. The area was so small and cramped that while sitting at the radio table his head touched the ceiling of the aircraft. When the pilot permitted it, the radio operator could tune the radio to music so the men could relax a little.[21]

Each gunner in a B-24 manned his respective .50-caliber Browning machine

Manuel Esquivel at his waist gun port on *Shadow*. He painted his wife's name (Rita) under his port for good luck. (Maurice H. Gilliam)

guns and informed the pilots of approaching enemy fighters. In addition, each gunner was responsible for the service of his guns and turret (if applicable) while in flight. Each was also cross-trained in another position if the need arose. The two waist gunners (left and right) protected the sides of the aircraft from enemy fighters. Because the waist windows were just wide openings, the exposure to the elements made them the most vulnerable to frostbite. Each manned a single, sixty-five pound, .50-caliber machine gun mounted on a swivel. During intense fighter attacks, the waist gunners were often side-to-side and back-to-back in their close quarters. Many times they bumped into each other. They had to be careful not to trip over empty shell casings, and in the heat of an attack, they had to be careful not to fire on bombers in their formation—including their own airplane.[22]

At a predetermined point upon approach of the target, the waist gunners threw out tiny strips of foil paper called "window"—now known as chaff. It resembled Christmas tree tinsel and was "the simplest of all electronic countermeasures."[23] The foil "reflected the enemy radar and gave him false readings on his instruments." Therefore, each bomber appeared as up to ten bombers on radar. During World War II there was no way for the radar operators to distinguish real from false targets. Window was most effective when used at night, because enemy fighters needed the radar fix to zero in on their intended targets. During daylight raids, the "bandits" could make visual decisions to attack. However, it was useful in misdirecting some of the enemy's flak batteries.[24]

Shadow's radio operator Manuel Esquivel at his desk in the bomber. (Maurice A. Erickson)

The ball turret was arguably the most precarious and vulnerable position to man in a B-24. The ball turret in a B-24 could be raised and lowered, unlike the one on a B-17. The gunner usually lowered and entered "the ball" as the formation approached enemy territory and exited it when clear of the same on the way home. A ball gunner's turret was so small that he could not wear a parachute while inside it. His job was to man two .50-caliber machine guns and protect the bomber from any enemy attacks from below.[25] *Shadow*'s ball turret gunner, Ted Morris, remembers that while in the ball he commanded the best view of the bombs dropping. His turret was directly behind the bomb bay doors. "When we reached the target I would turn my guns toward the front of the airplane so that I could see up into the bomb bay. I could see when the bomb bay doors opened and I was able to follow the bombs down to the target—conditions permitting."[26]

The next most hazardous and lonely position in the B-24 was that of the tail gunner. In his turret he manned two .50-caliber machine guns and protected the airplane's rear from attack. As Maurice Gilliam jokingly recalls, "I did not see where we were going, I was looking at where we had been."[27] His counterpart at the other end of the bomber was the nose gunner, who manned two .50-caliber machine guns in the electrically powered nose turret. His job was to guard the aircraft from a frontal attack. Since most attacks came from above, from the front and rear, these two gunners, along with the top turret gunner, remained active during most encounters with enemy fighters.

View from *Shadow*'s right waist gun over the Adriatic. (Grant D. Caywood)

As the bombers approached enemy territory the crews were on heightened alert. The contrails and roar of engines from the large formation of bombers could be seen and heard for miles by people on the ground. Airmen who had not yet donned their flak vests did so. Some waited because they were so heavy and cumbersome. The gunners strained their eyes looking for enemy fighters, while the pilot and co-pilot drove the plane under the careful guidance of the navigator. The Messerschmitt Bf 109 (ME-109) was the German fighter that the Allied crews faced the most in the skies above Europe. It was a single-seat, single-engine aircraft. Most models were equipped with Daimler-Benz (1200+ horsepower) motors. The armament included one 20mm cannon under the wing gondola and two 7.9mm machine guns in the nose. The second most encountered fighter was the single-seat, single-engine Focke-Wulf FW 190 (FW-190). It was armed with two 13mm machine guns in the nose, and depending on the model, either two or four 20mm cannons in the wings. The FW-190 was designated as a fighter-bomber, and each one could carry a 1,100-pound bomb under its fuselage. Another common German fighter was the Messerschmitt Bf 110 (ME-110). It was a two-seat, two-engine ship, with twin tails. The ME-110 was armed with two 20mm cannons and two 7.9mm machine guns in the nose. Some models also had bomb racks and two 7.9mm guns in the rear cockpit. Another fighter frequently encountered was the two-engine, four-seat Junkers JU 88 (JU-88). Depending on the model, it was armed with 13mm machine guns, 20mm cannons, and 7.92mm machine guns in various positions.[28]

All of the gunners were instructed to keep their turrets and guns in motion. This let any lurking fighters know that the crew was watching, alert, ready and waiting. Some gunners fired shots at fighters when the enemy was far out of range, just to deter an approach; however, this type of warning did not always work. "We never liked fighter interception," recalled Caywood, "but it came with the territory." An attack could come in an instant, seemingly from nowhere. A frantic call on the intercom let the rest of the crew know from where the "bandit" was approaching. Enemy passes lasted only a few seconds. Gunners could usually get off a couple of rounds before the attackers passed, but that was about it. If they were lucky, a fighter escort would deter the enemy, but they were not always available. It is no wonder that many B-24 crews, to this day, think that their escort fighters of P-38s and P-51s were "the most beautiful birds in the sky." Dogfights rarely occurred on bombing missions; it was usually one or two passes and out. Fighter opposition was just the first of many deterrents thrown up by the enemy.[29]

As the bomber formation neared the target, the fighter opposition (and escort) pulled back as the flak batteries began their solemn job—the fighters would usually reappear on the return home. Flak, the acronym for the German phrase "flugzeug abfall kanon, is translated as "aircraft downfall cannon," or antiaircraft gun. It was the most feared of all the enemy's opposition, because, for the most part, the airmen were helpless to its razor sharp shards of shrapnel. The mere mention of the word flak stirs strong emotions among airmen who had to fly through it. "Flak is a word that does not do justice to the damage and the anxiety the bloody stuff caused," remembers Jacobson. The old adage states, "there are no atheists in foxholes." Flak guaranteed that there were none in bombers. Gouldon somberly recalls that he was never very religious, but during the flak barrages, "I prayed to God for three more minutes just to get an even chance against the fighters on the return home." Radar allowed the enemy to throw it up with great accuracy, even through clouds. The most common antiaircraft gun used by the Germans was the 88mm, often called simply

Formation of 450th BG B-24s. Note the P-38 in the bottom center of the photograph. The nose section of the B-24 *Toni Gayle* can be seen at left. (Stan Butynski)

88. The guns came in several different forms. There were free standing models, which could be pulled behind vehicles and set in place where needed. Some were mounted on tank frames, while others were mounted on rail cars and deployed as needed around key marshalling targets. The guns were aimed at designated points in the bomber formation. The shells would explode at a predetermined altitude, based on how long or short the fuse was cut. They could be fired at a rate of 15 rounds per minute, but it took about 30 seconds for the shells to reach altitude. Flak was described in three categories. The first was the *caliber* of the gun, notated as "heavy," "moderate," or "light." The second was the *intensity*, which referred to the number of guns. Intensity was notated as "slight," "moderate," or "intense." The third category was *accuracy*, which described the ability of the flak to hit the target aircraft. It was designated as either "accurate" or "inaccurate."[30]

During this approach to the target, the navigator gave the pilot heading corrections and made constant reports on their position. Gilliam remembers, "The initial approach to the target always heightened our anxiety." Depending on the target, crews could face as much as thirty minutes of flak. This was especially true of heavily fortified and defended targets such as Munich, Ploesti and Bucharest—all of which were frequent missions for the 450th and the 15th AAF. Pilots could take some evasive action, which usually came in the form of turns about every fifteen seconds. Since it took approximately thirty seconds for the shells to reach altitude, "when we saw the flak guns flash below we would make a turn," Caywood recalled. Unfortunately

5. A Typical Mission

Flak: heavy, intense, and accurate. (Grant D. Caywood)

after the Initial Point (IP)—the designated point from which the bomb run was to begin—they could take no evasive action from flak, because the bombardier needed a stable platform. The aircrews could see the oily black residues left by the flak bursts. Gilliam recalls that when it hit the bomber it made an eerie sound, "like rocks thrown against a tin roof." The IP was usually an easily recognizable ground feature, such as a city, river, lake, mountain, or building, approximately ten to fifteen miles from the target. At this point in the mission it was imperative that all planes stay in formation and fly straight and level until the end of the bomb run so that all planes could drop on the lead bombardier's mark. The bombers had no choice but to fly through the flak.[31]

At the Initial Point, the bombardier controlled the plane through the bombsight, which was connected to the autopilot. "This was the most terrible part of the mission," Caywood wrote. The rest of the crew could do nothing else at this point, except listen to the intercom and watch flak bursts. "Now it is the bombardier's show—all his. The success or failure of the mission depends upon his training, ability, and cool head in the face of all this. Success or failure depends upon how deftly his fingers adjust rate and course in his bombsight. The airplane responds to the twist of his knobs, and the bombs drop automatically."[32]

In addition to the factors of flight, which had to be calculated, the bombardier's

B-24s from 450th BG in formation—note flak. (Grant D. Caywood)

accuracy also depended on the cloud cover over the target area. During World War II, as one historian described, "a fractional-notation system was used to denote cloud cover. The cloud coverage was expressed in 1/10ths. Thus, a solid overcast [was] denoted as 10/10 coverage. Heavy cloud coverage [was] denoted as 7/10 to 8/10. Light cloud coverage [was] denoted as 2/10 to 3/10."[33] By October 1943, some American bombardiers had radar equipment, known as "Mickey" or "Pathfinder," to curtail the cloud cover problem.

Only the lead bombardier in each element used the bombsight to drop his bombs. All others in the element opened their bomb bay doors when they saw the leader open his. The others, Caywood said, "dropped their bombs by watching the bomb bay of the lead ship and by operating a toggle switch when they saw the lead bombs fall. Since they were in formation, this was the only way possible."[34] Finally, over the target, after what seemed an eternity to the rest of the crew, the bombardier announced, "Bombs Away! Bomb bay doors coming closed." This was usually followed by "Let's get the Hell out of here!" from the rest of the crew. There was a "bit of an elevator feeling" upon the release of the bombs; some felt it more than others. This was the first of the "two best parts of the mission" for Richard Jacobson.[35]

After "bombs away," the entire formation turned "down and away, following the lead ship." They now had to negotiate their way back home; with the bombs dropped and the fuel tanks half empty, the return journey was always a little faster—but not easy. If the target was not obstructed, the crew was supposed to look for bombs hits;

5. *A Typical Mission*

Cottontail B-24s dropping bombs over a target. (Grant D. Caywood)

they would have to report these to the intelligence officer later. At nearly five miles up, it took about 30 seconds for the bombs to reach the ground—about the same time it took the flak to reach altitude and hit its target. They also still had to negotiate the flak and the enemy fighters. The groups, which had made individual bomb runs, would meet at a pre-designated rallying point afterwards to re-form the combat boxes for the return home.[36]

Sometimes on the way home, "Static" (Manny Esquivel), *Shadow*'s radio operator, tuned the radio to Axis Sally so that the crew could hear some music and relax a little. For members of the 450th, if the mission was to the east, to targets in Romania, Yugoslavia, Hungary or Austria, the sight of the Italian coastline on their return was always a welcome sight—they were almost home. It was at this point that many of the crew removed their flak vests and breathed a sigh of relief. They had survived another mission. However, they still had to land. Flak could cause damage that was not apparent until then, such as flattening tires or damaging the plane's landing gear. Erickson's most satisfying moment of a mission came when he "taxied in and parked safely after a mission."[37]

The ambulances were always standing by upon their return. Invariably someone needed medical attention. Whether the injury was received from fighters, flak, or frostbite, there was always a need. Once they disembarked their aircraft, crews headed to the Red Cross doughnut line located in front of group headquarters. There

***Shadow*'s crew at the Red Cross doughnut line after a mission. (Ted Morris)**

waiting for them were ladies with smiles, doughnuts, coffee or hot chocolate. A 2-ounce shot of 100-proof bourbon was dispensed by the squadron's flight surgeon to each airman who wanted it—most did. They knew they were safe again once they had their doughnut. After the "bomb's away!" call, this was Jake's favorite part of the mission. For many it was the first thing they had eaten since the night before. From there, it was off to debriefing.[38]

At debriefing, usually held in the hangar building, the crews gathered to answer questions from the group and wing intelligence officers. Invariably the first question was "Did you hit the target?" Often the crews could not answer this because of smoke coverage or cloud concealment. For most missions, photo recon airplanes were sent a few hours later, sometimes the next day, to confirm strikes. A sampling of the barrage of other questions includes: *How was the weather? Did you pick up the target from the IP? Did you have any trouble identifying the target? Were you on the correct altitude, speed, and time? How was the flak? How many flak batteries could you identify? Were they where they were supposed to be and were they mobile? How many and what type of fighter opposition did you encounter? Did the fighters seem to be experienced and aggressive? What type of attacks did they make and from what direction? At what time and where did you encounter them? How was your escort? Did anyone in your airplane get any photos? How many of our airplanes were damaged, failed to return, or returned early? How many wounded or dead? Did you see any parachutes from downed planes? How many fighters did you shoot down? How was your forma-*

tion? And the list continued. The questions, which seemed painful to some and pointless to others, were important. The answers helped in planning future missions and recording the success, or failure, of the day as accurately as possible. From this information, the intelligence officer would create his report (the S-2 Narrative or Special Narrative Report) of events, which was usually filed the next day. Today, these S-2 (Intelligence) reports provide historians and researchers with the only source material regarding some of these missions.[39]

After debriefing, the exhausted crews returned their parachutes and headed to their respective barracks. Some wrote letters home to loved ones; some recorded the day in their diaries and journals; others read; some played cards; they all said their prayers of thanks for a safe return. Everyone looked to see if they were scheduled to fly again the next day; many times they were. Then came sleep. Sweet sleep.

Radio operator Manuel Esquivel in full flight gear. Note the zippered A-6 sheepskin boots. Manny is standing in front of a tufa block building on the 450th BG's base in Manduria. (Grant D. Caywood)

For the crew of *Shadow*—and most other crews in the same circumstances—their bond intensified once they were overseas. They would soon be putting all of their training and preparation to the ultimate test. The changes in their daily interaction were small, almost imperceptible, but they all knew they would have to depend on each other to make it home alive. There was a bit of a stigma attached to being a replacement crew. To the veteran crews, replacements were a painful daily reminder of lost friends. Most crews kept to themselves; their best friends were their fellow crewmates.

6

March 1944: Baptism by Fire

Grant Caywood and the crew of *Shadow* had an uneventful hop from Tunis to Manduria. Like hundreds of airmen before them, they approached their new homes from the Bay of Taranto. Each one of the crew was filled with a mix of emotions. Some of them were curious; some were scared; some were excited, while others were just anxious to get their tour of duty completed. Whether able to admit it or not, all of them were intimidated by the inexperience. Maurice Gilliam recalls, "I was neither scared nor excited; I preferred to be at home, but that was not possible." They were a replacement crew; would there be a stigma with that? Would they be shunned or accepted by the veteran crews? These thoughts and more passed through their minds as they circled the ancient city below and began their descent to a runway surrounded by an old olive grove.[1]

Once they landed in Manduria, Caywood's crew knew that they would soon be flying combat missions. How much would combat differ from training? Did each really only have one in three chances of completing his tour? Their questions were understandable. But they were well trained; they were ready. Even though the crew probably did not realize it yet, in Caywood they had one of the most skilled and experienced pilots in the Mediterranean theater. Others would soon recognize this too. Just as in his primary flying school, he could not hide his ability.

Upon their arrival in Manduria on Wednesday, March 8, a "welcoming committee" greeted Caywood and his crew. The committee asked them for their K-rations, which consisted of chocolate bars, cheese, crackers, coffee, and chewing gum, among other American "staples." None of the crew realized their value in Manduria. (In the coming weeks, the men of *Shadow* welcomed as many new crews as possible to replenish their supply.) They were then shown to their quarters in the 720th Squadron's

6. March 1944

Aerial view of Manduria, Italy. (Ted Morris)

area. It really did not seem like a Wednesday to them, but days of the week had not meant anything to them for over a year now. As was customary, the four officers bunked together in a separate barracks from the enlisted men. For Caywood and his officers this was barracks "10B." Gilliam, Jake, Manny, Woody, Stan, and Ted took up residence in their new home, the "Cotton Club"—so designated by the wooden sign above their barracks door. Their arrival in camp was overshadowed by the frenzy to set up the new officer's club, which was slated to open the following night. It was appropriately named "The Cottontail Club." A light snow prevented the mission on March 9. The next one scheduled was Saturday, March 11. *Shadow*'s tail gunner, Maurice Gilliam, was the first of *Shadow*'s enlisted crew to fly a combat mission.[2]

Gilliam was drafted on the evening of Friday, March 10, to fly with 1st Lt. Reaford Charles McCraw's crew the next morning—they needed a tail gunner. McCraw, called "Mac" by his crew, was a happy-go-lucky boy from Oklahoma who was always telling a joke. Born on June 6, 1915, he was several years older than most pilots in the war. An aviation buff since a boy, he had taken some aeronautical engineering courses at Oklahoma University, but had to drop out due to lack of money during the Depression. Like Caywood, he took his job as pilot seriously and was a big-brother figure for his crew. McCraw was already something of a legend in the 720th Squadron. Just a few weeks before, on the February 25 mission to Regensburg, Germany, McCraw's B-24, *True Love*, experienced mechanical problems. Just after the bomb run, the bomber lost the supercharger in its number two engine. Upon return, this caused

Maurice Gilliam (left) and Richard Jacobson outside their barracks, dubbed the "Cotton Club." (Grant D. Caywood)

McCraw's ship to lag behind the rest of the formation. *True Love* was soon met by approximately forty ME-109s and FW-109s, which attacked aggressively in formations of six to eight planes. McCraw took what evasive action he could during the ninety-minute aerial battle, but the B-24 received extensive damage, which included "gaping holes in the wings, flaps, and fuselage rudder, and [the attack] holed the propellers. The electric, hydraulic, and oxygen systems suffered serious damage [that rendered] the heating, flaps, brakes, and gun turrets inoperable." McCraw was able to remain levelheaded. He took the ship down to an altitude where oxygen was not needed, but the enemy fighters continued their pursuit towards the Yugoslavian border. Realizing the gravity of the situation, McCraw took further evasive action, diving in a steep controlled spiral. This gave the enemy the impression that the bomber was in an uncontrollable dive. When the bandits finally broke off their pursuit, McCraw kept his ship low over the Adriatic and "skimmed" the water back to Manduria, where he returned his crew to safety. In 1998, two of *True Love's* enlisted men, Sgt. John Barnacle and Sgt. Charles Flanagan, petitioned successfully to have McCraw awarded the Distinguished Flying Cross posthumously for his heroism on this mission.[3]

Grant Caywood was also scheduled to fly his first mission on March 11. It was almost unheard of for a pilot to fly a combat mission (especially with a different crew) so soon. Usually there were test flights and some orientation, but Caywood's reputation preceded him. He was a leader, not a follower, and everyone in the 450th BG would soon recognize this.[4]

6. March 1944

Caywood (left) and Erickson outside of their barracks, "10B." (Grant D. Caywood)

The target for Saturday was the submarine repair facilities in Toulon, France.[5] Some questioned the effectiveness of bombing sub pens as a strategic target, because most, like those in Toulon, were covered with a twenty-foot concrete roof. The five hundred pound bombs just bounced off of them, causing little or no damage.[6] How-

Inside view of the 450th BG Officers' Club in Manduria, Italy. It was nicknamed "The Cottontail Club." (Grant D. Caywood)

ever, Toulon was an important harbor. In addition to the sub base, Toulon was the home of the Vichy fleet. The 450th BG started sending up its thirty-six B-24s at 0810. They were to rendezvous with the 98th BG, 376th BG, and 451st BG at 0840 about 6,500 feet above Manduria.[7] McCraw's B-24 had a flat tire that morning and was late to take-off.[8]

Once all of the groups formed up they would proceed to the Isle of Capri, then follow the prescribed course to the target. Twenty-eight of the 450th BG's B-24s reached the target at 1159 and released their bombs with some success. Bursts were seen in the target area at the marshalling yards and harbor installation. McCraw never caught up with the formation due to the flat tire, so he returned early, along with four other B-24s. His crew had to jettison their bomb load in the Adriatic upon return. Depending on the bomb load, this was common practice, because landing a B-24 full of bombs and fuel was treacherous. Maurice Gilliam had a lackluster first mission, but he did get credit for it—1 down, 49 to go.[9]

For the next five days the 450th BG "stood down" and flew no combat missions due to weather. On Sunday, March 12, Caywood flew an orientation flight with Capt. Floyd Robinson. Heavy rains that night prevented a mission on Monday. The crews passed the time as best as they could. Many of them found recreation in poker, craps, cribbage, or any number of other games. Airmen like Richard Jacobson found enter-

6. March 1944

A group of 450th BG officers relaxing at the Cottontail Club. *Shadow*'s bombardier Robert Stricklin is in the direct center of the photograph (just behind and to the right of the officer with his mouth open). Navigator Herb Gouldon is fourth from the left (another officer is leaning on his back). (Irene Stricklin Frazier)

tainment in music. Jake's saxophone, coupled with Red Mason's guitar and Harold Crevita's accordion, delighted all who heard them play. Everyone wrote letters home. Between Tuesday and Thursday Caywood managed to fly a few practice flights with his crew. He worried constantly about them; they were in his charge and he did everything in his power to make sure they were prepared.[10]

Their first combat mission as a crew came on Friday, March 17. Caywood and his crew were alerted of their flight status Thursday night; sleep did not come easy for most of the crew in their restless anticipation of the unknown. After breakfast and briefing, forty of the Cottontails' B-24s, including *Shadow*, began rolling down the runway at 0938. By 0947 they had rendezvoused with the 98th Bomb Group 4,000 feet above Manduria, and by 0952 they had met up with the 376th and 451st Bomb Groups to complete the formation. The target was the aircraft assembly installations at the Schwechat Airdrome (air base) in Vienna, Austria. The factory, twelve miles outside Vienna, assembled ME-109s. Vienna was a "double credit" target; it was the second best defended city on the continent, behind Berlin. It contained a number of strategic targets that included crude-oil refineries, oil storage depots, airdromes, aeroengines works, and marshalling yards. The German Air Force (GAF) put up a "ferocious resistance" to Allied attacks on Vienna.[11]

No enemy fighters were encountered on the way to the target and no flak was present in the target area; the enemy was not anticipating this mission. All seemed fine, except the weather, which was not cooperative. The skies were overcast and the target was obscured. Caywood and his crew had no trouble until they reached the target. When Stricklin tried to open the bomb bay doors they would not budge. The constant rain in Manduria caused the runway to be extremely muddy. Upon takeoff *Shadow's* belly was covered with mud. At 22,000 feet the mud had frozen the bomb bay doors shut. Ball turret gunner Ted Morris clearly remembers this first mission. "I could hear Stricklin tell Caywood over the intercom that the bomb bay doors wouldn't open." Without hesitation Caywood yelled back, "Drop 'em through the doors." Stricklin did. Morris remembers, "I could see every bit of it. The doors flapped in the wind all the way back to base." This made it even colder than it already was and Esquivel, whose radio desk was directly above the bomb bay, got frostbitten.[12]

The weather played havoc with the other B-24s. Only eleven of the 450th's initial forty bombers dropped near the target. Fourteen crews dropped their bombs on "targets of opportunity in Austria," while another five dropped on targets of opportunity at undisclosed locations. For most missions there was a primary and secondary target. When the primary target was covered, crews could hit the secondary.

1st Lt. Reaford McCraw, pilot of *True Love*, 720th Squadron, 450th BG. (Carol Ritter)

Some of the time when snafus occurred pilots chose a "target of opportunity" over enemy territory. The group returned to Manduria at about 1550. Despite the inaccuracy of the day's bombing and the bomb bay door mishap, Caywood's crew received credit for two missions. *Shadow* made it through her first mission and the crew gained some combat experience and confidence.[13]

Unfortunately, one of the 450th BG's bombers did not return. After extensive repairs from the February 25 mission, 1st Lt. Reaford McCraw's *True Love* experienced yet another mechanical failure, this time on the way to the target, somewhere over Yugoslavia. McCraw did his best to maintain control, but it was not possible. Sensing the futility of the situation, he demanded that his crew parachute to safety. McCraw

Music was one of the ways the men passed the time in Manduria. Here Richard Jacobson is entertaining some airmen with his saxophone, with Harold Crevita on accordion and Red Mason on guitar. (Richard M. Jacobson)

stayed at the controls until everyone was out. Sadly, just as McCraw made his way to the waist area to jump, *True Love* crashed into a mountain. His body was found just outside the bomber, beside the left waist window. Local partisans who aided downed American soldiers in the area helped the crew bury McCraw in a local cemetery. The partisans also helped the nine surviving crew members of *True Love* return to Manduria.[14]

Shortly after Caywood and his men finished the debriefing, they learned that they would be flying again in the morning. The ground crew repaired *Shadow*'s bomb bay doors that night. It was an early start for the airmen that Saturday; thirty-nine B-24s took off at 0730. The mission was to the Lavariano Airdrome dispersal area, near Udine, Italy, which was a key fighter field near Austria. The 450th BG rendezvoused with the 451st BG at 0810 over Manduria and proceeded to the target. The group had clear skies all the way to Lavariano, which was reached at 1104. For the second straight day no enemy fighters were encountered, but unlike Vienna the previous day, they did encounter flak. It was moderate, accurate and heavy. Jake got a hole in his top turret.[15]

The bombs for this mission were fragmentation, or frag, bombs. The target was hit with great accuracy as great concentrations of bursts were observed in the dis-

Shadow **taking off in Manduria. (Ted Morris)**

persal areas. Four enemy aircraft on the ground were hit—three fighters and one transport. The 450th BG returned to Manduria at 1325. Although the hole in Jake's turret was a little unnerving, the crew's second mission was a success. *Shadow*'s gunners had not seen any action yet, but that was fine with them.[16]

After dinner that night, *Shadow*'s crew was made flight ready for the third day in a row. The late briefing on Sunday morning, March 19, lulled everyone into believing that the target would be close or a milk run. They could not have been more wrong. The target was the Walzlagerwerke plant in Steyr, Austria, which produced 10 to 15 percent of Germany's ball bearings. AAF airmen dreaded Steyr, because it was heavily fortified with flak batteries. In addition to the ball bearing plant, the structure also housed the Daimler-Puch aircraft component factory, which "manufactured fuselages, undercarriages, cylinder crankcases, cylinder heads and other ME-109 components." The combined "sprawling factory complex [was] once the largest engineering works in Austria, employing 30,000 workers," as one account described it. Steyr was a key city in Hitler's war machine.[17]

The wait had been for the weather to clear over the target and the 450th BG did not begin sending up their B-24s until 1000. It was 1050 before they rendezvoused with the 98th BG over Manduria and 1057 when they met the 376th and 451st Bomb Groups to complete the formation. Cloud cover over Steyr prompted the group to hit the secondary target of Graz, Austria. About seven minutes from Graz, ten to fifteen enemy fighters, consisting of ME-109s and FW-190s, began attacking the formation at 21,000 feet. Maurice Gilliam, *Shadow*'s tail gunner, shot at his first fighter. The bandits were not aggressive, which suggested that they were trailing the formation, waiting for stragglers damaged by flak. The group's fighter escort, the first seen by Caywood's crew, also kept the enemy aircraft in check.[18]

Once over Graz, the group experienced "intense, accurate and heavy flak," which damaged sixteen of the 450th's aircraft. The target there was also covered in clouds, but a fortunate, momentary break in them allowed the lead bombardier to "make a short run and a factory area in the south center of town was selected as the aiming point," according to the mission's report. Clouds prevented photo confirmation

Shadow's bombardier, Robert Stricklin. (Grant D. Caywood)

and accurate visual observations, but several barracks were hit, as were some store buildings. Upon safe return, Caywood's crew had completed their fifth mission—the sixth for Caywood and Gilliam. They needed forty-five more missions to go home.[19]

The weather gave *Shadow*'s crew a much-needed rest for the next four days. Fog and drizzle kept most airmen in their barracks. Jake found his way to Bari and its small hotel. There he met up with some of the locals; he played his saxophone and they played their piano and violins. He recalls, "Playing the sax was a great outlet for me. I was able to discharge a lot of emotion." The 450th's recreation teams provided outlets for others. Boxing, baseball, and basketball were among some of the sports in which the Cottontails competed. In addition to music, Jake also boxed and played his favorite sport, baseball. The days of rest were always a nice break, but they did nothing to help the airmen reach their immediate goal of obtaining enough missions to go home. Too much idle time to think about the fifty-mission goal was detrimental to an airman's psyche.[20]

Shadow's crew was alerted on Wednesday night for a "big leaguer" on Thursday. After a 0430 briefing, the mission was scrapped due to weather. They were made flight ready again on Thursday night. It was another early start and the B-24s were rolling at 0732. The mission on March 24, for the second time in a row, was the Wal-

Crew of 450th BG B-24 *True Love*. Back row (left to right): 2nd Lt. William R. Taylor, navigator; 1st lt. Reaford C. McCraw, pilot; 2nd Lt. John S. Fulks, co-pilot; 2nd Lt. Ernest D. Connors, bombardier. Front row (left to right): S/Sgt. Thomas W. Netherton, tail turret gunner; T/Sgt. Dominique Juneau, engineer/top turret gunner; S/Sgt. Charles R. Flanagan, radio operator/waist gunner; S/Sgt. John F. Barnacle, ball turret gunner; S/Sgt. William H. Britton, nose gunner; S/Sgt. Harold J. Violet, waist gunner.

zlagerwerke ball bearing plant in Steyr, Austria. The 450th BG's forty-two B-24s could not rendezvous with the other groups due to weather conditions and lack of visibility. They took off in two attack units. The first unit, which consisted of only sixteen bombers, turned at Trieste in the northeast corner of Italy and headed for the alternate target at Rimini, an Italian port city on the Adriatic. The second unit turned back early due to "nearly solid overcast skies." The visibility was so bad that two of the second unit's bombers collided on the way to the target over the Adriatic; no parachutes were seen. In the area of Trieste the first unit was "aggressively attacked" by nearly forty enemy fighters, including ME-109s, FW-190s and JU-88s. The intensity of the attack was amplified by the fact that the group did not have a fighter escort. Gilliam wrote that night in his diary, "We sure would have like to have some P-38s [today]." Jake got another hole in his turret and Gilliam got the first one in his. Gilliam saw three B-24s go down, "one in flames." Of the sixteen B-24s in the first unit, thirteen made it to the marshalling rail yards at Rimini—Caywood and his crew were among them. There they were greeted with flak. The right side of Stan's nose turret was shot way. The main marshalling yard was hit, but cloud cover prevented any detailed accounting of the mission's success. When *Shadow* returned to Manduria in a slight drizzle at 1418, the crew breathed a sigh of relief. This had been their toughest mission yet. Unfortunately, it was more typical of bomber missions

Grant Caywood (left) and Manuel Esquivel survey flak damage to *Shadow* after a mission. (Grant D. Caywood)

than the ones they had experienced up to this point. The 450th lost six bombers on the mission; ten of the sixteen that made it to Rimini received flak holes. Each of Caywood's crew began to doubt seriously if he could survive forty-plus more missions like this one.[21]

Friday's rain continued through Monday. Monday night *Shadow*'s crew was placed on the list to fly the next day, March 28. The crew was a little uneasy with the posting because Caywood, Erickson and Gouldon were replaced with others for the mission. In their five months together Caywood had become a father figure to them. They trusted him and Erickson at the controls. However, Caywood had been ordered to run an errand up in Rome that day. Upon his return to Manduria he was able to view the last day of Mount Vesuvius' two-week eruption—its first major one since 1874. It was a magnificent and violent scene, a once in a lifetime experience; it was much like his crew's tour of duty.[22]

The briefing was later than usual that morning. The 450th BG's thirty-four bombers did not take off until 0845 because the target for the day, Mestre, Italy (near Venice), was relatively close. There was also the thought that by waiting, the muddy runways would dry out a little—they did not. The group was to bomb the marshalling yards, which connected an industrial and chemical plant. The weather, for the first time in weeks, was beautiful.[23]

The 450th BG met up with the 98th BG over Manduria at 0930 and together

Mt. Vesuvius (Naples, Italy) erupting—March 1944.

they comprised the initial wave of the attack force. The second wave consisted of the 376th BG; the 449th and 451st Bomb Groups were in the third wave. Their formation was complete over Ostuni. Eighteen minutes from Mestre six ME-109s were spotted a few thousand feet above the formation. They dove down and under, but did not make an attack. The fighters' "wings and fuselages were painted a mottled brown and they had red noses." They remained in sight until the target was reached at 1234. Heavy head winds en route put the formation twenty-four minutes behind schedule, but they were not penalized; the flak over the target was light and inaccurate. This, along with the lack of fighter interference and beautiful weather, allowed the group to make some very accurate drops on Mestre's marshalling yards. There were several direct hits on the chemical plant and industrial plant, as well as on some warehouses and other storage buildings. The railroads connecting these warehouses were also hit, as were some rail cars containing oil and gasoline. The mission was a complete success and it gave a tremendous boost of confidence to the crew of *Shadow*.[24]

Caywood, Erickson and Gouldon were back on the bulletin board with the rest of *Shadow*'s crew that evening. They would be flying together again in the morning. The mission for Wednesday, March 29, was to Bolzano, Italy; a town nestled in the Alps near the borders of Italy, Switzerland, and Austria. The 450th BG, along with the 451st BG, was to bomb the marshalling yards there. Albeit obscure, it was a vital

Part of *Shadow*'s crew after an Air Medal presentation. Back row (left to right): Maurice Erickson, Vincent Olney, Herb Gouldon, and Grant Caywood. Front row (left to right): Maurice Gilliam, Stan Butynski, Norman Woodward, and Richard Jacobson. (Richard Jacobson)

target due to its location. As in Mestre the day before, the object was marshalling yards. They were the arteries for Hitler's Third Reich. Targets like these were the central hubs in the system. The Allies believed that by crippling these strategic targets they were impeding Germany's ability to wage war. They were.[25]

It was an early takeoff, 0740, but it was another forty-five minutes before they rendezvoused with the 451st 3,000 feet above Manduria. They then joined the rest of the 47th Wing en route at Ostuni and flew up the Adriatic coastline of Italy. Upon turning inland at Padova (modern-day Padua), the group encountered twelve ME-109s. Another ten were picked up at Verona, south of the target. As they approached the target another thirteen joined the attack. The 47th Wing had a good fighter escort of P-38s above their formation that prevented any effective passes at the bombers. Gilliam recorded in his diary that "one of those beautiful P-38s was shot down." In addition, flak over the target shot the left wing off of a B-24 just ahead of *Shadow*'s combat box. The bomber immediately caught on fire—none of the crew had a chance to bail out.[26]

The bomb run commenced at 1214. The hits were concentrated and accurate. There were "ten direct hits at the choke point of the marshalling yard," the mission report said, with others knocking out two bridges. The locomotive depot and car repair shops were also hit. "The entire target area was smoke covered as the formation made its rally." Caywood and his crew returned safely back in Manduria at 1450. This was a double credit mission. With the six actual missions they had flown together to date, most men of *Shadow*'s crew now had received credit for nine of their fifty missions.[27]

That evening Caywood's airmen checked the board; they were scheduled to fly the next day. It would be their third mission in as many days. Exhaustion was more powerful than their fear or nerves that evening, so most of them slept well until the pre-dawn wake up. Forty-two of the 450th's B-24s, including *Shadow*, started down the runway at 0722. They met up with the 98th BG over Manduria at 0821 and then rendezvoused with the rest of the 47th Wing near San Vito Di Normannie. Their target for the day was the marshalling yards and industrial area in Sofia, the capital of Bulgaria. The target was a strategic and political one. Aside from damaging a key German rail center, an attack on Sofia was intended to increase the "dissatisfaction among the Balkan people with their Axis alliances."[28]

At about 0940, nineteen minutes from the target, thirteen enemy fighters (11 ME-109s and two FW-190s), approached the 47th Wing's formation. They made an uncoordinated pass and were easily handled by the fighter escort. The flak over the target was heavy, moderate, and accurate; however, the bombardiers made good runs at the target. Direct hits were recorded at the key choke point at the end of the marshalling yard and its adjacent buildings. Another 180 or so bombs fell in the south and southeast portions of the city, causing great destruction. "We blew it off the map," bragged Floyd Robinson that night in his diary. On their return another seven bandits made wide passes at the formation over Skopje, Yugoslavia (capital of modern-day Macedonia), with no success. Flak was also encountered over the city; five Liberators were hit.[29]

Caywood's crew and the rest of the 450th BG ended the month with a stand down; it rained once again. They had learned a lot in a short time. In just fifteen short days, *Shadow* had flown seven actual missions and had been credited with 10. It was a fast and furious pace, but it was the best thing for them. If an airman relaxed too much or had too much free time to think about the fifty-mission goal, he could lose his nerve.[30]

7

April 1944: "Goodbye Shadow"

"Sunny Italy" was anything but that on April Fool's Day 1944. "The usual continuous rain soaked the camp and added to the waters of *Lake Manduria*," reported the 450th BG's historian in the *War Diary*. "The successful advance of the Russian Army across Romania[1] during the latter half of March forced a complete reorganization of the entire German transportation and supply system. Much of the material needed to support the German forces in Romania was now being routed through northeastern Italy." A mission had been scheduled on Saturday, April 1, for Treviso, Italy (just northwest of Venice), which was one of the newly active rail hubs in the Axis war machine. However, bad weather prevented take-off. It was an eventful beginning to one of the costliest months of the war for the Cottontails. The group had only flown ten missions in March. With the coming of spring, the weather would clear, and they would nearly double that number in April. A new group also joined the fray in April. The Royal Air Force's 205th (Bomb) Group began nighttime raids on the same targets as the 15th AAF. This two-pronged plan of attack had the 205th hitting the same, or nearby, targets as Gen. Twining's men. Sometimes the 205th struck the night before the 15th AAF, while other times they bombed afterwards. It became a very effective method.[2]

Saturday night, for the second in a row, *Shadow*'s crew found their names on the board to fly the next morning. They were anxious to get back up again. The anxiety of a cancelled mission was more than some could bear. The mental preparation and sleepless night were seemingly wasted; each airman's spirit was drained. Each knew the more often he flew, the quicker he could complete his fifty missions and go home.

The 450th BG's crews were awakened at 0400 for breakfast and by 0445 the officers were in the briefing. The target for April 2 (Palm Sunday) was the Daimler-Puch ME-109 aircraft component factory in Steyr, Austria. This would be the 15th AAF's third attempt in two weeks at the city. The missions of March 19 and 24 had to hit the secondary targets of Graz and Rimini due to weather. Steyr kept coming back on the list, because it was such an important target. The complex was heavily defended with 61 heavy flak guns.[3]

Forty-one of the Cottontails' B-24s began taking off at 0730. This was a big mission. The 15th AAF was sending three wings (the 5th, 304th and 47th Bomb Wings) against the city in three separate intervals, ten minutes apart. Because Steyr was so far from their bases, the bombers' fighter escorts had to rotate every thirty minutes to ensure coverage in enemy territory. The 47th Wing, which attacked in the third interval, also planned to strike in three waves with a total of nearly 200 bombers. The first wave consisted of the 449th and 451st Bomb Groups whose B-24s were loaded with 500-pounders. In the second wave, the 98th BG would drop incendiaries. Both the first and second waves were to attack the ball-bearing plant. The third wave, composed of the 450th and 376th Bomb Groups, carrying twelve 500-pounders and incendiaries respectively, was to hit the Daimler-Puch aircraft component factory. The Cottontails rendezvoused with the 376th BG at 0809 at 3,000 feet over San Pancrazio and with the rest of the 47th Wing over San Vito Di Normannie.[4]

As the 47th Wing's formation passed into Yugoslavia two JU-88s were spotted. They flew abreast of the formation for a few minutes then moved to its rear, trailing approximately 4,000 feet behind; for whatever reason they did not engage. Shortly thereafter, at 1045, the 47th picked up its fighter escort. About forty-five minutes later, still an hour from the target, the B-24s of the 450th BG were jumped by approximately 40 ME-109s. The Cottontails' S-2 narrative for the mission vividly describes the action; *Shadow*'s element bore the brunt of the attack in which six of the 450th BG's B-24s were individually attacked. The bandits' "tactics were to attack in line astern at 5, 6, 7, and 9 o'clock." They closed to within 300 yards and then broke off in diving turns. "One flight of six ME-109s, rocket equipped, flying two abreast, closed to within 100 yards before breaking off on either side." These six came after *Shadow*. They fired rockets from 400 yards and closed using their machine guns. They were "almost close enough to hit with a rock," Gilliam recorded in his diary that night. He was able to get off several rounds from his tail turret during the passes. He was later told he hit a fighter. Although not listed as destroyed in the S-2 report, Gilliam's hit is recorded as "probably destroyed." *Shadow* was damaged in the attack; the antenna and radio compass in front of Jacobson's turret was shot away. Fortunately, Caywood and Erickson were able to hold on and keep up with the formation. The enemy fighters resumed their attack around 1200. This one was less aggressive; it was obvious they were waiting for stragglers.[5]

The 450th BG was flying in the last wave; *Shadow* was flying "tail end Charlie." This precarious position was the last plane in the last element, and it was the most dangerous one. Unlike the others in the formation, they had no protection from behind. They were also the last to cross the target. The first bombers to cross a tar-

7. April 1944

Shadow in flight. (Ted Morris)

get usually did not feel the full brunt of flak, because the flak batteries had not zeroed in on the correct altitude or angle, or these bombers passed before the flak shells reached altitude. In a large attack such as the one on April 2, the bombers that crossed the target later were more vulnerable. By the time these airmen approached the IP and target, the batteries had accurately gauged the formation and made adjustments. These ships were also more open to attack from enemy fighters, who were always on the prey for stragglers or unprotected bombers. Strong headwinds on this mission slowed the formation and gave the enemy even more time to get their flak calculations right. The 450th BG did not reach the target until 1234.[6]

Intense smoke from the bombs dropped by "the 5th and 304th Wings just minutes earlier,"[7] as well as the intense flak over the target, made it impossible for the 450th BG to make any accurate damage assessment of the target. But it was "believed that a good coverage resulted." Just over the target *Shadow*'s crew saw a B-24 go down; it was one from the 376th BG. Caywood then made the sharp left turn for home. On the way back another group of fighters made a pass at *Shadow* and flak was encountered over several other cities in Austria, including Graz. Thirty-four of the 450th BG's forty-one B-24s returned to Manduria at 1504; three had returned early, two were reported missing, and two landed at other fields. "Rough isn't the word for it," Jacobson recorded in his diary that night. The double credit for Steyr was earned. This had been their toughest mission yet, but it was only the beginning.[8]

After dinner that night, the men of *Shadow*'s crew found their names on the board again. Their restless night of sleep ended at about 0300. Shortly before 0400 the officers learned that the target for Monday, April 3, was the main marshalling yard in Budapest. The yard was a large target which covered an area one mile long and a quarter mile wide. It contained a "locomotive depot and a large repair shop." Budapest, the capital of Hungary, located on the Danube, was yet another vital city in Hitler's war machine. It contained many strategic targets that included crude-oil refineries, aircraft factories, and rail targets. Because Hungary was located between Austria and Romania, the marshalling yards at Budapest were a key link in the Third Reich's rail network. Successful attacks on the rail yards prevented oil shipments and other much-needed supplies from reaching German troops. Budapest's importance had recently increased due to the Russians' advance into Romania. The two main German communication routes now had their origins in Budapest.[9]

Grant Caywood turned twenty-six on April 3, but his mind was on other things. That morning at 0630 *Shadow* and thirty-six others of the 450th BG's B-24s began roaring down the runway. The task would be another three-wave attack for the 47th Wing, whose bombers were all loaded with 500-pound general purpose bombs. The 450th and 98th Bomb Groups were in the first wave; the 451st BG comprised the second; and the third consisted of the 449th and 376th Bomb Groups. The radar countermeasure, window, had been used with some success over Steyr the previous day. Because of that success, operational orders for this mission advised that each bomber in the first element of each bomb group was to dispense window. The waist gunners in each designated bomber were to begin throwing out their three cartons of window approximately "two minutes before the IP and continue until three minutes after bombs away."[10]

The 450th BG rendezvoused with the 98th BG at 0750, 6,000 feet over Manduria, and with the rest of the 47th Wing at 0940. Approximately 20 ME-109s approached the formation at 1059, but no attack was made until 1110 when 5 FW-190s approached from the rear. They fired their 20mm cannons, but did not close in on the bombers. The fighters' attacks continued up until the target, at which time they disengaged. Over the target, the waist gunners in the B-24s dropped the window. The flak was heavy, intense, and accurate and holed 16 of the 450th's bombers. The fighters engaged the formation again as the bombers made the rally for home. The enemy fighters now included several JU-88s carrying rockets. One of the JU-88s closed in on *Shadow*. It first appeared as a speck in the sky, but the crew could soon see the rockets coming their way. All of their gunnery training had paid off. *Shadow*'s gunners were able to turn seven guns on the fighter (Gilliam's two tail guns, one of the waist guns, Morris' two ball turret guns and Jacobson's two top turret guns). They shot down their first (confirmed) fighter as a team. "I emptied my whole turret on him," wrote Jacobson that night. "You could see the tracers go right through him," recorded Gilliam. Most of the group returned to Manduria at 1352. It was another double credit mission. A major portion of *Shadow*'s crew had now completed 14 missions. Slowly but surely, they were plugging away at the fifty-mission goal, but according to the odds they could only survive a few more missions.[11]

Shadow's crew flew its third mission in as many days on Tuesday, April 4, but they did so without their steadfast pilot Grant Caywood; the 450th BG's commander had other plans for him. For this mission, the farm boy from Nebraska, Vincent Olney, replaced him. The target for the day was the marshalling yards in Bucharest, the capital of Romania. Like the rail hub in Budapest, the target was a vital one. It was the key link for the two main supply routes for the German Army in Romania. It also served as a key hub for exporting the petroleum products produced in Ploesti, located just 30 miles north. Bucharest was also the home of several crude-oil refineries, an airfield, and a large POW camp. Most AAF airmen shot down over Romania ended up in the POW camp outside Bucharest. This made the need for precision over the target even greater; stray bombs over the city could potentially hit their fallen comrades.[12]

The mission started late. The 450th BG's forty-one B-24s did not begin taking off until 1010. As had become common practice for the 15th AAF over the past few missions, three wings would attack the target at ten-minute intervals. First, the 47th Bomb Wing was to attack the target in three waves—the 376th and 449th Bomb Groups in the first wave, the 451st BG in the second, and the 98th and 450th Bomb Groups in the third wave. The 5th and 304th Bomb Wings, each with their respective waves, would follow the 47th at ten-minute intervals. The Cottontails rendezvoused with the 98th BG at 1059 over Manduria; they then met up with the remainder of the wing en route to the target.[13]

All was quiet until the group approached the IP, thirty miles northwest of Bucharest. In the target area, the 450th BG encountered approximately 35 enemy fighters that made "moderately aggressive" attacks on their formation. The 449th BG faced the brunt of the bandit attacks, because they had lost several bombers from their formation on the way. The flak was minimal over the target due to the heavy concentration of fighters in the area. The bombardiers hit the mark and caused great destruction to the target. Direct hits were recorded on the "choke point leading north to Ploesti." Many hits and several large explosions were seen in the northwest corner of the marshalling yard. Warehouses, storage buildings, and other industrial structures were rubble. Reconnaissance a few days after the attack showed that, in addition to the above hits, "at least 1,500 railroad cars and 10 locomotives were destroyed."[14]

For the crew of *Shadow*, the mission had been a complete success. The flak was not a problem, they did not encounter any enemy fighters, and the target was hit with great precision. Stricklin had done a great job. It was a good first mission for Olney with the crew. Unfortunately, the 449th BG did not fare as well. April 4, 1944 (ominously remembered as 4–4–44 by veterans of the 449th BG), turned out to be the most costly day of the war for them. They lost seven B-24s, while another thirteen received damage. This illustrates just how much luck (and chance) was involved in completing the fifty-mission goal. The 450th BG and 449th BG had flown the same mission with vastly different outcomes.[15]

Wednesday, April 5, 1944, opened a new chapter in the history of the 15th AAF and the 450th BG. That day their focus turned on a new target: Ploesti, Romania. This marked a change in strategic bombing strategy. From its start, the 450th BG had focused primarily on transportation targets: marshalling yards and airdromes.

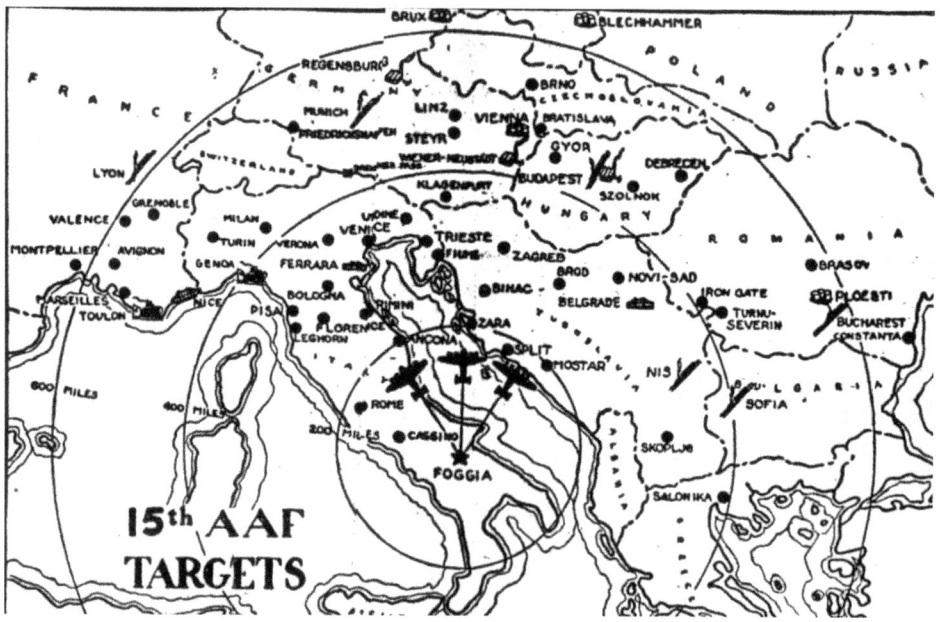

Targets of the 15th AAF. (Samuel Stein)

By the end of February 1944 the "victorious nature of POINTBLANK operations" made it evident that a new strategy was needed. For the better part of a year the Army had been planning the invasion of France, code-named OVERLORD. The AAF was now being asked to support this effort. Lt. Gen. Carl D. Spaatz, the commanding officer of the strategic AAF in Europe, concluded that the best way to support OVERLORD (and POINTBLANK) was to attack Hitler's oil supplies. This would keep the GAF engaged so that they would not be diverted to France. It would also diminish petroleum production and deprive the Germans of much-needed oil supplies.[16]

Early in the war, the Allies had discussed an oil campaign. However, the German oil production centers were "widely scattered … in more than eighty different localities." Most were "entirely out of the range before the 15th AAF was established in Italy." Fifty-four crude-oil refineries and synthetic petroleum plants accounted for over ninety percent of Germany's total production. Twenty-seven of these "had been grouped about Ploesti, in Silesia, and in the Ruhr in the overconfident expectation that the Luftwaffe could protect them." Ploesti, Romania, was home to the most "invaluable cluster" of refineries. It was the third best-defended city in the entire Third Reich behind Berlin and Vienna. The city, which was only nineteen square miles with a population of 100,000, was located 30 miles north of Bucharest. The thirteen refineries that ringed the city produced nearly one-third of the petroleum products for Hitler's war machine—Hitler's black gold. The best fighter squadrons and the most accurate and deadly flak batteries guarded them. The targets there were obscured with hundreds of smoke pots, which were lit as soon as the Allied bombers crossed the Axis' warning radar in Yugoslavia. Ploesti was the site of the famous low-level raid in August 1943. However, repairs were quickly made and production at the refineries steadily rose in the months following the attack. So beginning in April 1944, the crippling of Ploesti's refineries became the number one priority for the 15th AAF's commanding general, Nathan F. Twining. It would become the most dreaded target on the 450th Bomb Group's list.[17]

Shadow's crew did not fly the April 5 mission to Ploesti; it would have been their fourth mission in four days. However, forty crews from the 450th BG did. It would be "the first of twenty-four hammer blows" delivered by the Cottontails and the 15th AAF over the next five months. The target for the day was the marshalling yards — the intricate rail web connecting the city's refineries. The baptism of Ploesti was costly for the 450th BG; five B-24s were lost (only seven chutes were seen) and another twenty-four were damaged. The damage was not one-sided. The Cottontails shot down 27 "confirmed" enemy fighters, with another two listed as "probably destroyed."[18]

The next day the group stood down to make repairs. The missions over the previous four days had taken their toll on the bombers and the crews. "After an early squall, the day turned out to be very pleasant," reported the 450th's *War Diary*. Awards were presented to some airmen in front of group headquarters. Some of the airmen made their way to Lecce and Brindisi, while some others just slept. Richard Jacobson headed to Bari to play saxophone with the locals at the Hotel Miramar. It was also a time of reorganization. A new wing, the 49th Bomb Wing, was beginning operations. To reach its complement of groups, the 451st Bomb Group was transferred to the 49th on April 6. With this change "the 47th Wing would consist of 98th, 376th, 449th, and 450th Bomb Groups for the remainder of the war." The 15th AAF, which had been adding to its strength over the past three months, was now approaching full complement. A new fighter wing, the 306th, would begin operations in April. The wing consisted of the 31st and 52nd Fighter Groups, "both of which were equipped with the new, long-range, P-51 Mustang. The P-51 [was] capable of providing continuous fighter escort even for the deep penetration missions; [it] would change the character of the air war over Europe."[19]

During this break, Grant Caywood also made preparations for a change. Caywood had a natural ability to lead and he always seemed older and wiser than his age would suggest. His popularity and presence served him well in this regard. When he entered a room, it was his. Caywood's men trusted him completely; they would follow him anywhere. The 450th's group commander recognized his talent and on April 7, Caywood was promoted to squadron operations officer for the 720th. The ops officer worked closely with the squadron commander, maintenance, armament, and others. He kept track of all the squadron's bombers and assigned the crews and planes for each mission. The promotion had other consequences for Caywood. As was the custom, the operations officer or squadron commander lived with the flight surgeon, so he left "Barracks 10B"—and his fellow officers, Erickson, Stricklin, and Gouldon. Caywood was sent to "Lead School" at headquarters, where he learned about German tactics and other things vital to his job. The promotion also meant that he would only fly every third or fourth mission, which would more than double the time to complete his fifty mission goal. But Caywood, always the dutiful son and consummate soldier, readily accepted the challenge.[20]

The promotion came as no shock to the rest of *Shadow*'s crew. They all knew what a capable leader Caywood was and they were proud of him. Leadership of the crew fell to co-pilot Maurice Erickson, who had been with them since Clovis. He was an excellent pilot and a quiet leader in his own right. Eric made the transition an easy one. Vincent Olney joined the crew as an interim replacement to Caywood. Olney was gregarious and outgoing with a good sense of humor and was a welcome addition to the crew.

Shadow's crew was on the board Thursday night. The mission for Friday, April 7, was to the marshalling yards at Mestre in northeastern Italy. The Russian advance into Romania in late March made targets in northeastern Italy strategically important. The marshalling yards throughout the area now served as the main artery of "military traffic" from Hungary and Romania for the Germans. The scrubbed mission to Treviso on April 1 had the same objective. On April 7, the 15th AAF planned to attack most of the strategic transportation targets in the area. The 47th Wing would attack the rail yard at Mestre; the 5th Wing would hit Treviso; the 304th Wing would strike at Bologna; while the 49th and 55th Wings moved on Ferrara.[21]

For the 47th Wing, "the Mestre marshalling yard was particularly important since it controlled all the traffic for Porto Marghera and the port of Venice." The adjacent area also included several industrial targets, including a chemical plant. At least twenty-eight anti-aircraft guns, as well as some aggressive fighter units, protected the target area. The 450th BG began sending up its thirty-five B-24s, each loaded with twelve 500-pound general-purpose bombs, at 1003. They rendezvoused with the 98th BG at 1018 and

Grant Caywood was promoted to operations officer for the 720th Squadron on April 7, 1944. (Grant D. Caywood)

together comprised the second wave to the 47th Wing's attack. The first wave consisted of the 449th and 376th Bomb Groups. The formation was escorted by a group of P-38 Lightnings.[22]

The first wave of the formation had sporadic encounters with enemy fighters, but the escort did its job. Crews from the 450th BG spotted a dozen or so ME-109s at some distance, but they did not engage the group. The flak at the target, which was heavy, light and inaccurate, did not pose a problem for the bombers. The IP and target were obscured by smoke, but photo reconnaissance afterwards revealed great precision and success on the mission. A heavy concentration of bombs hit the "railroad station and adjoining yard areas," and several direct hits were recorded on adjacent industrial buildings. The 450th BG arrived back in Manduria at 1533. It was one of their most successful missions to date. Olney and Erickson made a good team and *Shadow*'s crew gained confidence on the mission. That afternoon "gas chamber exercises were held for all personnel."[23]

Even though the April 5 mission to Ploesti had marked a shift in strategic priority to oil targets, the destruction of the German Air Force was still high on the 15th AAF's list. Chief among these were the aircraft component production and assembly plants like the one in Wiener-Neustadt, Austria. A mission was briefed and took off on April 8 for Wiener-Neustadt, but it was cancelled over the Adriatic due to bad weather. That evening Capt. Floyd Robinson of the 720th Squadron was in charge of the entertainment at the Cottontail Club. He coordinated "music, skits, and impersonations" much to the delight of the audience. The show was toned down quite a bit and was more tasteful than some in the past, due to the Easter service planned for the next morning.

Maurice Erickson took leadership of *Shadow*'s crew when Caywood was promoted to operations officer for the 720th Squadron. (Stan S. Butynski)

720th Squadron HQ building. (Grant D. Caywood)

No mission was scheduled for Sunday, April 9, because it was Easter. It was a beautiful morning, and a silver B-24 provided a dramatic backdrop to the service. This was a special day; most Sundays the group flew missions, but for this service there was a general stand down. The entire group was in attendance. The choir, of which Robinson was a member, had practiced for weeks. Their songs echoed out over the PA system and field organ set up for the occasion. The service conducted by Chaplain Paul Stevens remains one of the strongest memories of many Cottontail veterans. That afternoon the nine survivors of 1st Lt. Reaford McCraw's crew returned to base and reported that Lt. McCraw had been buried in Yugoslavia.[24]

Bad weather returned on Monday and no mission was attempted. Another mission to Mestre was planned for Tuesday, April 11, but it was cancelled prior to take off because of bad weather. Caywood was scheduled to lead the formation. It would have been his first as squadron operations officer. Also on April 11, Capt. Floyd Robinson was appointed flight leader and he was to fly with *Shadow*'s crew as their new pilot. Even though the mission was cancelled, Robinson took the crew up with others in the group for a practice mission.[25]

Four consecutive nonoperational days ended for the Cottontails on Wednesday, April 12. Their target was the large Messerschmitt aircraft assembly plant in Wiener-Neustadt, Austria, south of Vienna—the same one attempted on April 8. It was an important target in one of the most heavily fortified cities in the Third Reich. The plant at Wiener-Neustadt along with those in Regensburg (in southeastern Germany) produced half of Germany's fighters. Photo reconnaissance during the previous six weeks revealed over eighty heavy flak guns in the area. In addition, it was estimated that the Luftwaffe could concentrate up to 300 fighters to counter a strike on Wiener-Neustadt. At the 0530 briefing Caywood and the other officers learned that the 450th BG would be flying in the second wave of the day's formation with the 449th BG, and that they would carry 100-pound, clustered, fragmentation bombs. The lead wave of the 47th Wing, consisting of the 98th and 376th Bomb Groups, would carry 500-pound general-purpose bombs and would attack the target first.[26]

Vincent Olney. (Marilyn Siebels)

At 0811, the first of forty-one of the 450th BG's B-24s started down the runway. By 0900 all were airborne and the group rendezvoused with the 449th BG 6,000 feet above Manduria. They met up with the rest of the formation seven minutes later. For Robinson and his new crew in *Shadow*, the mission was routine until 1105, when the P-38 fighter escort joined them. A few enemy aircraft were spotted northeast of the 450th's formation, but surprisingly they did not engage. Because of the flak and fighters anticipated over the target, the bombers climbed to 25,000 feet as they reached the IP and started the bomb run. At that altitude the temperature was more than 50 degrees below zero. Both Gilliam and Jacobson recorded in their diaries that the thermometers in *Shadow*, which could record temps as low as 48 degrees below zero, broke on the mission. As the bomb run commenced at 1207, it was evident that the temperature was also having other effects.[27]

Stricklin opened *Shadow*'s bomb bay doors on the lead bombardier's mark. After dropping the bombs, he gave the familiar call, "Bombs away! Bomb bay doors coming closed." However, something was not right. From his turret, ball gunner Ted Morris always tried to count the bombs as they dropped; at this point in the mission it was all that he could do. They were carrying forty bombs. Less than thirty came out by his count. He looked up to discover twelve still lodged in the bomb bay. The cold temperature had frozen them in place.[28]

Ted immediately alerted the rest of the crew via the intercom; Stricklin left the

Easter Sunday, April 9, 1944, in Manduria. The 450th BG's chaplain, Paul Stevens, conducted a memorable service. An unpainted, silver B-24 provided a dramatic backdrop. (Grant D. Caywood)

doors open. Ted knew how dangerous it could be if the bombs remained in the aircraft. Without hesitation he got out of his turret and headed for the bomb bay. On the way, he grabbed one of the portable oxygen bottles. At 25,000 feet he could not survive very long without it. Ted then straddled the catwalk and without a parachute he made it to the bomb bay. He knew he had to be careful. It was going to be hard to maintain his balance while carrying the oxygen; it would be impossible with a parachute. After leaving his turret he had no way to communicate with the rest of the crew. He was on his own.[29]

Once in the bomb bay, Ted braced himself against the side of the bomber and held on to the shackles of bombs already released. The rush of air into the bomber's belly was intense. Ted swayed back and forth as he clung to the shackles. He desperately held on to the oxygen. He quickly flipped the manual toggle switches that held each of the remaining bombs. These switches were a backup feature that permitted the bombs to be released from inside the bomb bay. All but one dropped safely out of the plane. The last one fell from its shackle but wedged between a control cable and a hydraulic line. This one was "fused and could have exploded at any moment, so he had to get rid of it fast." Ted carefully worked his way down to where the bomb was lodged. He wrapped one arm around a bomb shackle and put the oxygen bottle under it. He then braced his leg against the side of the ship. "With a rush of adrenaline I was able to pick up the bomb with one arm," Ted said, "It came back and hit inside the bomb bay, but it fell out." In an interview after the incident, Ted was asked what he thought as he saw the bombs stuck in the bomb bay. "In a predicament like that, one really doesn't have time to think of danger," he replied. When asked what he would have done if he had lost his hold, he grinned and said, "I don't know. All I can remember is that I had icicles over my eyebrows."[30]

After Ted watched the bomb drop out of the plane, he leaned back to breathe a sigh of relief. The ordeal, which seemed to last an hour, had transpired in a matter of minutes. As he began to make his way back up into the waist area he saw his bombardier, Robert Stricklin, crouched in the hatchway leading to the front of the airplane. Ted did not know it, but Strick had watched it all; he was there to help if needed.[31]

The group's other bombs hit their marks. As noted in the mission's S-2 report, "The target area was heavily hit and a concentration of bombs was noted on railroad and highway overpasses south of the target area.... A large work shop received many hits, and direct bomb strikes were noted on the Henschel and Sohn Factory." Another heavy concentration of bombs hit the north portion of the airdrome.[32]

The flak over the target was heavy, intense, and accurate and tracked the formation throughout the bomb run. Enemy fighters aggressively attacked several of the 449th BG's B-24s after they passed the target; three were lost. Flak was also encountered over Mostar, Yugoslavia. The 450th BG returned to Manduria at 1435. Fourteen of its Liberators were damaged, five severely. *Shadow*'s crew had a close call on the mission, but they had a new hero, Ted Morris. They would all later learn that Stricklin put Ted in for the Distinguished Flying Cross (DFC), which was awarded "for extraordinary heroism in connection with military operations against the enemy." Ted would later receive this medal, and another one.[33]

Shortly after returning from this harrowing mission, Ted Morris and the other crew members of *Shadow* saw their names on the board to fly the next morning. Each man retired to quarters and began to "mentally prepare to do it all again the next day." The wake up call came early. At the briefing, Robinson and Erickson learned that the target for the day was the Vesces airdrome, located just southeast of Budapest. The installation there "was believed to be engaged in modification and repair work, but was also known to be capable of final assembly work on airframes." The 450th BG's thirty-seven B-24s began roaring down the runway at 0900. Accompanied by the 449th BG, they would lead the first wave of the 47th Wing's attack. The second wave was composed of the 98th and 376th Bomb Groups. Fighter escort was to be provided by the 306th Fighter Wing, which was comprised of P-38s and P-47s. The secondary target was the industrial center of Budapest, to be bombed by ETA. All of the bombers were loaded with clusters of 20-pound fragmentation bombs.[34]

After meeting up with the 449th BG at 0953, and the remainder of the wing at 1000, the 450th BG led the way to Budapest. The escort did its job as Jacobson recorded in his diary, "no fighter trouble." The flak also was not a problem. Despite this fact, one B-24 blew up over the target. The bomber was that of 2nd Lt. Warren N. Rustad of the 449th BG. It was accidentally struck from above by elements of another group. As one account described it, "A single bomb struck [Rustad's] ship squarely between the number-3 and number-4 engines, 'knocking off the right wing and setting the ship on fire.' … All ten crew members died." The exhausted crews of the 450th BG arrived back in Manduria at 1510. Poor weather on April 14 gave the Cottontails a well-deserved rest.³⁵

It was back to business on Saturday, April 15. An 0600 briefing revealed that their target was once again the marshalling yard at Bucharest, Romania. The mission there on April 4 had been a total success, virtually destroying the entire rail yard. But because the target was so vital, the 15th AAF was going back "to further complicate German transportation and communication problems by disrupting whatever repairs were in progress." Its importance was further demonstrated by the fact that the 15th AAF sent four heavy-bomber wings (47th, 49th, 55th, and 304th) against the target—more than 450 B-24s. It was also an important mission for *Shadow*'s crew. For the first time they would not fly their beloved B-24 into combat. Today they would lead the 450th BG and fly a "Pathfinder" ship.³⁶

Pathfinder was one of the nicknames given to a new radar bombing system used by Allied bombers in World War II. Early in the war it became apparent that due to the poor weather conditions in Europe, and enemy countermeasures such as smoke pots, that visual bombing was not always possible. But radar technology (radio detection and ranging) could enable bombers to track, chart, and destroy unseen targets.

In 1941, the British developed the first radar navigational device called "Gee." As one historian described it: "Sets in the [specially equipped] aircraft received pulse transmissions from ground stations made up of one master and two slave transmitters. Differences in the arrival of signals from these three points enabled the navigator to *fix* the position of his aircraft by referring to two *Gee* coordinates. These were printed on special *Gee* charts—*Gee* derives from *G* for Grid."³⁷

The British also developed two other precision radar-radio bombing aids, *Oboe* and *H2S*. Oboe was very accurate. It used a master (cat) station and a slave (mouse) station. Signals transmitted and retransmitted between the two stations allowed the controller to pinpoint the bomber's exact location. "H2S was an airborne radar scanner which displayed a rough outline of the terrain

Ted Morris, *Shadow*'s ball turret gunner. (Ted Morris)

below on a cathode ray tube"—like the one in a television receiver. The device was dubbed H2S after remarks made by one of Churchill's top advisors, Professor Lindemann. He said that it was "'stinking that it had not been invented sooner.' (H2S, hydrogen sulphide, smells like rotten eggs)."[38] Users later gave H2S the nickname "Home Sweet Home."[39]

These led to the creation of a special USAAF group in August 1943. The 482nd "Pathfinder" Group, formed at Alconbury, was "the first and only American heavy bomber group to be formed on English soil." It consisted of three squadrons, two B-17s and one B-24. Its bombers were equipped with the British radar devices and its airmen were specially trained in their use.[40]

Meanwhile, back in the United States, scientists at the Massachusetts Institute of Technology's Radiation Laboratory tried to develop an improved version of the British H2S. Since the Army knew that the new, complex, secret device would need to be produced in mass quantities, they approached Philco, a leading manufacturer of radios, to help in the design. Philco's research engineers teamed with the M.I.T. scientists, and together they completed the project in record time. "Using a new and shorter microwave length than had ever been used before, [they] built a radar set that would give a sharper and more faithful picture of the ground. The new device, called H2X, was [put] into production by Philco in the summer of 1943." Twelve bombers equipped with the new H2X technology joined the 482nd BG in October 1943.[41]

The first factory-built H2X sets began to arrive in January 1944, "replacing the virtually home-made radar sets" constructed at M.I.T. Building upon the cat and mouse analogy of the British Oboe system, these new American H2X sets (AN/APS-15) were called "Mickey," after Mickey Mouse. The H2X units, which had over 80 tubes and weighed over 300 pounds, were housed in a pod that replaced the bomber's ball-gun turret. A specially trained operator who replaced the crew's bombardier on the designated missions operated the radar. The Mickey sent out ultra high frequency radio waves "that bounced back from solid targets and were picked up by the radar receiver and transformed into a radar picture on a screen like the one in a home television receiver." By early 1944, this new radar bombsight came to be known by various, interchangeable names that included Pathfinder, PFF, Mickey, or H2X—most commonly Pathfinder or Mickey.[42]

The 8th AAF flew the first mission with this new technology on January 11, 1944. For some, this marked the beginning of all-weather bombing capability.[43] But Caywood stresses, when Pathfinder was utilized "the navigator would use it only as a secondary means of cross checking his position." When conditions permitted, the bombardiers sighted the targets visually through the bombsights; the Pathfinder was used only if the target was concealed. They had to be careful, because if the Pathfinder bomber dropped on the wrong target, so did the entire group.[44]

The 15th AAF utilized this new radar technology for the first time on April 15 at Bucharest. On this mission to Bucharest the 720th Squadron led the 450th BG, which in turn led the 47th Wing. Floyd Robinson and Maurice Erickson took up Caywood's old crew. Since they were flying a Pathfinder, ball-turret gunner Ted Morris and bombardier Robert Stricklin stayed in Manduria.[45]

The 450th BG's forty-two B-24s started taking off at 0818. Each carried ten 500-pound general-purpose bombs. At 0910, the Cottontails rendezvoused with the 449th BG, 6,000 feet above Manduria. They joined the remainder of the wing at 0917 en route to the target. Cloud cover over Yugoslavia was fairly dense and it worsened as the formation neared the IP. Over fifty enemy fighters were spotted in the target area under the formation and above the clouds, but they were engaged by the P-38 escort and did not attack the bombers. With each passing mission, the bomb crews' respect and love for their escorts grew. Jacobson wrote later that night of the mission's P-38s, "I love 'em."[46]

By the time they reached the target, the cloud cover had increased to between 8/10 and 10/10. At 1210 the 450th BG dropped its deadly cargo through the solid cloud cover. Two minutes later the 449th BG, also guided by Pathfinders, dropped its bombs. Flak over the target was heavy, light and inaccurate and was not encountered until after the bomb run. Clouds prevented any assessment, but as Gilliam recorded in his diary, "The Pathfinder found the way to the target." Later reconnaissance showed that the mission was a success with heavy hits in the southwest corner of the city. The 450th BG returned to Manduria at 1520. Upon their return, *Shadow*'s crew told Ted and Strick about the mission. After dinner, they discovered that a mission was scheduled for the next day, Sunday, April 16. But, uncharacteristically, they were not on the list—there was a shortage of bombers.[47]

The mission for April 16 was to the marshalling yard at Brasov, Romania, located northwest of Ploesti.[48] One historian has noted it was a "key point on the Bucharest-Ploesti-Budapest railroad network ... that crossed through a pass in the Carpathian Mountains. The Brasov marshalling yard—on the north side of the mountains—was a base for spare engines used to assist the heavily loaded trains over the top of the pass and down the south side into Campina."[49] It was a rough but successful mission for the 450th BG. *Shadow*'s crew spent the day off relaxing as best they could. Some attended chapel; most wrote letters home. Robinson flew to San Pancrazio to pick up another Pathfinder. After dinner, the men of the crew found their names on the list for the next day. They also discovered a welcome surprise—Caywood was scheduled to be their pilot for the mission. That evening, as the show at the Cottontail Club was winding down, a B-24 (number 443) exploded in the parking area. The explosion caused another bomber, 150 feet away, to catch fire. But thanks to the brave efforts of Tech. Sgt. Julian C. Clark and PFC Marquis Cedeno of the 720th Squadron, the second B-24 was saved. They were able to extinguish the blaze on its wing before it also exploded.[50]

The next morning everyone was a little shaky because of the explosion. Robinson went over to inspect Shadow and discovered that some of her windows had shattered from the blast. Other bombers were also damaged—a total of seven from the 720th Squadron alone. At the morning briefing Caywood and the other officers learned that the target for the day was Sofia, Bulgaria. The 450th BG had hit the marshalling yard there on March 30, but extensive repairs made another mission necessary.[51]

On Monday, April 17, for the second time in three days, the Cottontails would

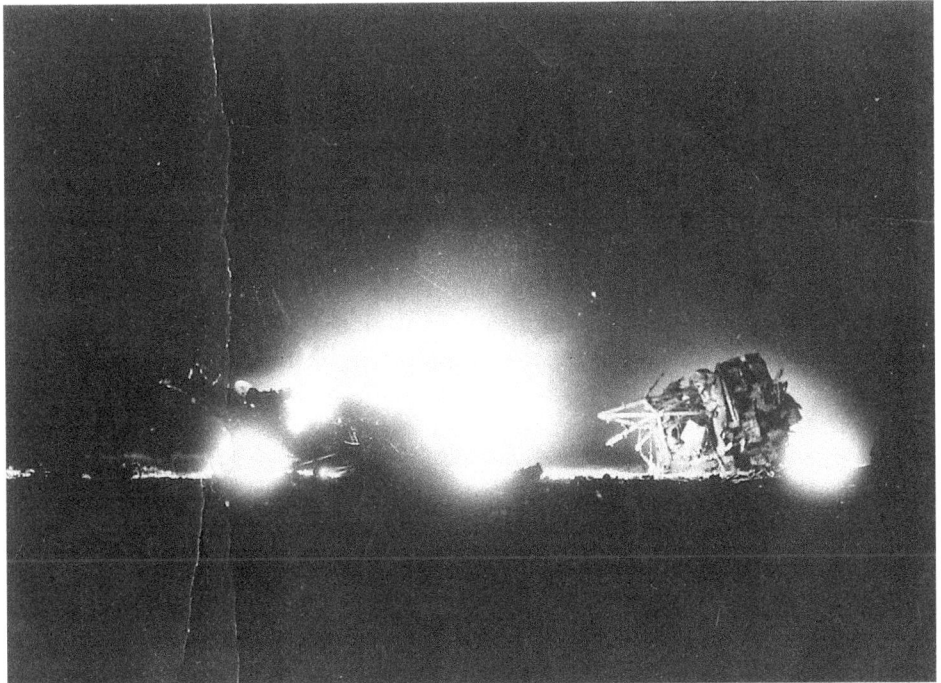

The remains of the 450th BG B-24 number 443 that exploded on the evening of April 16, 1944. (Maurice H. Gilliam)

utilize Pathfinders to bomb the intended target. Because Caywood was the squadron's operations officer, he was asked to lead his element in the radar ship. Since he was flying with his old crew, this once again bumped ball-turret gunner Ted Morris from the mission.[52]

Just before take-off a smoke grenade went off in Caywood's airplane. With the events of the previous night still fresh in their minds, the crew immediately exited the B-24. "I ran about a half-mile," jokes Gilliam. But the fire was quickly extinguished, and the smoke soon cleared. At 0916 thirty-nine of the group's B-24s started to take off. They met up with the 449th BG at 1019, and with the remainder of the formation en route. The Cottontails' first P-51 escort joined them at 1045. The first enemy fighters attacked the group at 1220, eight minutes outside Sofia. Two of the bandits made a pass at Caywood's bomber; one of them was shot down. The P-51s handled the rest and by 1240 all enemy fighters pulled back. None was seen on the way home.[53]

The flak was much more of a problem than the fighters. Over the target it was heavy, intense, and accurate and damaged eight of the group's B-24s. For this mission the 450th BG was instructed to select the center of Sofia as its aiming point, while the 449th BG focused directly on the marshalling yard. The Pathfinder method was effective. The 450th's S-2 report for the day noted approximately 200 bursts in the city, southwest of the cathedral. Bursts in the marshalling yard and adjacent industrial area were also seen. Bombs hitting the tracks and cars sparked other fires, which included some at the yard's repair shop and warehouse. The mission was a complete success. Despite its inauspicious beginning, it turned out to be a fairly easy one.[54]

The 450th BG returned to Manduria at 1415. That afternoon and evening, some of the group saw a movie at the theater in nearby Oria. Weather prevented a mission on Tuesday, April 18, so the group caught up on much-needed repairs. A mission was scheduled for Wednesday, April 19, against the shipyard and harbor at Montfalcone, Italy (located on the border between Italy and Yugoslavia), but it was cancelled prior to briefing due to bad weather at the target. *Shadow*'s bombardier, Robert Stricklin, took advantage of the morning off to write a letter to his sister. In it, he told her he now had twenty-two missions. He apologized for not writing more often. He asked her to send "a big box of Baby Ruths or some sort of candy, preferably chocolate." Airmen craved chocolate; it was a comfort from home that they rarely received. That afternoon Robinson led the group on a practice mission in which they "camera bombed" for four hours. After dinner Robinson and his crew found their names on the board for Thursday's mission.[55]

A late briefing indicated that the target was fairly close, and it was. The 450th BG was to attack the marshalling yard at Treviso, Italy. The "accumulation of rolling stock" in the rail yards of northern Italy made Treviso a strategic target. In their attack on April 20, the 15th AAF hoped to disrupt the German supply and communications network in central Italy. The 450th's forty Liberators began taking off at 0940. They rendezvoused with the 449th BG at 1044 and followed them to the target.[56]

No enemy fighters were seen. The formation had its best escort to date, which consisted of P-38s, P-47s, and P-51s. "They sky was full of them," Gilliam wrote. "The P-38s came in so close you could almost touch them." As they approached the target a large cloud cover obscured the entire area. The coverage was so widespread that alternate targets were also blocked. This bad weather forced the 450th BG to abort the mission. On the return to Manduria, twenty-three of the Cottontails' Liberators jettisoned their bombs in the Adriatic. Fifteen B-24s, including *Shadow*, returned to base with their bombs at 1550.[57]

The mission was disappointing, but the crews did receive credit for it. The day would mark an important milestone for *Shadow*'s crew. For most of them, especially the enlisted men, it marked their twenty-fifth mission; they had completed half of their combat tour. Each began to wonder when and if the odds would catch up with them. The second half of their journey would be much more difficult than the first from both mental and physical standpoints.[58]

That night *Shadow*'s crew slept well. In fact, many of them slept late; they were not scheduled for the Friday, April 21, mission. They were lucky. The target for the day was once again the marshalling yard at Ploesti. But "adverse weather conditions" at the target forced the wing commander to abort the mission. All forty of the 450th BG's B-24s returned with their bombs at 1047. A steady rain that night did not hamper the opening of the 720th Squadron's "day room." It was like an officer's club for enlisted personnel. It contained a bar and a reading and writing room, as well as card and dice tables. All in attendance enjoyed the new facility. Heavy rains continued throughout the night and the muddy runway prevented a mission on Saturday, April 22. *Shadow*'s crew was not on the board that night and did not fly to Vienna, Austria, on Sunday with the rest of the 450th BG. But they wanted to fly; it was the only way to get back home. They did not have to wait long. The men of *Shadow*'s crew found their names on the board Sunday night.[59]

The events of Monday, April 24, 1944, have been seared into the memories of all of *Shadow*'s crew—it was a most memorable mission. The day started out like any other. By now it was routine. There was the uneasy sleep from the previous night, because each knew he was going to fly the next day. The early wake up call, the rush to make the bed and head to the mess hall for breakfast. The usual mix of dehydrated food was served; some could tolerate it while others detested it. After finishing their coffee, it was back to the barracks to suit up. The officers attended the briefing, while the enlisted men waited outside prior to heading over to the parachute building. The target for the day was Ploesti, Romania. They were advised that there were 150 heavy (flak) guns in the area and to expect enemy fighters upon approach. The mere mention of the target raised the hair on the necks of most airmen.[60]

The 450th BG flew its first mission to Ploesti on April 5, and the April 24 mission there was their third in as many weeks. For *Shadow*'s crew the April 24 mission was their first trip to the dreaded target. The luck of the draw had kept them out of the rotation on April 5 and April 21.[61] As *Shadow*'s crew loaded their gear through the bomb bay and entered the aircraft, their normal banter was missing. There was a reverence with this target. Robinson and Erickson would be their pilots for the day. Robinson was fairly new to the crew, but he had not gotten them into trouble yet. They were beginning to trust him and call him by his nickname, Robbie. Erickson had been with them since Clovis, and there was comfort in that.

The 450th BG's thirty-eight B-24s began rolling at 0824; all were airborne by 0900 to begin the 600-mile trip. It was a beautiful day. The group joined the 449th BG over Manduria at 0919, where they proceeded on course to San Vito Di Normanni. There they met up with the 98th BG and 376th BG to complete the 47th Wing formation. As they were approaching altitude, *Shadow*'s ball turret gunner, Ted Morris, realized that he had forgotten his oxygen mask. This could be detrimental to the mission. Without an oxygen mask he could not remain in the ball and the emergency portable oxygen tanks could not be substituted for two reasons. For one, they would not last long enough and secondly, he could not fit one into the cramped quarters of the ball turret and operate his guns. Ted decided to gather the other gunners in the rear of the airplane—Gilliam, Esquivel, and Woodward—and tell them of his predicament. All agreed that he had to go up front and advise Eric and Robbie.[62]

Ted made the perilous trip up to the cockpit of *Shadow* across the "catwalk" through the bomb bay. It was the only walkway connecting the front and rear of the bomber. It was extremely narrow and at altitude, in full flight gear, it was like walking on a trapeze. On the way up front, Ted thought that maybe he could just suck on the end of his oxygen hose. Once he reached the pilots he told them, "I forgot my oxygen mask."

Robinson replied, "Oh damn. We'll have to go back."

Jacobson, the engineer, took a deep breath. He knew that they could not go back. This was Ploesti. The mission was too important.

"Let's not do that. I'll just pull the metal off the end of the hose and suck on it as needed. I'll be all right."

"OK, try that," Robinson advised.

Erickson piped in, "But Ted, you're the ball turret gunner. You cannot do that."

Robinson agreed and told him to trade places with one of the waist gunners. "Let him man the ball with his mask and you can suck on the oxygen hose as needed in the waist." With this plan, if Ted was having a hard time with the hose, he could trade off the mask of another waist gunner and they could go back and forth as needed. It was a good compromise. It also proved that the cross-training was necessary.

Ted headed back to the rear of the aircraft; once again he traversed the treacherous catwalk. The other gunners were anxiously waiting for him. He thought it was time for a little fun.

They all asked, "What did the pilot say?"

"He told me to get my ass out of the airplane," whereupon Ted grabbed his chute, hooked the harness, and headed for the rear hatch. He opened it and squatted as if he were going to jump. "I'll see you later," he yelled. At the last minute he turned around and smiled at his tense crewmates. "Oh, I'm just kidding." The little joke, characteristic of their daily interaction, helped to break the tension. Ted then told them the plan.[63]

Without hesitation, Norman Woodward volunteered to go into the ball and let Ted man his left waist gun. Everything went well until they approached the target. None of the crew saw any fighters that day, which corresponds to official reports. There were twenty-four enemy aircraft in the area, but they stayed well away from the formation, "apparently looking for stragglers"; the group did not have an encounter with them. At the waist gun, Ted was seeing a view of combat he had not seen in the ball turret. "I never got to see any action above; all I saw was below the aircraft and there wasn't much action down below." Most fighters came in high and attacked the bombers from the front or rear. Therefore most fighters and accurate flak bursts were out of the view of the ball turret gunner. It was different for Ted this day, at about 1200, just as the formation reached the IP, about five miles south of Ploesti, he got to see the "whole show." "As we approached the target, it was really the first time that I had seen all the flak. It was so thick that it seemed to me you could almost walk on it like stepping-stones." Gilliam recorded in his diary that the flak that day "was the heaviest I had ever seen." For Jake, it "looked like a solid stone wall up ahead of us."[64]

Ted vividly recalls, "Almost all of the bursts were black, but I remember seeing several white bursts of flak. As I watched these white bursts I was mesmerized. There was one off of us quite a distance, and then another one came a little bit closer, and then another even closer. I turned around to tell Static that I was frightened. Just as I turned, the last burst hit me and the airplane, and knocked me down."

When Ted fell he lost the oxygen tube on which he had been sucking. Static immediately looked down at Ted and called on the intercom, "Jesus Christ! Ted's been hit! Ted's been hit!" Ted heard the call, because his earphones were still connected. Static then gave Ted his oxygen mask and took the hose for himself. Unfortunately for Ted, the bomb run had just commenced and everyone had to remain in his position until "bombs away." The formation had to endure another 17 minutes of flak. After Strick dropped the bomb load, at approximately 1217, their attention turned to Ted. Strick brought the medical kit. The remaining gunners had to stay in their positions for a few more minutes to ensure that there were no enemy planes in the area. After a few minutes all seemed clear, so they rushed to check on their friend. "Ted was a bloody mess, " Stan clearly recollects of the scene when he arrived in the waist area from the nose guns. Moe Gilliam came out of the tail turret to find his friend calm considering the circumstances. "I don't remember feeling any pain and I don't remember being scared," Ted recalls. Strick pulled out one of the small morphine tubes with a needle and told Ted that he was going to give him some morphine. Ted replied, "I don't think I need any." They all knew that he did; Ted was in shock.[65]

Strick's first attempt at administering the shot failed when the morphine's seal would not burst. The second failed because the vial was frozen. He was more careful, and successful, with the third attempt. Strick warmed it up in his hands for a few moments, and then carefully inserted the needle. The morphine and shock soon put Ted to sleep. Static, Moe, Stan, and Woody administered to his injuries. They tore away the clothing and could see that the flak had "dug a hole in his back." They applied sulfa dust and direct pressure to the wounds. Luckily for Ted, with the help of the direct pressure, the bandages froze to his wounds in the cold temperature of *Shadow*'s exposed waist gun area. This stopped the bleeding. Ted emotionally recalls, "I would have bled to death had it not been for the crew." They would later discover that five pieces of shrapnel had struck Ted, creating six holes—one went clean through him. He had a broken femur, broken pelvis, and several broken ribs. One of the pieces completely penetrated the back left side of his flak suit.[66]

Meanwhile, up front, Erickson and Robinson had some trouble of their own with which to contend. The flak had hit two of *Shadow*'s engines, the number 1 and number 2. Robinson ordered Erickson to feather them both. Just before the number 1 stopped Erickson noticed its oil pressure gauge flicker. "I unfeathered and restarted it. Fortunately it continued to run." Jake cut off fuel to the number 2 engine, which kept spurting flames. *Shadow*'s pilots did an impressive job staying in the formation, without lagging behind, on the three-hour return to Manduria. If the bomber had shown any sign of weakness, she would have been an easy target for enemy fighters.[67]

Jacobson checked all of the instruments and gauges for which he was responsible. Before going back to the waist area to check on Ted, he headed to the bomb bay to check on things there. On the way, Jake caught the ripcord of his parachute on part of the bomber's narrow passageway. It pulled clean out. Nothing happened. The chute did not open. If the crew had to bail out, he would not make it.[68]

The steadfast crew took turns comforting Ted, who slept the whole way back. As they approached Manduria, at about 1530, Maurice Gilliam held him. He leaned over to wake him up and told him to brace himself for the landing. He had to shake him a little.

"Steady yourself."

"OK," Ted replied. Maurice clutched him tightly.

No one knew it, but the flak burst over Ploesti had flattened the left main tire. This became all too clear when *Shadow* touched down on the runway. The force of landing with a flat tire caused the left landing gear to snap off and crash into the bomb bay. The tattered airplane was then forced into a severe ground loop. She skidded on her belly into the mud and muck adjacent to the runway. Suddenly the number 1 engine caught fire.[69]

The crew then hurriedly tried to exit *Shadow*. Jake remembers, "The guys up in the nose headed for the bomb bay to get out, but that was impossible, because *Shadow* was on her belly. I grabbed Gouldon and pointed him to the upper hatch and the others followed. I shut off the remaining gas lines and began to run as fast as I could—wishing the whole time I wasn't wearing those damn heavy fur-lined flying boots."

Ted, with his head in Gilliam's lap, remembers looking up from the floor of the airplane. He saw the rest of the crew exiting. He also saw smoke and asked Moe to

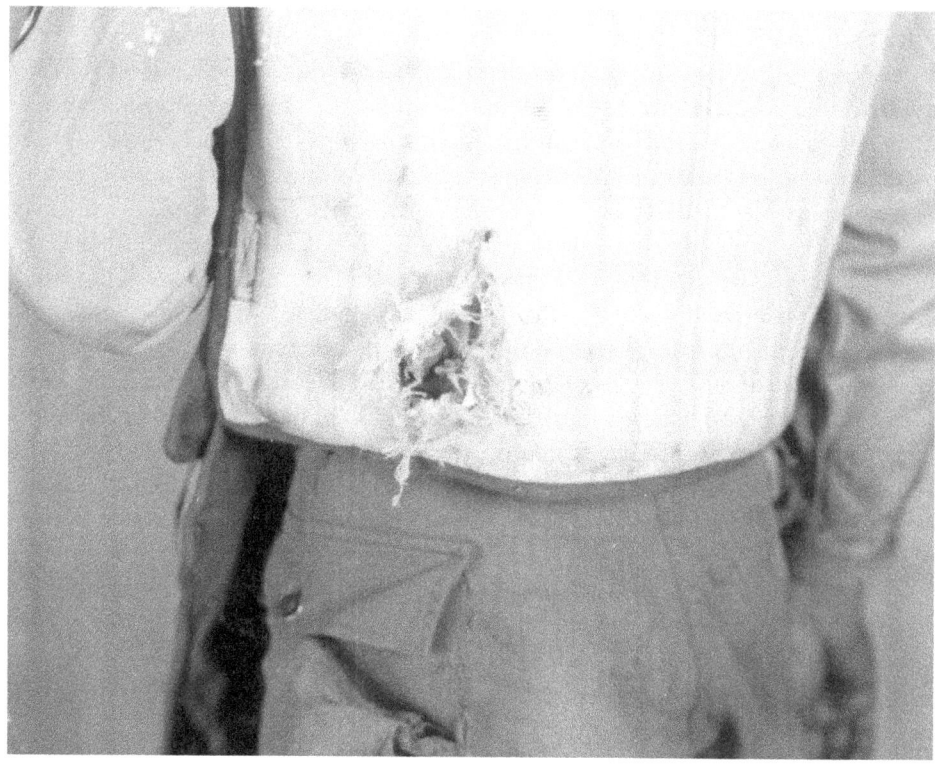

Ted Morris' flak jacket (inside out view). (Ted Morris)

get him out of the bomber before it exploded. Gilliam looked around and thought that the smoke was just dust that had been stirred up upon their crash landing. He did not know that the number 1 engine was on fire. He assured Ted everything would be all right. Gilliam started to get up to get help, but Ted pleaded, "Don't leave me! Don't leave me!"[70]

Gilliam then attempted to move him out of the airplane. The pain was too much and Ted hollered, "Put me down!" Maurice started to leave the bomber a second time to get help, which resulted in another cry from Ted, "Don't leave me! Don't leave me!"[71]

"I stood perplexed," Gilliam recalls. By now, he knew the engine was on fire. "I looked at him and looked out of the waist window. I realized the distance to the ground was too far for me to get him out. I was afraid to leave and afraid to stay."[72]

Ted recalls that he asked again about the fire. "Maurice cradled me and once again assured me that everything would be 'OK.'"[73]

At that moment, Jake came back to the waist area to check on Ted before he exited—the rest of the crew, except for Erickson, were safely out at that point. "I will never forget the sight!" Jake remembers. "Moe Gilliam had never left *Shadow*. He was sitting there with Teddy bleeding in his arms. He looked up at me through a haze of dust and smoke and firmly, but calmly said, 'Can we get Ted out of here?' I

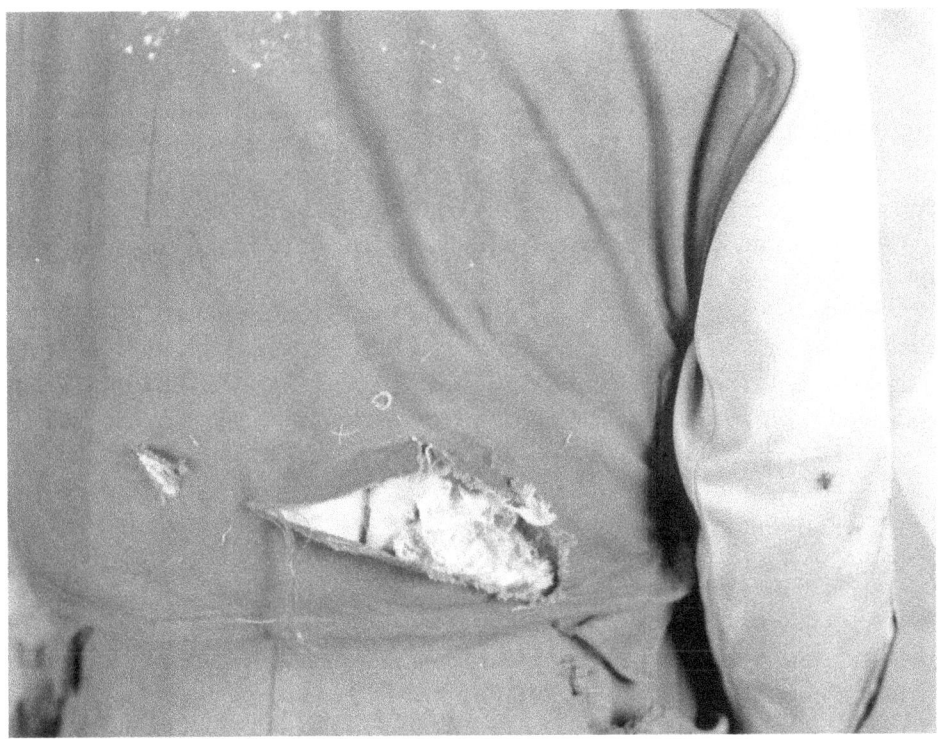

Ted Morris' flak jacket with a hole. Thanks to the diligent efforts of *Shadow*'s crew, Ted was able to survive the injuries he sustained on April 24, 1944, over Ploesti. (Ted Morris)

Aerial view of bomb strikes over Ploesti, Romania, on April 24, 1944. (Grant D. Caywood)

saw the fire trucks and ambulance coming and I did not think that we could get him safely out of the waist window without causing more serious damage to him." Eric also came back to the waist area about this time. He still has emotional flashbacks of the sight of Gilliam holding Morris in his arms. Eric and Jake then exited *Shadow* and signaled to the rescue personnel.[74]

Within a minute or so the ambulance and fire truck arrived. A red flare had been fired; thus the tower had been notified of Ted's injury and of the engine trouble. Emergency crews were at the ready; crash landings often ended in explosions. The firemen soon put out the flames on number 1. Maurice called out to the ambulance and told them that an injured man was aboard. "Help him!" he screamed. The medics were able to get Ted safely out with a stretcher and ladder. Maurice Gilliam, whom Jake felt "not only had great compassion, but nerves of steel," then left *Shadow*; he was the last one out. Although he got updates about his condition, Maurice never saw Ted Morris again. The experience uniquely tied them together as heroes in each other's eyes.[75]

Ted still wonders that if he had not forgotten his oxygen mask, "Would Woody have been injured or killed?" It is a question that will always haunt both men.[76]

The crew had one hell of an experience at Ploesti, but they were all still alive. Unfortunately *Shadow* would never fly again. There was some salvage potential to her, but that was about it. That night the crew attempted to go about their normal routine. Jake, Gilliam, Robbie, Stan, and the others briefly recorded the events of the day in their diaries, but words seemed inadequate to describe what they had experienced. Maurice Gilliam closed his entry with the simple eulogy, "Goodbye, *Shadow*." Jake recalls that the mission had a "resounding effect on the reality of what we were all facing each day. The loss of *Shadow*, our seemingly indestructible flying machine, that had carried us safely over oceans, mountains, and through impenetrable black walls of anti-aircraft fire" was no more. Her loss and Ted's injury compounded the anxiety and tension of the crew. Each was beginning to seriously doubt the chances of completing his tour of 50 missions.[77]

Ted was taken to the 35th Field Hospital in nearby Erchie, Italy. Caywood, Robinson, and some other officers visited him there the next day. Several pieces of flak remained in his body. Meanwhile, as Robinson recorded in his diary, "*Shadow* is a pitiful sight resting on its nose by the service squadron." Because of Ted's injury and the loss of their bomber, the crew was not scheduled for the April 25 mission to the aircraft factory in Varese, Italy. But the day did hold some news for them. Robinson was moved over to lead Ed Ley's crew and Erickson officially took over the pilot seat for *Shadow*'s crew. Vincent Olney, who had flown with the crew on a few missions, now rejoined the crew as Erickson's co-pilot.[78]

Shadow's tail gunner, Maurice Gilliam. (Maurice H. Gilliam)

The events of the last few days created a lot of change. The first order of business was to get the crew a new Liberator. Caywood exercised his power as squadron ops officer and procured *Sleepy Time Gal* for them. They inherited the bomber, name and all. "I will always remember the curvaceous girl painted on the nose," Jacobson said. Characteristic of later-model B-24s, *Sleepy Time Gal* was aluminum in appearance, without the olive drab paint job that had been on *Shadow*. After a few test flights Erickson concluded, "It was a better handling plane than Shadow."[79]

Another matter at hand was to replace Ted Morris. Norman Woodward, one of *Shadow*'s waist gunners, moved to the ball-turret. Another gunner replaced Woody in the waist. He is remembered as a "nice guy." His face is familiar, but unfortunately the bond with the new gunner was not as strong as with the original members. His name has been lost to the memory of the crew.

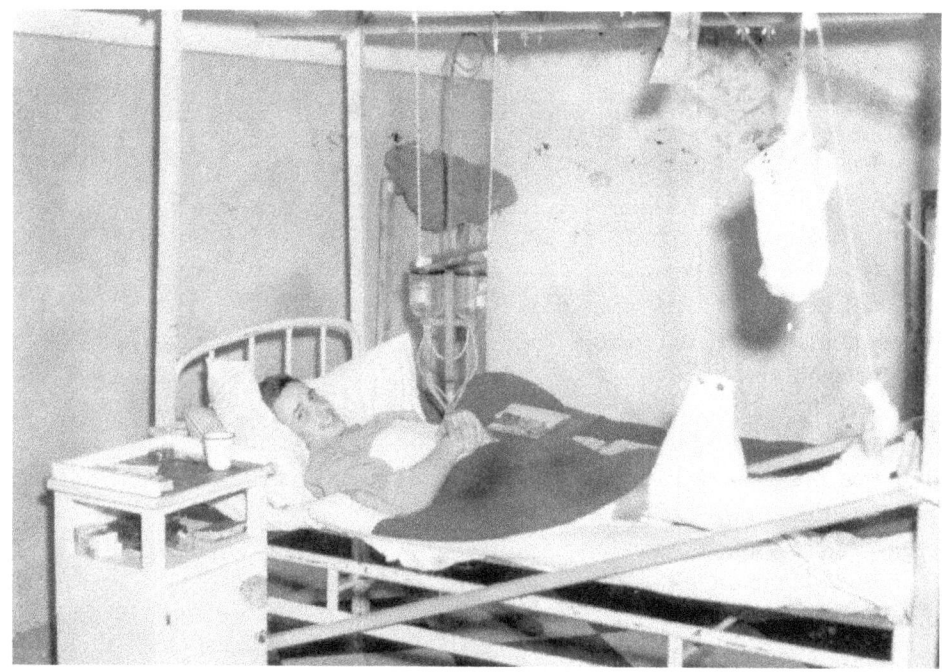

Ted Morris in the 35th Field Hospital in Erchie, Italy, in late April 1944. (Grant D. Caywood)

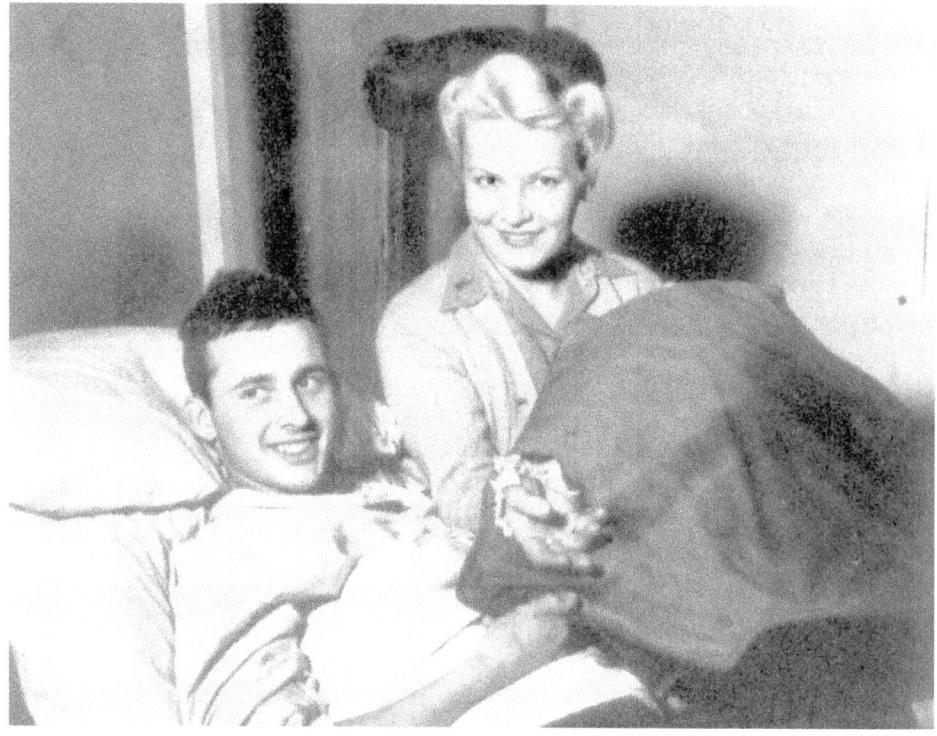

Ted Morris with a nurse in the 35th Field Hospital. (Grant D. Caywood)

Views of *Shadow*'s crash landing, April 24, 1944. (Grant D. Caywood)

Views of *Shadow*'s crash landing, April 24, 1944. (Grant D. Caywood)

Bad weather prevented the scheduled mission to the airdrome at Wiener-Neustadt on Wednesday, April 26. Conditions did not improve on April 27 so no mission was attempted. That evening, the men of Erickson's crew found their names on the board for the next morning. Weather continued to play a factor on Friday. The officers were briefed late, and the 450th BG's B-24s did not start taking off until 1115. Each Liberator carried ten 500-pound general-purpose bombs. Their target for the day was the communication and harbor facilities in Orbetello, Italy, north of Rome.[80]

The 450th BG picked up a P-38 escort at 1335, "about thirty miles inland from the Italian coast," that protected the formation all the way to the target. The clouds, which delayed take off, were now over Orbetello and hindered precision bombing. In fact, this mission would prove to be one of the poorest on record for the 450th BG. Most of the bombs dropped fell left of the aiming point into Lake Orbetello. Photo coverage later revealed that there was no visible damage to the target area. Unfortunately, the enemy anti-aircraft was more accurate. One of the 450th's B-24s was lost over the target due to the heavy, intense, accurate flak—nine chutes were seen. Flak also hit Erickson's new ship, *Sleepy Time Gal*, during the bomb run. He was forced to feather the number 4 engine. The crew worried all the way to Manduria; each wondered if they had another flat. At 1655, as they approached the base for landing, their anxiety heightened. Every member of the crew braced for another crash. But the flak had not hit the tires and *Sleepy Time Gal* landed safely. In all, thirteen Cottontail B-24s were damaged by flak; this included the one lost over the target. Erickson's crew was unnerved. Each man made his way back to his quarters after the debriefing. Hardly a word was spoken.[81]

The damage to *Sleepy Time Gal*'s number 4 engine prevented Erickson's crew from flying the 450th BG's April 29 mission to the harbor installations at Toulon, France. But they were back in the rotation on April 30. An early briefing revealed that the target was the marshalling yard at Alessandria, in northwestern Italy. The 15th AAF made repeated attacks on the Brenner Pass. This was the main German supply and communication route in and out of Italy and the attacks had forced the Germans to shift some of this traffic west. Alessandria was a key center in this new route. It, and the other rail yards in northwestern Italy with ready access to the ports of Genoa and La Spezia, had taken on added strategic significance in the past month.[82]

Sunday, April 30, would be an important one for the 15th AAF. It was sending nineteen bomb groups to these various transportation targets in northern Italy. Because of the incredible number of bombers in the area, "instructions went out to all units that times must be adhered to and courses must be followed closely to avoid forcing someone out of proper position." The 450th BG's B-24s, leading the 47th Wing, roared down the runway between 0802 and 0830. The 449th BG joined them at 0859 and they rendezvoused with the 98th and 376th Bomb Groups on the course to San Vito Di Normannie at 0905. The formation was joined by forty P-38s at 1115 near Rimini, which escorted them until 1350. Flak over the target, which was heavy, light, and inaccurate, caused no damage to the 450th's ships. Clear weather, the lack of fighter opposition, and inaccurate flak enabled the group to hit the target with

Sleepy Time Gal's enlisted crew with Ted's replacement in front of 720th Squadron building in Manduria. After Ted's injury, Woodward moved to the ball turret and a new gunner replaced him in the waist. The new man's name has been lost to the memory of the crew. Left to right: Ted's replacement, Manuel Esquivel, Stan Butynski, Maurice Gilliam, and Richard Jacobson. (Richard M. Jacobson)

450th BG B-24 *Sleepy Time Gal*. (Grant D. Caywood)

precision. Over fifty hits were recorded in the marshalling yard, as well as direct hits on a munitions plant and some state buildings. The mission was a success and all of the group's bombers returned safely to Manduria.[83]

Although April ended on a positive note, the heavy losses for the month were beginning to affect morale and confidence throughout the 450th BG. Replacement crews joined the group almost daily. Friends were lost on nearly every mission. It was a numbers game and most believed that if one played too long his number would come up. Erickson and his crew were veterans now. They understood the coolness shown to replacements. Each wondered if his luck was running out.

8

May 1944: Ploesti—Again!

Monday, May 1, 1944, marked the first anniversary of the 450th BG's activation at Gowan Field in Boise, but now the group was in Italy fighting the war. The day was clear, bright, and cool, but the group did not have a scheduled combat mission. It was "defense day." This drill was scheduled at regular intervals, and all personnel were required to "wear or carry their respective arms, gas mask, and helmet." Pilots in the group flew two practice flights "in search of new leaders," which were being lost in combat at an alarming rate. At the same time, Stricklin and other bombardiers participated in target identification instruction led by headquarters. This training was designed to make assessment of target damage more accurate. Gilliam and the other enlisted men in the 720th Squadron attended the squadron surgeon's (Capt. Al Wagner) lecture on malaria control. For the enlisted men of the 720th Squadron, this day of training and drills ended on an upbeat note with the opening of their new day room. The room was nicely appointed with painted tables, white walls, and a concrete floor. It gave the enlisted men a place to relax away from their barracks, away from B-24s.[1]

There was no scheduled mission for May 2. Instead, it was another day of training. This time the entire group practiced formation and bombing flights. Col. John Mills, group commander, continued to stress the importance of maintaining the prescribed formation on missions. "Anyone flying loosely is not [only] making a vulnerable gap in the formation … but also he is a clay pigeon for the ME-109s," Mills reminded his airmen. In the afternoon, the 720th Squadron held several boxing matches at their new ring, which they dubbed "Manduria Square Gardens." Jacobson boxed there to relieve stress and for the "prize money," which invariably was paid in "terrible GI dehydrated chocolate…" "That was about all we could get; so it tasted pretty good when I was able to win a match," he remembered.[2]

8. May 1944

That evening Jacobson, Gilliam, and the rest of *Sleepy Time Gal*'s crew found their names on the board to fly again in the morning. For the airmen, the early morning wake-up and briefing foreshadowed a tough target. Their instincts were right. The target for the day was Ploesti. But the mission was scrubbed before takeoff due to weather in the target area. Taking advantage of the down time, Col. Mills ordered more practice missions. That afternoon Mills was presented the Silver Star in the monthly awards ceremony for his leadership on the April 5 mission to Ploesti.[3]

In that same ceremony Erickson, Gouldon, Stricklin, and Butynski received the second oak leaf bronze clusters to their Air Medals. In April, each of Erickson's (then Caywood's) crew had received the Air Medal, which was given for distinguished "meritorious achievement while participating in aerial flight."[4] Subsequent achievement was noted with the addition of an oak leaf cluster to the Air Medal—the equivalent of another air medal. By May, most of Erickson's crew also had at least one oak leaf cluster. Unfortunately, the medal was given out with "two-fisted generosity," writes author Geoffrey Perret—especially in the 8th and 9th Army Air Forces.[5] For those who knew about this prodigality, its meaning was diminished.

There were no hard and fast parameters for distribution of the Air Medal, so a rule of thumb was used to determine the frequency. For some groups an Air Medal, or cluster, was given out for every five missions flown. For others they were given for a certain number of hours flown. They were distributed less liberally in the 12th and 15th Army Air Forces, where some attempt was made to distribute the medal according to the original intention of the executive order that created it. They were given out monthly, usually in a formal ceremony like the one on May 3, and most of the airmen were justifiably proud when they received them. There was no doubt that *Shadow*'s crew had earned their medals.[6]

The airmen had a wonderful treat for dinner that night—hot dogs and Coca-Cola. Afterwards, on the way back to their barracks, the men of Erickson's crew found their names on the board again. The early briefing on May 4 revealed that Ploesti was once again the target. But all of the 450th BG's bombers returned within three hours due to bad weather; no credit was earned for the mission. That evening, Caywood assigned himself to fly with his old crew the next day. It was his prerogative as squadron operations officer. Perhaps he sensed the target would again be Ploesti, since the last two scrubbed missions had been. Maybe he wanted an experienced crew to go with him, or maybe, like a big brother, he felt he could protect them if they had to go back to Ploesti. His intentions have been lost to memory, but he was the pilot that day, and the crew was excited that he was back. It would be Caywood's first time flying *Sleepy Time Gal* and it would be one of the last missions he would fly with his original crew.

At about 0200 on Friday, May 5, the sealed orders arrived at headquarters. Caywood had just fallen back asleep; he had gotten up at 0100 to see if they had arrived. The flight crews were awakened at 0400, and the briefing was set for 0500. When the briefing curtain was pulled the target was revealed: for the third day in a row, it was Ploesti. The briefing officer said, "We have plotted 142 heavy guns at Ploesti; there are probably more. Flak is expected to be heavy, intense, and accurate. The enemy has a capability of 225 to 250 fighters, both single and twin engine. We expect attacks en route from the Nis-Belgrade area to the target, heavy interception over the target area, and possible second sortie attacks on the route home. Gentlemen, your work is cut out for you." For Erickson and the rest of Caywood's original crew, it was an unnerving shock. They had still not recovered from the April 24 mission to Ploesti, in which Ted Morris was injured and *Shadow* was lost. Flying with Caywood again, however, provided them some comfort.[7]

As usual the ground crews worked through the night preparing the bombers for the mission. They fueled them, ran checks on the radios, loaded the bombs and the .50-caliber machine guns, and performed the myriad other tasks for which they were responsible each mission. By the time the crews picked up their parachutes, the bombers were ready to fly. But the ever-worrying ground personnel could always be seen making last minute checks and rechecks.[8]

There was already a reverence for Ploesti. The 450th BG had flown there three times in April, and crews knew what to expect from the Hitler's third best-defended city. Caywood felt that Ploesti was actually the best defended. Berlin and Vienna may

Vincent Olney, Herb Gouldon, and Richard Jacobson in Manduria after receiving the Air Medal. (Richard M. Jacobson)

have had more heavy flak guns and fighters, but they were distributed over a much larger area. Ploesti's were concentrated in a small city, with great effect. As Caywood and his crew boarded *Sleepy Time Gal* they focused on the task at hand. For Caywood, this would be his first mission to the dreaded target. But the crew knew that Stricklin could drop the bombs in the "pickle barrel" and that Caywood and Erickson could get them home safely.

For the May 5 mission, the 15th AAF planned a large attack on the marshalling yards around Ploesti. The 450th and 449th Bomb Groups represented the 47th Wing in the offensive. Between 1015 and 1042, thirty-nine of the 450th BG's B-24s roared down the runway at Manduria. Each one was loaded with ten 500-pound bombs. They rendezvoused with the 449th BG at 1116. An escort of thirty P-38s and P-47s joined the formation at 1232. This escort broke away at 1340 and was replaced by ten P-51s at 1350 near the IP (Targoviste).⁹

As the group neared the target, the flak guns opened up on the bombers. As predicted, it was heavy, intense, and accurate. The accuracy was further aided by an

Manuel Esquivel, Stan Butynski, and Maurice Gilliam in Manduria after receiving the Air Medal. (Maurice H. Gilliam)

Manuel Esquivel (left) and Stan Butynski in front of *Sleepy Time Gal*. (Richard M. Jacobson)

ME-109, flying 2,000 feet above the formation, which dropped various colored flares as signals to the flak guns below. Twenty-one of the 450th's thirty-eight bombers, including *Sleepy Time Gal*, received holes from flak. At 1359 clouds and smoke pots completely obscured the target over the aiming point. But momentary breaks in the clouds during the bomb run allowed Stricklin to see the target, "which gave a concentrated pattern" of bombs over the marshalling yards and refinery.[10]

About a minute later, just as the formation turned away from the bomb run for the rally home, approximately twenty ME-109s attacked. They came in from out of the sun at the 6 o'clock position, singly and in pairs. Gunners in both bomb groups turned their .50-caliber Brownings on the bandits. Most of the attacks were over by 1411, when the P-51 escort rejoined the formation. At about 1430, the ten P-51s were replaced by thirty P-38s, which escorted the group all the way back to the Italian coastline. The first of the 450th BG's B-24s returned to Manduria at 1700. All made it home safely, but over half of the bombers had received flak damage. Two airmen received minor wounds. The 449th BG did not fare as well. They lost five bombers over the target.[11]

Post-mission aerial reconnaissance confirmed that the attack was, at least in part, a success. A large column of smoke over the target area that extended nearly 12,000 feet signaled a significant oil fire at the refinery. But continued cloud cover, smoke from the oil fire, and the enemy smoke pots "prevented any detailed evaluation of the accuracy of the bombing."[12]

For Caywood and the crew of *Sleepy Time Gal*, despite thirteen flak holes, the mission had been a complete success—they made it home from Ploesti alive. After debriefing and doughnuts, the crews went back to the barracks exhausted. There was little conversation. The mission had been draining, emotionally and physically. After dinner the men of the crew found their names on the board once again. They would be flying in the morning. Before he went to sleep that night, Gilliam wrote, "I hope we never have to go back to Ploesti." It was a sentiment echoed by all of the airmen. But they would have to go back.[13]

On Saturday, May 6, the 15th AAF continued its attack on Hitler's oil distribution in Romania. At that morning's briefing, the officers of the 450th BG learned that they, along with the rest of the 47th Wing, would attack Romania's third largest rail yard at Brasov. It was a major hub for distributing the petroleum products refined at Ploesti and other oil centers in Romania. At the same time, the 15th AAF's other B-24 wings would attack Pitesti, Craiovi, and Campino, while its B-17 wings bombed the aircraft factory and airdrome in Brasov. In all, the 15th AAF sent over 300 bombers to Romania on May 6. There could be no doubt now that the 15th's strategic bombing strategy was now focusing on Hitler's "black gold."[14]

Thirty-nine of the 450th BG's B-24s, each loaded with ten 500-pounders, thundered down the runway between 0800 and 0828. They rendezvoused with the 449th BG at 0856, 6,000 feet over Manduria. En route to the target they joined the 376th and 98th Bomb Groups. The latter led the 47th Wing. The formation had sporadic fighter escort on the way to the target. About forty P-38s were observed for a short while around 0945, but they quickly withdrew. They were followed by a group of twenty-five P-47s that stayed with the formation until 1330.[15]

The 450th and 449th Bomb Groups dropped their bombs over Brasov between 1147 and 1150. The 450th's S-2 Intelligence Narrative for the mission reported, "The greatest concentration [fell] about 600–800 feet north of the aiming point. The target area was hit hard, and many fires were seen among the cars in the marshalling yard." Photos later indicated the following results: 45 bursts at the northeast end of

450th BG B-24s returning from a mission to Ploesti, Romania. (Grant D. Caywood)

the marshalling yard at the choke point; 30 hits in southwest of portion of the yard that extended across two-thirds of the tracks; direct hits on "shop type" buildings; 40 strikes at the north choke point of the south marshalling yard; and 75 bursts at the southwest choke point of the north marshalling yard. Unlike many other missions, the destruction on this mission was clearly visible to the airmen after the bomb run. "We really tore the place up today," Gilliam wrote in his mission diary.[16]

The flak and fighter opposition over Brasov was light. All of the 450th BG's B-24s returned home safely to Manduria around 1700. Although the mission had been a complete success, it had been a grueling day for the airmen. They had been in their bombers for over nine hours. Most of them barely had the energy to make it to their barracks after debriefing. Unfortunately for Erickson's crew, they were on the board to fly again the next morning.[17]

Caywood was conspicuously absent from the mission to Brasov, but with good reason. His talent and ability had once again been recognized. On May 6 he replaced Capt. Gordon T. Colley as the 720th's squadron commander (CO). The commander was the chief executive officer of the squadron. He was supposed to know everything, and he was responsible for everyone in his unit. All of the squadron's communications "come to and go from him—even if he never sees them." The CO assigned duties to those who would take action. He relied heavily on the squadron operations officer—the role Caywood held at the time of the promotion. The promotion meant that he would fly less than he did as ops officer, and this would prolong his tour even more. But, as before, Caywood readily accepted the duty. Capt. Floyd Robinson, one of *Shadow*'s replacement pilots, was promoted to squadron operations officer to fill the vacancy left by Caywood's advancement.[18]

Erickson's crew was up early for breakfast and briefing on Sunday, May 7. The target was, once again, the marshalling yards at Bucharest, Romania. *Sleepy Time Gal* was one of the forty B-24s from the 450th BG that took off that morning between 0735 and 0815. They were joined by thirty-five B-24s from the 449th BG. The 15th AAF bombing strategy was working. The German rail lines were severely strained, especially on the Russian front. This mission sought to destroy the repairs made since the two previous raids to Bucharest in April. About "two hours after take-off, in the vicinity of Bor, Yugoslavia, the escorting fighters, which were well ahead of the bomber force, called back and informed the 450th Group leader that the 'weather was too bad [and] they [the fighters] were turning back.'" Both groups heeded the warning and aborted the mission. They returned to their respective bases with their "bomb loads intact." No credit was given for the mission.[19]

Not completing a mission was emotionally draining, but there was not much time to think about it; *Sleepy Time Gal*'s crew was on the board again for May 8. Monday's mission was scrubbed before briefing. There was a collective sigh of relief—the Concordia Vega oil refinery at Ploesti had been the intended target. Officers from the 47th Wing headquarters used this down time to inspect the 450th BG. Caywood's presence as CO was already in effect; the 720th Squadron was noted as the best in the group. Later in the day "practice bombing and gunnery flights were flown by some replacement crews." Some airmen, including Robinson, saw *Reveille With Beverly* at the theater in Oria. Others played softball; the 720th lost 7–5 to the 450th Group HQ team.[20]

A mission was scheduled for Tuesday, May 9, but it was cancelled before the briefing due to weather. The bad weather gave most of the group an opportunity to see the USO show in Oria. The day also marked Richard Jacobson's twenty-first birthday, and the crew celebrated accordingly. That evening, for the sixth in a row, the men of Erickson's crew found their names on the board to fly the next morning. The briefing on Wednesday, May 10, revealed the aircraft complex (Werk No. 1) at Wiener-Neustadt, Austria, as the target. Thirty-nine B-24s from the 450th BG joined forty from the 449th BG; each was loaded with ten 500-pounders. A few hours into the mission the weather turned bad. Once again they had to turn back. This time the crews jettisoned their bombs in the Adriatic before landing. The aborted missions started to affect the morale of the group. Airmen began to wonder how long the war would last. Some speculated that the 450th BG would have to spend another Christmas in Manduria—they would.[21]

That evening the airmen were restricted to base. They did not know what was going to happen the next day, but they found out soon enough. The wake-up call on Friday, May 12, came at 0130, with a 0230 briefing. The briefing was so early because the 450th BG planned to fly two missions to the same target: the harbor installations at San Stephano, Italy. The mission served a dual purpose. First, it was routed past the Allied front lines to boost morale in the area. Second, of course, was to destroy

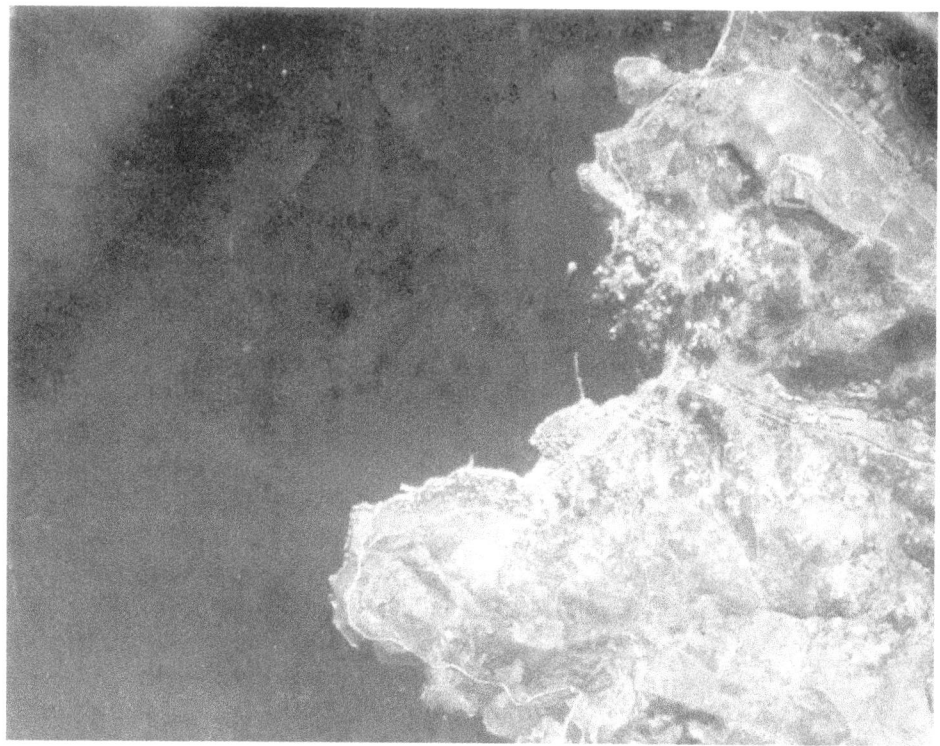

Aerial view of bomb strikes over Porto San Stefano, Italy. (Grant D. Caywood)

the facilities at San Stephano that supplied the German forces. Caywood and Robinson were scheduled to fly both missions in the "double-header."[22]

In the first mission, forty-two B-24s from the 450th BG took off in the dark at 0511. *Sleepy Time Gal* was among the group's bombers that rendezvoused with the 449th BG at 0556. No fighters were encountered on the way to the target, but the formation experienced moderate flak over Marzano and Villetta. The flak intensified at San Stephano, and it was extremely accurate. There flak hit the left vertical stabilizer on one of the 450th's B-24s, causing it to spin into another bomber. The first B-24 "cut the other in two," wrote Gilliam that night. They only saw six chutes. It was the type of image that haunted crews. Each airman reasoned that it could just have easily been his plane, and there was not a thing anyone could do to help.[23]

Substantial damage was done to the target—but at a cost of two bombers. The 450th BG returned to Manduria at 1046. The second mission took off, but bad weather made them return before the rendezvous with the 449th BG.[24]

With the May 12 mission, most of Erickson's crew had completed thirty-four of their fifty-mission goal—Gilliam had thirty-five. The crew was showing obvious signs of stress and fatigue. The Army Air Force knew that airmen needed a break from the rigors of combat flight; so they designed rest leaves (also called "flak leaves") for crews when needed. The leave usually came at about the halfway point of a tour. For some reason, however, Erickson's crew had been overlooked until now. This all changed on May 13 when the enlisted men of *Sleepy Time Gal* went to rest camp at Santa Cesario.

Enlisted men and officers attended rest camps separately. In England, the 8th AAF leased English castles and mansions for their airmen. In Italy, the 15th AAF rented out either lavish resort hotels overlooking the Adriatic or cabins in quaint villages. The leave usually lasted a week and was meant to get the airman away from combat and allow him time to relax. Depending on the camp, recreation ranged from swimming to horseback, boat, or bicycle riding to hunting and fishing. Women from the Red Cross staffed most of the camps. There was no schedule. Each man could sleep as late as he wanted and plan his own day. Uniforms were only required at dinner.[25]

Gilliam, Jacobson, Butynski, Woodward, and Esquivel were assigned this leave at Santa Cesario. On their first full day there (May 14), they had cause to celebrate; their radio operator, Manuel Esquivel, turned twenty-two. The day-to-day routine at Manduria ranged from sheer terror while flying through flak alley to complete boredom on the rainy days that they did not fly. At Santa Cesario they could do whatever they wanted to. "All I remember doing was sleeping, eating, and reading," recalls Maurice Gilliam.

But Jacobson remembers that it was only a "theoretical rest." While they were at Manduria they were working towards their goal of getting home. Each day in Santa

Rest camp at Santa Cesario. (Maurice H. Gilliam)

Rest camp at Santa Cesario. (Grant D. Caywood)

Cesario delayed the promise that they would safely complete another mission, and thus be one step closer to home. Although the rest camps were nice (and necessary), things were different there. For that week they had no chance to get closer to the fifty-mission goal. Ironically, the leave gave them even more time to think about the odds of their survival.[26]

"We all began to show signs of nervousness at the rest camp," Jacobson recalled. "I vividly recall the dinner on the second or third night—and maybe having more 'Rooster Blood' [Chianti] than usual. You could see your buddies tremble a little. I know at one point my teeth began to chatter, and I had to clamp down on them. We were all experiencing some kind of nervous withdrawal. I don't think the rest camp did us much good at all. I know, from my perspective, that I felt more tense when I returned to action than when I was flying just about every day."[27]

Jacobson, Gilliam, and the others returned to Manduria the next weekend. While they were at rest camp, the 450th BG had flown five missions: Piacenza, Italy, on May 13; Vicenza, Italy, on May 14; Porto San Stefano, Italy, on May 17; Ploesti, Romania, on May 18; and Spezia, Italy, on May 19. On Sunday, May 21, the crew of *Sleepy Time Gal* was back in the rotation. Rest camp was over. They were set to fly again in the morning; once again they could begin chipping away at the fifty-mission goal.[28]

The briefing on Monday morning was a little later than usual. There, the officers learned that the intended target for the day was the railroad bridge over the Tagliamento River near Latisano, in northeastern Italy. Thirty-nine of the 450th BG's B-

8. May 1944

Rest camp at Santa Cesario. (Richard M. Jacobson)

24s took off between 0915 and 0940. Each was loaded with ten 500-pound GP bombs. The Cottontails rendezvoused with the 449th BG 3,000 feet above Manduria at 1006. According to D. William Shepherd in his history of the 449th, the "two groups headed out over the Adriatic where they encountered a densely-clouded weather front. The formation proceeded to make three 360o turns in an attempt to gain altitude to get above the clouds. Unable to get above the clouds, the formation then flew east as far as the Yugoslav coast [to a point] some twenty miles south of Zara in an unsuccessful attempt to go around the weather front. The decision was then made to head for the Italian coast and to make an attempt to bomb an alternate target." At this point the 450th and 449th Bomb Groups split up. Most of the 449th BG dropped their bombs on the rail line and highway bridges in the coastal town of Giulianova, but five jettisoned theirs in the Adriatic. The 450th BG found their target of opportunity in Montesilvano, five miles north of Pescara. There they bombed the railroad and highway with accuracy. But they missed the bridge over the Saline River.[29]

No fighter escort was present for the mission, and, thankfully, it was not needed. Flak, however, was heavy, intense, and accurate over Pescara. Eighteen Cottontail Liberators sustained flak damage in the attack; two were severely damaged. All thirty-nine of the 450th's bombers returned to Manduria by 1353. The mission was confusing for the airmen. Jacobson wrote in his diary that night, "Damned if I know where we went. We flew all over Italy and up into Yugoslavia." Gilliam recorded in his, "We went around in circles so long everyone got disgusted." Despite the frustration and somewhat mixed results, Erickson's men had completed another mission.[30]

That evening the men of the 450th were in for a treat; the new open-air theater opened. Construction of the 2,000-seat theater had begun in April in an effort to help boost morale. Now, the men would no longer have to find a ride to Oria to catch a movie or be faced with an "S.R.O" (standing room only) sign. All seats were taken on opening night, and the airmen were entertained with *Sweet Rosie O'Grady* starring Betty Grable. "It reminded me of the drive-in theaters back in the States—without cars," recalls Maurice Gilliam. From that day on, weather permitting, movies were shown nightly at "The Cottontail Theater." Later in 1944 the 450th BG could also boast of having its own radio station, "The Voice of the Cottontails."[31]

Erickson's crew could enjoy the movie more than some, since their names were not posted to fly the next morning. But the 450th BG did fly a mission on Tuesday, May 23. The target was German troop concentrations at Grataferrata, Italy, in support of the Allied efforts on the Anzio beachhead. It was one of the few tactical missions flown by the 450th, but as the 720th Squadron War Diary recorded, "Our men are always enthused about aiding the infantry. Men of the AAF have a very wholesome respect for the soldiers up on the front." The crew of *Sleepy Time Gal* also stood down for the May 24 mission to the Wollersdorf Airdrome in Wiener-Neustadt, Austria. Navigator Herb Gouldon celebrated his twenty-first birthday.[32]

Erickson's crew was back in the rotation for the Thursday, May 25, mission to the oil storage facilities in Porto Marghera, Italy. *Sleepy Time Gal* was among the 450th BG's thirty-six B-24s that took off between 0920 and 0946 that morning. They rendezvoused with the 449th BG over Manduria at 1004. The Liberators in each group were loaded with ten 500-pound GP bombs. No enemy fighters were observed or encountered on the way to the target—or upon return. The flak over the target was heavy, scattered, and inaccurate. Three ships in the port's harbor fired rockets at the formation, but all missed their mark. The 450th dropped its bombs first at 1240; this was followed by the 449th at 1245. Both groups recorded direct hits on the storage tanks. The S-2 (Intelligence) Report for the mission stated that "concentrations of bombs into target areas ignited oil storage tanks, and smoke rose 10,000 feet as we left the target." "Old Strick really put his bombs in there," Jacobson proudly wrote that night of his bombardier's accuracy. All of the 450th's bombers were safely home by 1503; it had been a very successful mission. That night a large barbeque was held in honor of the airmen with forty or more missions. All in attendance enjoyed a large feast of barbequed sheep, goat, and pig, as well as "hard boiled eggs and potatoes with skins." At this point most of Erickson's crew had 36 missions—Gilliam had 37; Caywood had 25; Robinson had 31.[33]

That evening the men of *Sleepy Time Gal* found their names on the board once again. Sleep was minimal; the crews were aroused early, at 0300. The briefing was scheduled for shortly after 0400. The target for the day was Nice, France. All four groups in the 47th Wing were scheduled to attack targets in southern France which were helping to supply enemy troops in Italy. Their primary objective was the Main Riviera Line, the coastal railroad that connected Marseilles, France, to Genoa, Italy.

Aerial view of bomb strike over Porto Marghera, May 25, 1944. (Grant D. Caywood)

The 450th, 376th, and 98th Bomb Groups were to attack the main marshalling yards in Nice, while the 449th BG was to bomb the railroad bridge across the Var River, four miles west of the city.[34]

The crews boarded their bombers in total darkness. Between 0600 and 0635, thirty-nine of the 450th BG's B-24s rolled down the runway, each loaded with ten 500-pound GP bombs. They rendezvoused with the 449th BG over Manduria at 0647 and proceeded to meet up with the rest of the 47th Wing. Both Gilliam and Jacobson commented in their mission diaries about the wonderful P-38 escort that the formation had to and from Nice. The presence of an escort and the lack of fighter opposition in the target area was a welcome relief to the airmen. The only flak encountered was over the defenses at the Var River Bridge. It was heavy, moderate, and inaccurate and was fired in a barrage as the formation flew over. Although none of the 450th BG sustained damage from the flak, the 449th BG did. A direct hit to Capt. Gerald W. Warner's B-24 (Ship number 21) caused the "aircraft to break into several pieces which were seen falling in flames, and crashing into the water just offshore. No chutes were seen. All ten members of Warner's crew died as ship #21 disintegrated in mid-air."[35]

Despite the tragic loss for the 449th BG, the mission was successful. At 1031 the

450th BG dropped 95 tons of bombs on the car repair and machine shop area of the Nice marshalling yards. "An excellent concentration of hits was effected on the target area. Many fires and heavy smoke were visible as the formation withdrew," the mission report said. Many bursts were recorded across the tracks and station as well as in the military camp area. Most of the 450th's Liberators returned to Manduria by 1332—two returned a few hours later after stopping to refuel.[36]

Although he had washed out of pilot training, Robert Stricklin had proven himself to be one of the 450th BG's best bombardiers. For this reason, he was given the opportunity to become the lead bombardier. The first mention of this promotion was in his May 26 letter home. He was to attend a bombardier school for a week at the 15th AAF HQ in Bari, Italy. Stricklin was pleased with the recognition, but was apprehensive about the delay the promotion would cause in completing his 50-mission goal.[37]

After debriefing and dinner, Erickson's crew checked the board. For the third night in a row they were on it; they would be flying again in the morning. It was another early wake-up call for the airmen; this time it was 0330. An hour later at the briefing, the officers learned that they would be going back to France. The Saturday, May 27, target was the St. Charles marshalling yard in Marseilles, and it represented the continued effort to cripple the Main Riviera Line.[38]

As they did the previous day, the crews boarded their ships well before sunrise and thirty-nine of the Cottontails' bombers began thundering down the runway at 0600. They met up with the 449th BG at 0651 and proceeded to rendezvous with the 376th and 98th Bomb Groups en route to the target. The scarcity of flak on Friday's mission indicated that the Allies had caught the Germans off guard. On Saturday, however, the enemy was better prepared. Flak batteries were first encountered over Cannes, just west of Nice, nearly 100 miles from the target. Several more batteries were encountered over other cities on the way to Marseilles. *Sleepy Time Gal* received a few direct hits. One piece hit Maurice Gilliam's tail turret just below his seat. Other pieces punctured two of the bomber's gas tanks, but luckily they did not explode. The crew, obviously shaken, called out the hits to Erickson, who calmed the crew and kept a steady course. The only fighter opposition came from six ME-109s that flew above the formation. They unsuccessfully attempted to drop aerial bombs on the group.[39]

At 1050 the 450th BG dropped nearly 76 tons of bombs on the target. Smoke obscured the target at the aiming point, but the bombardiers dropped on the leader's mark. As the formation turned for home, some bursts could be seen at St. Charles Station and its nearby warehouses. Later, bomb strike photographs revealed the group's precision in and around the target area. By 1415, most of the 450th BG had returned to Manduria. None were lost on the mission, but five of the group's B-24s were at friendly fields due to refueling or minor damage. In total, nine of the Cottontails' Liberators, including *Sleepy Time Gal*, received damage.[40]

The flak hits had a tremendous impact on Erickson's crew. It brought back the feelings and emotions that haunted them after their April 24 mission to Ploesti when Ted was injured and *Shadow* was lost. Despite good weather, the group stood down on Sunday, May 28, for maintenance and training. The three consecutive days of missions had taken a toll on the bombers. Most of them needed at least some repairs or maintenance. While the diligent ground crews were busy at work, 720th Squadron Ops Officer Floyd Robinson and others trained some of the green replacement crews in formation flying. Repairs to *Sleepy Time Gal* were not complete when Robinson made the assignments for Monday's mission, so Erickson's crew had another free evening. A bright moon Sunday evening made the movie almost indiscernible on the open-air screen. Excitement for the evening was provided by an air raid, which scattered the crowd from the Cottontail Theater into the shelters. The base's British flak crew fired at the recon planes overhead, which dropped flares to light up the base. Fortunately no other enemy planes appeared and the all-clear signal was given shortly after midnight.[41]

The next morning, Monday, May 29, Major Snaith led the 450th BG on a mission to the Wollersdorf Airdrome in Wiener-Neustadt, Austria. It was the group's second trip there in six days. But this time the mission was strategic, not tactical. That evening the men of *Sleepy Time Gal* were surprised when their names were not on the list to fly on May 30. That mission took the 450th BG back to Austria for the second day in a row, this time to the aircraft factory in Ebreichsdorf. Erickson and his crew were back in the rotation for May 31—but they would not all fly together.[42]

Maurice Gilliam was on guard duty that night and did not know he was scheduled for the May 31 mission. "When I came in at 0500 to eat breakfast Static [Manuel Esquivel] said, 'You are flying.' I didn't know what to do. I could not find anyone to fly in my place, so I flew." Gilliam had been placed as the tail gunner in the lead ship with Col. Robert Gideon, who would take command of the 450th BG in July 1944. Jacobson was also placed with a different crew; the only member of *Sleepy Time Gal*'s crew with him was the co-pilot, Vincent Olney. The rest of Erickson's men flew on the mission with various other crews.[43]

The splitting up of the crew for the mission could not have happened at a worse time. At the briefing the target was revealed as Ploesti. For Gilliam, Jacobson, Erickson, and most of the rest of the crew, it would be their third trip to the treacherous city, and this was to be a big one. For the Wednesday, May 31, mission, the 15th AAF was mounting a massive attack against Ploesti's network of refineries. It was sending all five of its heavy bombardment wings against the city, with each one attacking a different refinery. The 47th Wing was to lead the mission, followed by the 304th, 55th, 49th, and 5th Wings. The 450th BG would lead the 47th Wing against the Romano Americana Refinery. The rest of the wing's formation consisted of, in order, the 376th, 449th, and 98th Bomb Groups. This would be a Pathfinder mission, and all bombers were to load three cartons of window to be dispersed "three minutes before the IP until clear of the flak area."[44]

The 450th BG rendezvoused with the 376th BG at 0644 and with the remainder of the wing at 0652. No enemy fighters were encountered on the way; the formation had an escort of P-38s and P-51s. About fifty miles out, the smoke pots around Ploesti could be seen. The 450th BG reached the target at 0953. Since the entire area, as expected, was covered in smoke, the bombardiers dropped on the Pathfinder's mark. Just as they came out of the bomb run, approximately 30 enemy fighters pounced on the formation (15 to 20 ME-109s and FW-190s; 5 to 7 JU-88s; and 5 ME-110s). They attacked from 10 o'clock high, coming out of the sun. The first wave of approximately fifteen fighters made a wide, swinging pass about 200 yards out. It was the only coordinated attack reported. After that initial pass, the bandits broke into elements of two or three and made attacks from various angles for nearly twenty minutes.[45]

Flak was by far a bigger problem. Over the target it was heavy, intense, and accurate. It holed twenty of the 450th's bombers, five of them severely. Flak claimed two of the group's B-24s; only 11 parachutes were seen. One pilot was killed, and a bombardier from another crew was seriously wounded. Jacobson and Olney were facing their own perilous situation. Their crew was green. According to Jake, "They couldn't get their guns going. The bombardier couldn't release his bombs, and we started to fall back from the formation. The bombs finally had to be toggled out by hand." Jacobson made his way down to the bomb bay to manually release the bombs, just as Ted Morris had done on *Shadow* seven weeks before.[46]

All of Erickson's crew, most in different bombers, returned safely to Manduria. They were really beginning to defy the odds. As May came to an end, most of *Shadow*'s original crew had forty missions. Most of them secretly felt that they could not survive another mission to Ploesti—but they would be going back within a week.

9

June 1944: Fifty and Home

In accordance with time-honored tradition, airmen were paid on the last day of the month. The May 31 mission had been to Ploesti; so most of them were too exhausted to celebrate or even get their pay. Thursday, June 1 was a stand down day, and no combat mission was flown. Instead, according to the 720th Squadron's War Diary, it was a day of "maximum maintenance and training. New crews were indoctrinated at Group S-2 (Intelligence), and practice gunnery and bombing missions were flown, morning and afternoon." Some used the brief respite to take a swim in the Mediterranean at the beach, while boxing fans watched some excellent matches in the 720th's ring. For others, card playing passed the hours. Since most of the combat airmen had been paid recently, money changed hands swiftly.[1]

On the way to the movie that night, the men of Erickson's crew found their names on the board for the next day's mission. According to the posting, they would, thankfully, be flying as a crew again. The crews were awakened early for breakfast and briefing on Friday, June 2. Everyone complained of "fighting this damn war in the middle of the night." When the curtain was pulled, the target for the day was revealed as the marshalling yard at Simeria, Romania. No one had heard of Simeria, but any target in Romania increased the airmen's anxiety. The crews assumed that it must be a key location for petroleum and supply transport. It was. This mission marked the beginning of Operation FRANTIC, which was a shuttle-bombing campaign of Axis–controlled targets along the Russian front. In addition to the 47th Wing's attack on Simeria, the 15th AAF sent wings not only to attack targets in Brasov, Oradea and Cluij in Romania, but also to Miskolc, Debreczen, and Szolnok in Hungary.[2]

Sleepy Time Gal and thirty-four other B-24s took turns down the runway in

Manduria at 0525. Each was loaded with the now standard and lethal package of ten 500-pounders. They rendezvoused with the 376th BG over San Pancrazio at 0624, and then joined the remainder of the wing en route to the target. No fighters or flak were encountered on the way to the target. It was apparent that Germany was having trouble putting up an intercept, much to the relief of the American airmen. The 450th BG dropped 75.75 tons of bombs over the target at 0926. Despite the absence of flak and fighters, perfect navigation, and good weather, the bomb results were poor. Visual observations revealed that only three strings of bombs landed in the target area. The 449th BG reported that many of their bursts landed in the open fields adjacent to the marshalling yards—a few houses were hit. All of the bombers returned home safely to Manduria shortly after noon. It had been an easy mission and was a good reprieve from the usual horror of combat flight, but a great opportunity had been lost.[3]

That evening the men saw *Let's Face It*, the musical comedy with Bob Hope and Betty Hutton. The crew of *Sleepy Time Gal* was scheduled to fly the next morning to a marshalling yard in Romania, but just after an early morning briefing, low clouds over the target scrubbed the mission. Instead, the day was used for inspections. Once again, Caywood's squadron received the best marks. He brought the needed logic to the unit, which was tempered with an uncanny ability to know when to let things go. For example, Caywood recalls, "My flight surgeon, Al Wagner, was very resourceful. He dispensed 2 ounces of 100-proof government bonded bourbon to all members of the flight crews after they returned from each mission. Somehow, there was always enough bourbon left over to trade the British for their issued gin, scotch, rum, etc. I never asked him how he did this, but he was accountable for the booze. One day I had to sign a *report of survey* sheet to replace three cases of bourbon 'broken in transit.'" Caywood signed it and did not ask any questions. On another occasion, one of his sergeants (whom he called "my sergeant") brought in a local Italian man with a donkey cart full of "dressed chickens and several boxes of eggs." For some reason the Italians loved C rations and the Italian wanted to make a trade. Caywood told the man that it was against regulations and that he could not do it. He then advised his sergeant to get the man off base. "I had an idea how he would get rid of him, and I was right. For days and days we had real eggs and chickens when no one else had such."[4]

On the way to the movie Saturday night Erickson and the men of *Sleepy Time Gal* saw their names on the board for the Sunday, June 4, mission. They were all sitting in the outdoor theater when the soundtrack turned off and a voice broke in: "Everyone go to the shelters in an orderly fashion. Enemy planes in the area." After about an hour of "watchful waiting," the all clear sounded. The plane was actually a lone aircraft, more than likely conducting a reconnaissance flight. It had also appeared several nights in a row over the 449th BG's base at nearby Grottaglie Field. The men of the 449th nicknamed the pilot "Fearless Freddie."[5]

The wake up call on June 4 came shortly after 0400, with a briefing an hour later. The sun was just beginning its ascent when Erickson and his crew loaded *Sleepy Time Gal*. They, along with the thirty-five other B-24s, took off from Manduria

Caywood's flight surgeon, Al Wagner (driving) and part of the 450th BG medical staff. Flight surgeons had to fly at least four hours a month to keep their rating. (Grant D. Caywood)

between 0715 and 0810. Each bomber carried thirty-six 100-pounders. The target for the day was the west marshalling yard in Genoa, Italy. The 47th Wing attacked in two waves on June 4, 1944. The first wave, consisting of the 450th and 376th Bomb Groups, was to attack the marshalling yards in Genoa. The second wave, consisting of the 98th and 449th Bomb Groups, was to destroy the marshalling yards in Novi Ligure. For the second mission in a row, the 450th BG met up with the 376th BG over San Pancrazio and rendezvoused with the rest of the wing en route. An excellent P-38 escort deterred any fighter opposition, but the P-38s could not control the flak over the target. Approximately 15 flak guns sent up several barrages of heavy, moderate, and accurate anti-aircraft fire, and ten of the 450th BG's Liberators were damaged. Cloud cover obscured the 449th's target, so they bombed the alternate, the harbor at Savona.[6]

The 450th BG dropped 66 tons of bombs on the rail yard in Genoa at 1203. Photos showing a "heavy concentration of bombs on the aiming points" evidenced the success of the attack. Over two hundred bursts were recorded in the marshalling yards. In addition, bursts were seen not only hitting adjacent station buildings and installations, but also the Ansaldo Plant northwest of the yard. By 1458 all but two of the 450th's Liberators had returned to base. Two were at a friendly field in Corsica getting fuel.[7]

That evening the crew of *Sleepy Time Gal* enjoyed the boxing matches and movie;

they were not posted to fly the next morning. Bombardier Robert Stricklin celebrated his twenty-eighth birthday at the officers' club. He was the "old timer" of the crew, but he did not celebrate too late. He was scheduled to fly the next morning, with a 0245 wake up call. Those alerted for the Monday, June 5, mission bombed the Castel Maggiore marshalling yards in Bologna, Italy. It was one of Strick's first missions as lead bombardier and was yet another successful mission in the campaign against the German communication and supply lines in northern Italy. News of the U.S. Fifth Army's June 4 capture of Rome arrived at headquarters that afternoon. The news was a great morale boost. Erickson and his crew checked the board that evening and found themselves scheduled to fly in the morning. None of them were aware of the momentous event that was to take place the next day: the Allied invasion of Normandy (code named OVERLORD).[8]

Robert Stricklin wrote two letters home on June 5, one in the morning and one in the evening. It is obvious from their content that he was feeling a mix of emotions. At this point, he had flown 35 missions, which was almost ten missions behind the rest of *Sleepy Time Gal*'s crew. Stricklin knew that he would have to finish out his missions with another crew; this made him very uneasy. "I'm dog tired. I'll be so damned glad when it [his tour of duty] is over that I think I'll just set down and cry," he wrote. However, the two letters were not all full of trepidation. Unknown to his family, he had been courting a girl. "Merle, don't be surprised if I get married when I get home. Don't say anything about it. You will all be surprised when you find out who it is—so don't speak of it."[9]

Tuesday, June 6, 1944, was to also big day for the 15th AAF. The crews knew something big was happening when the wake up call came so early: shortly after 0200. Sure enough, Ploesti was once again the target. The 15th AAF was dispatching all five of its heavy bomber groups. B-17s of the 5th Wing were to bomb the marshalling yards in Buza, while the 304th Wing was to bomb the yard in Brasov. At the same time, the remaining three wings were each assigned a separate refinery in Ploesti. The 47th Wing was to attack the Romano Americana; the 49th Wing the Xenia refinery; and the 55th Wing the Dacia Roman. The Romano Americana was the most important of the targets, because reconnaissance revealed that it was still operating at or near full capacity. "It was estimated that this plant alone was capable of producing over 3,000 tons of [oil] products each day," according to historian William Shepherd.[10]

Each B-24 had a bomb bay full of ten 500-pound GP bombs. It was now routine for the crews to load their bombers in the dark and prepare for take-off. Thirty-seven of the 450th BG's Liberators began taking off at 0510. About the same time in France, the Normandy invasion began. The 450th rendezvoused with the 376th at 0611 over San Pancrazio and joined the rest of the 47th Wing on course to the target. At 0830 a much welcome escort of thirty P-38s began swinging back and forth over the bombers.[11]

About twenty miles from Ploesti, the crews could see that the entire target area was covered with smoke. The enemy's chloro-sulfuric acid smoke generators were so efficient that they concealed not only the targets, but also most of Ploesti. The target's exact whereabouts could only be estimated. The waist gunners began to throw out the little aluminum strips of "window," or "carpet," as the B-24s left the initial point on the bomb run. These little metal strips were very effective in deceiving the enemy's radar-directed heavy guns. The flak, which started out as heavy, intense, and accurate, soon became inaccurate. But because of the sheer number of flak guns (more than 200), eight of the 450th BG's bombers received flak damage over the target. Another five were hit when a navigator goofed and took the formation over Belgrade by mistake.[12]

It was 0920 when Stricklin and the other 450th BG bombardiers laid their explosive eggs "through the smoke at the place where it was presumed the refinery would be located." Strick had used a method called "offset bombing" in his Sperry bombsite. At that same time a group above *Sleepy Time Gal*'s element mistakenly dropped their bombs right through the 450th's formation. Floyd Robinson was piloting one of the bombers in the same element and reported, "As we passed over the target, with bomb bay doors open, ready to drop our bombs, a stick of bombs passed down by my window. I looked up into the empty bomb bay of several B-17s, which were bombing the same area, but were about 1000 feet higher." By some miracle none of the B-24s were hit, but it scared everyone. As the formation started the rally to the left, they could see a thick black column of smoke ascending through the lighter smoke screen. This told them that there were direct hits on the oil facilities. The smoke of the bomb strikes and that of the generated smoke screen prevented any accurate assessment of the mission at the time. All of the 450th BG's B-24s were safely back in Manduria by 1236. It was a harrowing run, but very successful by Ploesti standards. No planes were lost or missing.[13]

After the crews got their doughnuts, went through debriefing, and turned in their parachutes and escape kits, they collapsed in the barracks. Each airman knew he had defied the odds again. For Erickson and his crew it was their fourth mission to the foreboding target. No one was aware of what was transpiring in northern France. That is the way war is played out. At the time, very few know the master plan. Each unit focused on its microcosm of the war and was unaware of the big picture. The men of the 15th AAF had unknowingly been helping in the preparation of the Normandy invasion for months. Their missions against Hitler's soft underbelly in southern Europe diverted men and resources needed to defend the French coast. Additionally, the continued attacks on Hitler's petroleum fields hampered the Germans' ability to supply its troops with much-needed fuel, oil, and grease.

That evening the airmen could enjoy the beautiful moon overhead at Cottontail Theater, since there was no mission scheduled for June 7. The crew of *Sleepy Time Gal* was cautiously optimistic. Each of the enlisted men was nearing the completion of his fifty-mission goal. Then too, with another Ploesti mission safely completed, there was a minimal likelihood of returning there before finishing the tour.[14]

On Wednesday, the news of the Normandy invasion reached Manduria. This further increased the hopeful spirit. "The S-2 War Room was the most popular place in camp. Officers and enlisted men crowded the maps." Everyone wanted to know the details of operation OVERLORD. The crew of *Sleepy Time Gal* took time on June 7 to help Stan Butynski celebrate his twentieth birthday. All of the men were surprised when a mission was not scheduled for Thursday, June 8. But, as the *720th Squadron War Diary* recorded for that day, "[We] are not in a position to see the big picture." Instead, June 8 was used for what was sarcastically called "our new secret weapon: close order drill." It began at 0900 and consisted of 400 men from each squadron. The men were especially bitter about marching in the muck in the wake of "the invasion." It seemed pointless to them. It was beyond pointless; it was ridiculous. In addition to the drilling, S-2 held an aircraft recognition class in the briefing room. "In a quest for new unit and box leaders," the group commander ordered a high altitude formation practice. A fine vaudeville show, with a strip dancer, increased spirits that evening. For the men of *Sleepy Time Gal* it was back to business; they were on alert to fly the next morning. They did have one surprise, Olney had been bumped; Caywood would be their pilot in the morning.[15]

For the Friday, June 9, mission the 450th BG was to lead the 47th Wing; Caywood was to lead the Cottontails' second attack unit. Crews were awakened around 0300. After a hurried and indigestible breakfast with a briefing, about an hour later, the officers learned that the target for the day was Munich, Germany. Sighs and gasps filled the room. A bombardier broke the tension with the remark, "Oh my aching G.I. ass." This would be only the second mission that the 450th BG had flown to Germany; the first had been on February 25 to Regensburg. In the coming weeks and months, as the Allies pushed foot by bloody foot eastward through France, targets in Germany would become part of the standard rotation for the 450th.[16]

Gen. Nathan Twining and his staff of the 15th AAF had an ambitious plan on June 9. It was "to strike airfields and aircraft production facilities in the Munich area of southern Germany." First, B-17s from the 5th Wing would drop fragmentation bombs on the Oberpfaffenhoffen airdrome installation, fifteen miles southwest of Munich. "Five minutes later, B-24s of the 47th Wing would hit the same target with 500-pound GP bombs. Simultaneously, the 304th Wing would attack the Bayeriche Motorenwerke and the Milbertshofen ordnance depot. The 55th and 49th Wings would follow shortly thereafter with attacks on the Allach Motorenwerke and Neuaubing airframe works," said the unit's intelligence report. The operational orders gave the attack unit leaders, as was Caywood, the leeway to bomb visually or via radar (Pathfinder) methods. They were to make the decision when they made the turn at the IP. The orders were specific, however, on one point. "If any doubt exists, use PFF [Pathfinder] on center of city. Bring no bombs back."[17]

Upon learning the target for the day, most of the airmen were visibly shaken. Maurice Gilliam wrote his feelings in his combat diary, "Today was the biggest shock I'd had since I've been flying. The place I dreaded most came up today. When they said Munich, I nearly fainted." There was good reason for trepidation. A mission to Munich meant a long trip over the rugged Alps and flying directly into the city's nearly 300 heavy flak guns. Moreover, the Germans could dispatch some 200 fighters in the area to intercept the Allied formations. But there was no time to be scared; there was a mission to fly. Thirty-nine of the 450th BG's B-24s roared down the runway in Manduria between 0505 and 0558. Since Caywood was flying a "Mickey" plane, ball turret gunner Woodward did not fly with the crew. His turret had been replaced with radar gear. The 450th BG first rendezvoused with the 376th BG over San Pancrazio, then with the 449th and 98th Bomb Groups en route.[18]

Once in the air, the crews settled into their routine. As the engines droned on, they made all the necessary equipment checks. Over Udine, Italy, enemy flak guns opened on the formation. The flak did not cause a problem for the 450th BG, which was in the lead. The anti-aircraft fire did, however, hit one of the 449th BG's B-24s (ship number 66—*Ghost o' the Omar*). This was only the beginning of trouble for the 449th. A navigational snafu forced the group off of the planned course. Estimates placed them reaching the target nearly thirty minutes late. This would have been suicide, so the group leader aborted Munich and decided to attack the second alternate target: the oil storage facilities at Porto Marghera, Italy.[19]

Meanwhile, the 450th, 376th and 98th Bomb Groups continued on towards Munich. The crews were pleasantly surprised by the lack of enemy fighters as they neared the target. They could see their escort of beautiful P-38s—30 of them—in the target area just as the bomb run commenced. A 9/10 cloud cover completely obscured the target, so at 1004, the formation bombed the secondary target, the center of the city, by PFF. Flak over the target increased in intensity as the bombing continued. Caywood and his crew passed over just before it got bad; Munich's heavy guns claimed two of the 450th's B-24s and damaged four others. Second Lt. Lloyd O. Osborne piloted one of the downed planes. His crew consisted of 1st Lt. Barney H. McClure, 2nd Lt. Irving B. McNulty, 2nd Lt. John F. Flannery, S/Sgt. Eugene L. Watkins, S/Sgt. Lawrence H. Cugine, S/Sgt. Sidney D. Benjamin, S/Sgt. Philip A. Smith, S/Sgt. Lloyd T. Smith, and S/Sgt. Chester Wojcik.[20]

The cloud cover prevented any accurate visual assessment of damage. "Photo coverage indicated sufficient check points to determine the strike area as being in the eastern part of the city." None of that mattered to *Sleepy Time Gal*'s nose gunner Stan Butynski. The mission to Munich was his fiftieth. He was the first of Caywood's original crew to complete the daunting goal. Stan had volunteered for and had been drafted on a couple of extra missions on days when his crew was on stand down—just as Maurice Gilliam had done on his first mission back on March 11. This practice became more common for the 450th BG as men began to complete the fifty-mission goal in late May and early June 1944. S/Sgt. John Mason, the ball turret gunner from the crew of *Ten Fighting Cocks*, became the first man in the 450th BG to complete 50 missions on May 6, 1944. Of note, *Ten Fighting Cocks* was the only B-24 that arrived with the initial group in Manduria in December 1943 to survive the war. As it stood now, Erickson would have to find another nose gunner for the crew's next mission. The rest of the crew was excited for Butynski and each of them knew that, with a little luck, he too would soon finish his tour. Gilliam was the next closest with 48 credited missions. Jacobson and most of the remaining enlisted men of the crew had completed 47.[21]

Erickson's crew was not on the board for the next morning; this allowed them the opportunity to celebrate with Stan. The 450th BG did, however, have a scheduled mission on Saturday, June 10. The target was the oil storage and loading facilities in the harbor at Trieste, Italy. Saturday night the men of *Sleepy Time Gal* were alerted of their flight status for Sunday.[22]

The Sunday, June 11, mission marked a slight turning point in strategy. By this time the attacks on Ploesti had begun to cripple its refinery facilities. "As a result, crude oil, formerly being refined at Ploesti, was now being piped to Giurgiu, and there pumped aboard barges to be transported up the Danube River for processing at several refineries in Hungary, Austria and Yugoslavia. Refined oil, bound for the south Russian front, was being moved [by pipeline] from the scattered refinery sites to the Black Sea port of Constanta, and from there, was transported by either railroad or marine transport to fuel depots near the front," according to Shepherd's historical account.[23]

For the June 11 mission, the 15th AAF turned its attention this reorganization of German petroleum production and distribution. All five of its heavy bomber wings, more than 540 B-17s and B-24s, would be sent against this new network of refineries, storage facilities, and transportation targets. The 5th Wing would bomb the marshalling yard at Smederevo, Romania, while the 55th Wing would attack the city's oil refinery and train ferry. The 49th and 304th Wings would destroy Giurgiu, Romania, which included both storage and transport targets. The 47th Wing would attack the vital oil storage installations at Constanta, Romania.[24]

It would be another early wake up call and briefing for the airmen of the 450th BG. When the target was revealed as Constanta, Maurice Gilliam was more than a little excited. Targets in Romania received two credited missions. If he could make it back alive, his tour would be complete.[25]

Sleepy Time Gal was one of thirty-eight B-24s which rumbled down Manduria's runway at 0548, just as the sun was beginning to rise over the field. They were all airborne by 0620, and at 0651 they rendezvoused with the 376th BG over San Pancrazio. Lt. Col. William G. Snaith, the 450th's operations officer, led the group, which in turn led the first wave of the 47th Wing's attack. The 376th followed. The wing's second wave consisted of the 98th and 449th Bomb Groups respectively. Each of the wing's bombers was loaded with twenty 250-pounders. No fighters were encountered on the way to the target, but ubiquitous flak was a problem. It was first encountered when the formation reached the IP (Medgidia). Fortunately, it was inaccurate. But over the target the enemy's anti-aircraft fire became very accurate and damaged six aircraft. At 0946 the 450th BG dropped nearly 85 tons of bombs on Constanta. The *720th Squadron War Diary* reports that the bomb results were poor; they "fell short and to the right." A closer evaluation revealed, however, that the bombing did cause a great deal of destruction. "Photo coverage showed several hits on installations at the northwest corner of the target area, including shop-like buildings, a railroad siding, and the probable destruction of one storage tank in the southwest corner.... Also [observed was] a concentration of bursts on buildings among trees on south side of target area ... several hits among [the] stores and warehouse area to the southeast started fires."[26]

All of the 450th BG's planes returned safely to Manduria by 1303. Maurice Gilliam said a prayer of thanks when *Sleepy Time Gal*'s wheels kissed the runway. He had finished fifty combat missions in three months. No mission was scheduled for Monday, so the rest of the crew could celebrate with him. Practice missions were flown on June 12 but Erickson's crew did not participate. They were the old-timers now. Jacobson now needed only one more mission to complete his fifty. He was not in the rotation for the June 13 mission to Munich. Jake did find his name on the board that evening. He was to fly with Lt. Col. Robert Gideon in the morning. Because of this assignment, Jake knew that more than likely his B-24 would be leading the group. His assumption was right.[27]

Maurice Gilliam's 50th mission photograph. (Maurice H. Gilliam)

The 15th AAF bombing strategy continued to adjust to the damage suffered at Ploesti. "As a result, the priority targets in the German oil-production system shifted to the synthetic-oil plants located in southeast Germany, the Standard refineries in the Vienna-Budapest area, and the other smaller refineries scattered throughout Hungary and Yugoslavia," Shepherd wrote.[28] The 15th AAF attacked "oil refineries and other targets in Hungary and Yugoslavia" on June 14. These included: Budapest, Petfurdo, Komarom, Osijek, and Sisak.[29] The Blechhammer Synthetic Oil plant in Budapest took the fury of the 5th and 49th Wings' hits that day. The 449th and 450th Bomb Groups of the 47th Wing were to strike the refinery in Osijek, Yugoslavia, while the 98th and 376th Bomb Groups were dispatched to the one in Sisak, Yugoslavia.[30]

So on June 14, thirty-nine of the 450th BG's B-24s took off between 0746 and 0828. The bomb load was once again twenty 250-pounders. The 449th led the way to the target and the 450th BG fell in behind them. No fighter escort was scheduled for this short mission. Visibility was good all the way to the target; there was no engagement from enemy fighters. As Jake recorded in his diary that night, "It was a perfect mission. No fighters. No flak. No nothing." This was mainly due to the fact that these had been secondary or tertiary targets, which had not had any need for such defense—until now. The 449th BG dropped its bombs first with great accuracy. At 1055 the 450th dropped its deadly cargo on the target area. It was smoke-covered from the 449th's run; "some bombs fell in the town area, and a few went long over the target." Photo reconnaissance, however, did show that many of the 450th's bombs hit their marks. Although some consider that there is no such thing as a milk run (easy mission), this one came as close as one could get. All of the Cottontails' bombers arrived safely back in Manduria by 1253. Jacobson become the third enlisted man from Caywood's original crew to complete his fiftieth mission. Due to the lack of surviving records for the group, the exact dates that Esquivel and Woodward completed their fiftieth missions are lost. But careful analysis of Gilliam's and Jacobson's diaries indicates that they either finished on the same mission as Jacobson, or on the next one. They truly were a statistical anomaly and could echo the final words of Jacobson's combat diary, "50 missions and now for home sweet home."[31]

They would not leave immediately. It would take a month or so for the military bureaucracy to process them back to the States. Most every airman in the 450th BG who completed fifty missions remained on base for a few weeks before flying to Naples. From there, each boarded a ship bound for a U.S. port. Some jokingly called the ship ride home their "51st mission." Most of the troop transport ships were round bottom "victory ships." They were very crowded, slow, and better for carrying a load than weathering rough seas. "It was a long and uncomfortable trip on the ship," recalls Erickson, "but it was headed in the right direction: HOME."[32]

Five officers with ties to *Shadow* would be staying in Manduria a while longer than their enlisted crewmates. Because of his promotions, Caywood was only flying about every five to seven days. By mid–June he only had 32 credited missions. Due to Olney's and Robinson's fill-in flights with the crew and Caywood's promotion, Maurice Erickson was a few short of the fifty required to rotate home. Eric's skill as a pilot and officer, however, was recognized and he was in line for a promotion. The Pathfinder missions and promotion to lead bombardier put Robert Stricklin several missions behind *Shadow*'s enlisted men. Vincent Olney and Floyd Robinson had been filling in with various crews and each still needed about ten more missions to finish their tour.[33]

As the men of *Shadow*'s original crew began to finish their tours, Robinson and Olney began flying together. Robinson had flown a few missions with Olney in *Shadow*. Olney was not only a good pilot, he had a wonderful sense of humor. Everyone liked being around him. For those reasons, Robinson, as squadron ops officer, assigned himself to fly with Olney whenever he could. For the past month or so, Olney had been the pilot for the crew of *Shoo Shoo Baby*, a B-24 named for the popular song by the Andrews sisters. His crew was in the final stages of becoming an element lead crew. On June 23, Robinson placed himself with the farm boy from Nebraska for the mission the next morning.[34]

Ploesti again reared its ugly head. The target on June 24 would be the Romano Americana refinery, the same one that the group had tried the day before and had aborted because of weather. Despite the recent successes at Ploesti, it was still the most dreaded target the group could face. The refineries were showing some signs of damage. Only the Romano Americana and Unirea Sperantza were still believed to be fully operational, which was a tremendous testament to the refineries' repair units that were able to patch up the bomb damage so well and so quickly. But, Ploesti's anti-aircraft guns and fighter intercepts were still formidable. Estimates placed the number of potential defending fighters at 130 plus. In addition, the target area was protected with over 230 heavy flak guns. It was still considered "the hottest target on the face of the earth."[35]

Thirty-nine of the 450th BG's B-24s roared down the runway between 0530 and 0606 for the group's sixth mission to Ploesti since April 5. Among these was the crew of *Shoo Shoo Baby*: pilot Vincent Olney; co-pilot Floyd Robinson; bombardier Louis Amster of New Jersey; navigator Marshall Samms; engineer and top turret gunner Armand J. L'Heureux of Connecticut; radio operator Richard Hackney of Minnesota; tail gunner and assistant engineer George Dobbs of Omaha; ball turret gunner James Cox of North Carolina; waist gunner Vernon Tanem; and nose gunner Edward Schwab. For this mission, the crew's regular co-pilot, Lewis Shackleford, "relinquished his spot to Major Robinson."[36]

Richard M. Jacobson's 50th mission photograph. (Richard M. Jacobson)

The 376th BG joined *Shoo Shoo Baby* and the rest of the 450th BG over San Pancrazio at 0659. Weather conditions forced them to rendezvous at 12,000 feet—double the normal altitude. Weather and mechanical problems also hampered the 449th and 98th Bomb Groups, which never fully completed their rendezvous with the lead elements of the wing. They trailed four minutes behind the 450th and 376th. Despite "turns made along course" to allow the trailing groups to catch up, "the distance was never appreciably lessened."[37]

Shoo Shoo Baby reached bombing altitude (about 22,000 feet) as the formation crossed the Danube River, just south of Bucharest. Olney noticed that their number-four engine was smoking a little, but it was "not bad enough to warrant turning back." *Shoo Shoo Baby* was "leading the low left box in the second attack group." About ten minutes from the target, approximately fifty enemy fighters (consisting of 30 to 35 ME-109s, 10 to 15 FW-190s, two JU-88s, and three ME-110s) attacked the formation.[38]

Part of *Shoo Shoo Baby*'s crew after the June 3, 1944, Air Medal presentation. Front row (left to right): T/Sgt. Armand L'Heureux; S/Sgt. George Dobbs; S/Sgt. James Cox. Back row (left to right): T/Sgt. Richard Hackney; Lt. Marshall Samms; Lt. Lewis Shackleford; Lt. Louis Amster. (Marshall Samms)

In a post-war article, *Shoo Shoo Baby*'s navigator, 1st Lt. Marshall Samms, described the fighter attack. A call came over the radio. "'Fighters coming in at twelve o'clock level. Get 'em. Get 'em.' And there they came, eight ME-109s on a head-on pass; puffs of white smoke came from their wings and spinners. Our engines whined as Robinson pulled into the center box. Schwab and L'Heureux cut loose with the twin fifties in the nose and upper turrets. Smoke filled the nose compartment and empty shell casings clattered down the window in front of the bombsight. One fighter zoomed over us leaving a trail of black smoke. Schwab and L'Heureux got him together. Luckily, we had not been hit seriously by this first pass of fighters."[39]

Samms continues with his description of events. "Then the flak started puffing up like little black mushrooms at one o'clock low and one o'clock level. None of it was too close. Below I could see a large white cloud that I knew was the smoke screen over Ploesti. And then (at 0932), 'Bomb's away.' I watched the little yellow lights on the bombardier's instrument panel flicker off as the bombs left the bomb bay. As soon as they were all out ... I closed the bomb bay doors. We could hear the flak as it burst close to the plane. Then we started our turn off the target. (There was) no flak up ahead, and I thought it was over, when WHAM! WHAM! and a bright flash burst a few inches above my head. I looked up and saw a hole about eight inches in diameter in the side of the fuselage a foot above me.

"Olney called out, 'What was that?' and I said, 'Just a hole up here in the nose.' L'Heureux yelled, 'My God!' and Louie, who now had his head up in the astrodome yelled, 'Look at number 3. Oil is pouring out; feather it quick!' Robbie then said, 'Prepare for emergency.' I opened the door to the nose turret, ripped off my flak suit and buckled on my parachute. Now Schwab was out of his turret and I handed him his chute. I felt the plane go into a dive and Dobbs called, 'Fighters, a whole slew of them, coming in at six o'clock, and my damn guns are jammed.' Olney called to L'Heureux to shut off fuel to the number three and number four engines. Down we went. Robbie cried, 'Olney slow down or you'll rip the wings off.' I looked down at the air speed [indicator] and it registered 290 M.P.H., altitude about 16,000 feet.

"By this time I had [made my way] to the bomb bay doors and crouched down by our emergency exit. Then I felt Louie kick me and I looked up to see him motioning me to bail out. I pulled the handle to open the doors but nothing happened. I gave the doors a kick, and they snapped open, letting in a strong blast of cold air. I swung my feet out and let myself down to my waist. Then I looked back at Louie once more and saw him motion again. Schwab was standing right behind him. So I shoved off and was hurled into the air. The shock was terrific, and I started tumbling over and over.

"I got my hand on the rip cord and pulled. I pulled again and again, but it would not budge. I let go of the cord and started to undo the flap that covered the pins. I got one side unsnapped, but my hands were so numb that I could not get the other side. I knew that I was not going to get that chute open. My life did not pass in front of me as is supposed to happen when you know that you are going to die; I just thought, 'This thing is not going to open, damn it!' But I pulled the ripcord once more and it came out of my hand. I completely relaxed and for a second nothing happened. Then WHUMPFH, I was jerked to a stop. A sharp pain caught my right thigh. I tried to pull myself up by the shroud lines so that I could slip the strap and sit on it, but I did not have the strength. So I just held on to the right shroud line with both hands to ease the pain. I could not let go, fearing that I would pass out. All was quiet—deathly quiet, save for the distant drone of the bombers as they roared home, the zoom of fighters, the staccato machine gun fire, and the thumping of the flak. Far below I could see the green and brown of the Romanian countryside.

"After what seemed hours, I watched the ground come rushing up to hit me. I was in hilly, farming country and I saw that I would land near, or in, a gully or streambed. A hill sloped steeply to the gully and a peasant was making his way down the hill to where I would land. I hit and rolled over backwards, ending up in a sitting position. My hands were numb from the cold, and I had to struggle to undo the parachute harness. I wasted no time in hiding the chute and immediately scrambled down the gully. Reaching the bottom I got to my feet and ran up the gully for about five minutes before I stopped to take off my heavy flying boots and Mae West. I waited a few more minutes to catch my breath and was just about to start on when I heard voices. I crept under some foliage and looked around. On the opposite ridge of the gully walked peasants armed with clubs. They were looking down the gully and I was sure they would see me. But they went past, and I began to [breathe] a little easier. Their voices died away; then grew louder. The peasants had climbed into the gully and were walking up on both sides. One of them finally saw me, and I crawled out with my hands in the air. One of them, an old, gray fellow smelling of garlic, smiled broadly and said, 'Nix, comrade, comrade.' Then he shook my hand warmly and saluted me. There were two other peasants with him and they did the same."[40]

Marshall Samms' bail-out experience was similar to that of thousands of other AAF airmen during World War II. Luckily, nine of *Shoo Shoo Baby*'s ten crew members parachuted safely out of the bomber. As Olney and Robinson made their way down to the bomb bay to jump, they found a lot of blood near where their engineer and top turret gunner, Armand L'Heureux, was last seen. L'Heureux never showed up in a POW camp and his body was never located. His parachute probably did not open or his injuries were so extensive that he died shortly after bailing out.[41]

Shoo Shoo Baby's pilot and co-pilot, Vincent Olney and Floyd Robinson, were among the last to jump. It seemed that Olney's chute had barely opened when he landed in a tree. With some difficulty, Vince got out of the tree and walked down a road adjacent to where he had landed. He heard loud noises coming from the other side of a hill. He climbed cautiously up to see what was going on. To his surprise, a small group of peasants had encircled his nineteen-year-old bombardier, Louis Amster, and they were beating him with "hoes and other objects." Vince's sister, Susan Rhynalds, recounts his description, "The only thing he could think to do was to run into the crowd yelling and waving his arms. All the peasants backed off except one old man who continued to hit Louie. Vince hit the old man to make him back off." Vince and Louie then began walking down the road, followed by all the peasants. Soon a German patrol came by and picked them up. They were taken to a holding area, where they were to be interrogated. The first thing that Vince's German interrogator did "was to offer him a Camel cigarette in a strong southern drawl. He told Vince that he had graduated from Georgia Tech in *Alabama* and how much he liked America and Americans." It was an obvious, albeit ineffective, attempt to gain his trust. Vince gave them his name, rank, and serial number, and then he was taken to a POW camp outside of Bucharest.[42]

Robinson landed near a vineyard. "I pulled my chute under a tree and sat down to gather my wits. I opened my escape kit and oriented myself," wrote Robinson, in what was to become his POW diary. He laid low for a while, but as the rest of the crew, he too was soon greeted by a group of local peasants. They walked him to town, where he was eventually interrogated at the same place as Olney and Amster. He and the rest of the crew were taken to the Romanian POW camp outside of Bucharest.[43]

The Romanian National Guard, which had a great dislike for both the Germans and Russians, ran the POW camp outside Bucharest. The prisoners were divided into two sections. Officers were housed in a schoolhouse, while the enlisted men were placed in a building near the marshalling yard. Both Olney and Robinson were able to hide some money from their escape kits, which contained $50 in $5 bills. They distributed it equally among men of the crew. The money was then used to bribe the guards for beer, bread, cheese, and other comfort items. Conditions in the camp were deplorable, but the Romanians treated their prisoners more humanely than did their counterparts in the Pacific theater. Officers could not be forced to perform manual labor; so playing cards (bridge) became a way for them to pass the time. Except for what they could purchase with the hidden funds, cabbage soup three times a day was their main staple. Olney's sister, Susan, remembers that her brother could not tolerate the aroma of cabbage after that.[44]

Meanwhile, in Manduria, the 450th BG continued its assault on the German war machine. In the three weeks after *Shoo Shoo Baby* was shot down, the Cottontails flew fifteen missions—eight days in a row during one stretch. By July 1944, Robert Stricklin had flown several missions as a lead bombardier. He had also been promoted to first lieutenant. In a letter home on July 5, he stated that he had completed 44 missions and was "sweating them out now." He had hopes of being home by Thanksgiving. He mentioned that he was having trouble with his tonsils and would have them removed upon his return to the States. But most of the letter expresses his concern about other family members. On the evening of Friday, July 14, Stricklin found his name on the board. He would be flying in the lead element with the 723rd Squadron. The 450th BG's operations officer, Lt. Col. William Snaith (Bill to his friends), was to be his pilot.[45]

It was another miserable wake up call well before dawn for the 450th BG's crews on Saturday, July 15. For the third time in as many weeks they would be going to the dreaded Ploesti. For old-timers like Snaith and Stricklin, there was a special dread as they saw the long red line to Ploesti on the briefing map. They knew the dangers, and both had lost good friends on missions there. Strick knew that fate could be tempted only so much. He had already had several close calls over Ploesti. Of all of *Shadow*'s original crew, Strick was the most worried about completing his tour of duty. He had confided his concerns to Jacobson on several occasions.[46]

The AAF's opinion of Ploesti, however, had changed over the past two months. Because of its diminished oil production, which was the result of the 15th AAF's three-month assault on the targets there, Ploesti had been taken off the list of double-credit missions. During the attacks in April, the 15th AAF had targeted Ploesti's marshalling yards in an effort to disrupt the shipment of petroleum products and supplies to the Russian front. By mid–May the focus turned directly to the oil refineries, and the strategy had paid off. As of late June, reconnaissance photos showed that only two of the city's refineries were still in production, the Romano Americana and Unirea Sperantza. The attacks of June 24 and July 9 resulted in no appreciable new damage; so the July 15 mission was scheduled.[47]

The 450th BG was to lead the 47th Wing to bomb the Romano Americana oil refinery. The 449th, 98th, and 376th Bomb Groups would follow them, in order. Between 0612 and 0659, thirty-five B-24s took off from Manduria and joined with the 449th BG at 0717. Each bomber was loaded with ten 500-pounders. Estimates placed the number of potential heavy flak guns in the target area at 241 and the potential number of enemy fighters at well over 100.[48]

The crew in Lt. Col. William Snaith's lead pathfinder bomber (number 42–51153) consisted of: copilot, 2nd Lt. Clyde O. Primrose, Jr., of Hemphill, Texas; navigator, Capt. Jerome R. Goldvarg of Chicago; bombardier, 1st Lt. Robert Stricklin of Dallas; engineer, T/Sgt. Woodrow W. Allen of Memphis; radio operator, S/Sgt. Penn W. Crawford of West Monroe, Louisiana; gunner, S/Sgt. Edward W. Evans of Bridgeport, Ohio; gunner, Sgt. John R. Reid of Chicago; gunner, S/Sgt. Andrew N. Johnson, Jr., of North Great Falls, Montana; observer, 1st Lt. Earl W. Tautfest of Kalispell, Montana; and radar (Pathfinder) navigator, 2nd Lt. George H. Fritz of River Edge, New Jersey. Each was handpicked because of his skill, ability, and coolness under fire. They were among the best and brightest men in the 450th BG.[49]

Everything was routine on the way to the target. Fortunately, no enemy fighters engaged the formation. One ME-109 flew parallel to the formation from the IP (Catrunesti) to the target, but since it was alone, it did not pursue any aggressive action. As they approached the target, smoke filled the sky. The combination of smoke pots and the 5th Wing's bombing of the target about fifteen minutes earlier completely obliterated the view of the target. As expected, Stricklin needed the help of the Mickey radar to lock in on the target. At 1018 he released his bombs and the rest of the formation followed on his lead.[50]

Lt. Col. William G. Snaith in front of a B-24. Snaith led the 47th Wing of the July 15, 1944, mission to Ploesti. (Suzanne Snaith Levy)

The flak over the target was heavy, intense, and accurate. Stricklin's trepidation of the past few months now seemed warranted. Just as Snaith made the turn out of the bomb run, his ship received a direct hit from flak. Corp. Carl L. Taylor, the nose gunner in ship number 282, was flying just behind Snaith in the number 3 position in the lead element. In his post-mission debriefing Taylor offered the following description of the horror that he witnessed. The flak hit in the bomb bay "causing a big explosion. The ship immediately dropped under our plane and headed straight for the earth in a mass of flames. I saw no parachutes leave the aircraft." In the same report, 2nd Lt. Otis K. Andes, the navigator on ship number 282 offered an almost verbatim description.[51]

Miraculously, Snaith was blown clear from the plane in the explosion. He had severe flash burns on his hands and face from the blast, but otherwise had his wits. "His first conscious thought had been the discovery that he was falling on his back, about two hundred feet below the flaming wreckage of his aircraft, and faced with a terrible dilemma. 'If I pull my ripcord, will the wreckage fall on me? If I don't…?' He'd taken the only option available. He grasped the D-ring and pulled. His body was instantly decelerated by the deploying parachute, and the wreckage passed harmlessly overhead before falling through his altitude."[52]

Taylor and Andes did not see Snaith's parachute, because he had waited until about 4,000 feet before pulling the ripcord. He landed about a mile southwest of the target near a low, bushy streambed. Snaith managed to shield himself as the bomb runs and fire continued for another hour and a half (until about 1200). When things began to settle down, he was spotted by a German patrol. As was the crew of *Shoo Shoo Baby*, Snaith was picked up and interrogated. On July 19, he was sent to the POW camp outside of Bucharest where Robinson and Olney were being held. Upon his arrival there, he became the senior officer for his fellow prisoners. In his casualty questionnaire, filled out upon his repatriation, Snaith advised the intelligence officer that he remembered feeling the hit and seeing the entire plane engulfed in flames just before it exploded. All of his crew were at their stations and perished in the blast.[53]

Ploesti had proven costly once again for the 450th BG. It had lost two bombers on the July 15 mission. The remaining thirty-three planes arrived back safely in Manduria by 1400. It would not be the Cottontails' last mission to the target. The 450th BG would return to Ploesti three more times before Romania capitulated in late August 1944. Ultimately, the 15th AAF's "hammer blows" against the vital target paid off. When the Russians secured the oil fields in August, production was at a trickle.[54]

By late July, Maurice Gilliam had been sent to Naples, where he boarded a ship bound for Norfolk, Virginia. Upon his arrival there in early August he was sent to Ft. Bragg in Fayetteville, North Carolina, for processing. At Ft. Bragg, he received a 30-day furlough. He took a bus from Fayetteville to his hometown of Reidsville. Maurice arrived in town about midnight and began walking home. No one in the family knew exactly when he would be coming home. A policeman saw him walking with his bag and stopped to question him. When he realized Maurice was a returning soldier, he gave him a ride home. His wife and parents were there to greet him. Stella was eight months pregnant with their first child. Maurice had made it home safely, but he was still in the Army Air Force.[55]

After his 30-day furlough was up he was sent to the Charleston Army Air Base, where he became an air-to-air gunnery instructor. In addition, he was placed in charge of a detail of German prisoners who were building sidewalks on the base. Stella remained in Reidsville with Maurice's parents. In late September, Maurice received word that Stella was about to give birth. He received an emergency leave and thumbed his way back to Reidsville. Their first child, a daughter, Sandra Kay, was born on September 21, 1944. Shortly after the birth, Stella and Kay joined Maurice in Charleston. He remained there another year until his separation and honorable discharge on September 10, 1945, at Camp Gordon, Georgia.[56]

Caywood's cabin at the rest camp in Villagio Mancuso. (Grant D. Caywood)

Caywood continued to serve as the 720th Squadron's CO until he completed his fiftieth mission on September 15, 1944. In July, he and Erickson went to the Villagio Mancuso Rest Camp for a week. After Robinson was shot down on June 24, Caywood promoted Erickson to the 720th's operations officer, which in turn, prolonged his tour. Unlike most of his crew, Caywood returned to the States via air, in a C-54. He arrived at La Guardia Field in New York on October 14, 1944, and was sent to Santa Monica, California, for reassignment. Upon his arrival in California, he spent a 30-day leave with Beo, George, and Shadow. He was then shipped off to Mountain Home Army Air Field in Mountain Home, Idaho, where he served as the director of supply and maintenance for the base, which dealt primarily with B-24s and P-38s. In April 1945, he was sent to Muroc Army Air Field in Muroc, California. Muroc was a "secret experimental aircraft base." It had all sorts of maintenance problems, and Caywood, who had gained the reputation as a trouble-shooter, was sent there to straighten things out. It was at Muroc that he flew his first jet. Within a month he was transferred again, this time to March Army Air Field ten miles southeast of Riverside, California. There he served as deputy of operations. He remained at March, except for a brief stint at Walker Army Air Field in Victoria, Kansas. Grant received an honorable discharge on October 27, 1945, but he remained in the Army Reserves. Maj. Grant Caywood would have had a wonderful military career, but he had to be his own boss.[57]

Maurice Erickson finished his fiftieth mission sometime in July, shortly after

Villagio Mancuso rest camp. (Grant D. Caywood)

his promotion to squadron operations officer. In August he flew to Naples, where he boarded a boat bound for New York City. From there, he was sent via train to Ft. Dix, New Jersey, for processing. He grabbed a train from Ft. Dix to Buffalo, New York, to see his wife, Lillian. They then took a bus down to Pennsylvania to see their families. Back home, Maurice purchased a 1940 Oldsmobile, which he and Lillian drove down to Palm Beach for "relaxation and reassignment." Afterwards, he was sent to Hondo, Texas, where he commanded a group performing B-24 maintenance. Erickson was then sent to Randolph Field, northeast of San Antonio, Texas. At Randolph he was a flight commander and instructor. The military suited him. Erickson had proven himself an able pilot and strong leader. Maurice remained in the service after World War II and participated in two more wars.[58]

Ted Morris spent the last week of April and the first few weeks of May 1944 at the 35th Field Hospital in nearby Erchie, Italy. On April 30, after several attempts, he wrote a letter home to his mom. The letter, which reached her, braced her for the news of his injury. Despite the tremendous pain and seriousness of his injuries, Ted played the role of the dutiful son; he did not want his mother to worry. He explained that he had been hit by flak and that "it really isn't anything serious. I know that it could be a lot worse.... They at once fixed me up and before long I expect to be good as new."[59]

But that was just a brave front for his mother. Ted had a broken rib, femur, and

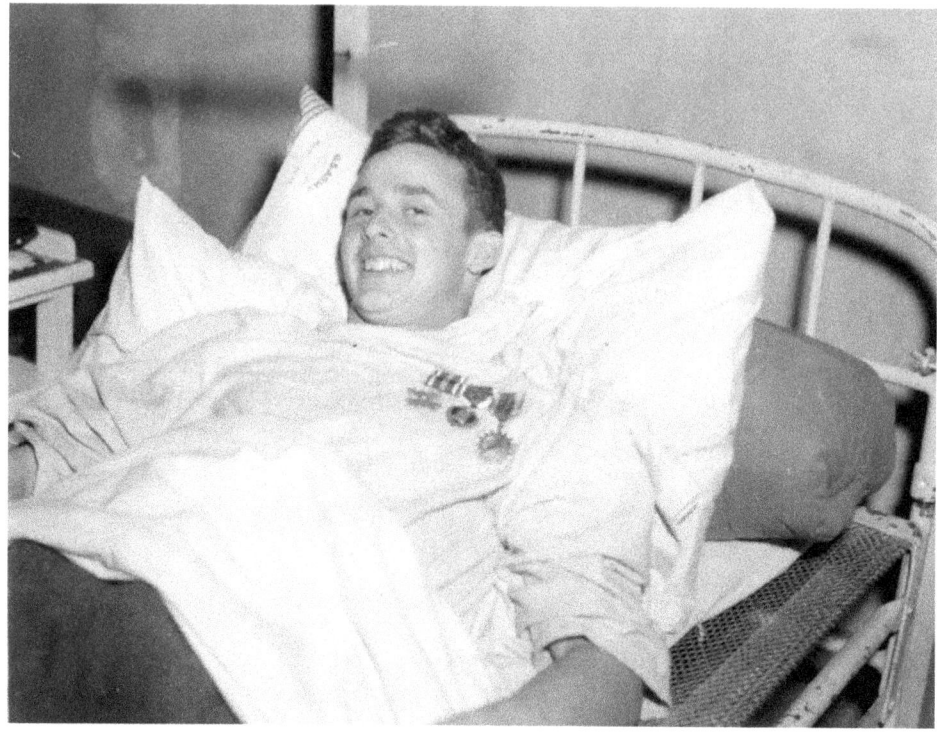

Ted Morris on May 9, 1944, in the 35th Field Hospital after receiving the Purple Heart, Air Medal, and the Distinguished Flying Cross. (Grant D. Caywood)

pelvis. He was in a body cast that ran from his chest all the way down his right leg and half way down his left leg. Due to the large amount of blood lost, he had numerous blood transfusions. Of the five pieces of flak that hit him, only two could be removed. The other three pieces remain in his body to this day. Caywood, Stricklin, Robinson, and some of the other officers visited Ted while he was at the 35th Field Hospital. There, on May 9, 1944, Ted Morris received the Purple Heart for his injury on April 24; the Air Medal for combat missions; and the Distinguished Flying Cross for his heroism in releasing the bombs by hand on April 12.[60]

On May 12, 1944, the day after his leg was put in a cast, Ted was sent to the hospital in Bari, Italy, where he could receive better treatment for his injuries. His brother-in-law, Louis Houlle (Ethel's husband), visited him there in late May. On June 27, Ted was sent to the Army hospital in Naples, Italy. From his room he could see Mt. Vesuvius. He stood up for the first time on July 7, and three days later he tried crutches. On August 21, he left Naples for the United States. He arrived in Newport News, Virginia, on September 1. After processing, he was sent to a hospital in Springfield, Missouri. There, he spent another few months healing. Ted then went to Santa Anna, California, to recuperate. Afterwards he was placed back on active duty. He received an honorable discharge in November 1945, but he would spend the rest of his life in and out of Army hospitals.[61]

In mid–July 1944 Stan Butynski flew to Naples where he boarded a ship for home. He arrived in Newport News, Virginia, on August 4, after three weeks at sea. After processing he received a furlough, which he used to go see Margie and his family. Stan was then sent to Courtland, Alabama, and later to Hondo, Texas, where he assisted with testing planes that were damaged and had been repaired. He received an honorable discharge on October 18, 1945, and returned home to Michigan.[62]

Manny Esquivel also left Manduria in July 1944 for Naples. Upon arriving back in the States, he and Rita spent two weeks of his 30-day furlough in Miami Beach at the Patricia Hotel courtesy of the Army. Due to the overwhelming numbers of soldiers to be trained during World War II, the government often rented out hotels to house the men, rather than building new barracks. When soldiers returned home from overseas they were often allowed to stay in them on furlough, on a space available basis. Manny was then sent to Galveston Army Air Field, five miles southwest of Galveston, Texas. As always, Rita accompanied him. There they rented a two-bedroom apartment. They also purchased a 1937 Plymouth and were able to make a few trips to Houston when Manny was not on duty. From Galveston, he was transferred to Casper Army Air Field in Casper, Wyoming. Just as Stan was doing, Manny tested damaged and repaired aircraft.[63]

In early 1945, they found out that Rita was pregnant with their first child. It was about the same time Manny was transferred to Pueblo, Colorado. He was still a member of a test crew. Test flying was more dangerous than most people realize. In July, Rita, who was six months pregnant, was advised by her doctor to go home to New Orleans to ensure proper care once the baby was born. Manny stayed behind in Pueblo and continued flying with a test crew. On one mission after Rita left, he was in his flight suit ready to board when another soldier asked Manny if he could fly in Manny's place, because he did not have enough flight time for the month. In his jovial manner, Manny agreed to be bumped from the flight. Just after the plane took off, it exploded, killing all on board. Shortly afterwards, Manny was sent to Camp Shelby in Mississippi, where he received an honorable discharge on September 7, 1945. That day he enlisted in the Reserve Corps.[64]

Unlike some of his friends, Richard Jacobson was given a choice for his return home: plane or boat. He was asked to fly as the flight engineer to ferry a B-24 back stateside. Jake declined. He had had enough flying for a while. "I thought I might enjoy a little boat ride," he jokingly recalls. He was wrong. Dick spent the next twenty-one days on a Liberty ship named the *Santa Maria*. "It might as well have been the original one," he said, "because that trip was like flying ten more missions." After a mishap leaving the Naples Bay, the convoy of seven or eight ships finally got under way. Jacobson had not been on board long when he was assigned a 20-millimeter cannon on the upper deck. He was also given "a fifteen minute class on how to use the damn thing in case of an attack." Jake just wanted a happy cruise home; he was not looking to be attacked. Despite seasickness and a few other mishaps on board, including one where he fractured his knee, he arrived at Newport News, Virginia, in August 1944. He then made his way home to Boston, where on August 29 he married Phyllis Harriet Ellis in a formal ceremony at Beacon House. Like Manny, Jake and his wife spent the 30-day furlough in Miami Beach in a hotel rented by the Army.

From Miami, he was sent to Chanute Field in Illinois to train on the B-29. If needed, he would soon be going to the Pacific theater. Shortly after arriving at Chanute, however, he came down with a serious flu-like illness. The doctors decided that he had had enough pressure and they reassigned him to Langley Field in Virginia. There he was put in charge of a flight line and all its equipment. He flew just enough to get flight pay. Phyllis and their new dog, Happy, joined him there.[65]

In early 1945, they found out that Phyllis was pregnant with their first child. They were still at Langley on July 20 when their daughter, Joanne, was born. Jake had to deliver the baby, because the doctor on call arrived about fifteen minutes too late. The family affectionately refers to the event as his "51st Mission." Shortly after Joanne's birth, Jake was sent to Ft. George Meade in Baltimore to begin the discharge process. He received his formal discharge at Ft. Devens, in Ayr, Massachusetts, on September 21, 1945.[66]

Norman Woodward finished his fiftieth mission in mid–June 1944, most likely on June 14 when Jacobson did. Like the other enlisted men of the crew, he was sent to Naples, where he boarded a ship bound for the United States. After his 30-day furlough, Woodward was shipped to various bases, where he served as a gunnery instructor. He received his honorable discharge on October 5, 1945.[67]

Shadow's navigator, Herbert Gouldon, left Italy on August 4, 1944. He had flown 32 actual combat missions, and with the "doubles," he was credited with 51 total missions. Because of his superior skill, Gouldon was promoted to first lieutenant and became group navigator. After a long ship ride back to the States and processing, Herb was sent to Miami Beach for 30 days of R&R. He lived in a hotel, and, except for morning roll call, he had no schedule. It was there that he met Mary Fay Baird from Alabama. After just two months of dating, Herb and Fay married in October 1944.[68]

Norman Woodward 50th mission photograph. (Maurice H. Gilliam)

After his furlough, Herb was stationed at the Boca Raton Army Air Field in Boca Raton, Florida. There he was a "check rider" navigation instructor at the radar school. His job was to make sure that the navigational students were ready to go out on their own. "I could tell within five minutes if a student was going to make it," Gouldon reflects. Herb and Fay rented a house in nearby Ft. Lauderdale. Herb had a great schedule while stationed in Boca Raton. He was scheduled to fly every other day from 0600 to 1200. He and Fay spent a lot of time on the beach. On October 25, 1945, Herb received an honorable discharge at Griener Field in Manchester, New Hampshire. He then transferred to the reserves.[69]

It was several weeks before Irene Stricklin learned that her son Robert was missing in action. At the time, the Army did not disclose the full nature of events that transpired on his last mission. It would take six months for the AAF to find and positively identify his remains, and to officially notify her that he had died in the explosion on July 15, 1944. As are most mothers who lose a son in war, Irene was never the same after she found out. The rest of the family was also devastated. On May 20, 1945, Robert Stricklin and the other graduates of Forest Avenue High School who died during the war were honored in a dedication ceremony. Stricklin was awarded the Distinguished Flying Cross and the Purple Heart posthumously. He was given a marker at Plot C, Row 39, Grave 13, in the Ardennes American Cemetery in Neupre, Belgium.[70]

Floyd Robinson, Vincent Olney, and the crew of *Shoo Shoo Baby* remained in the POW camp outside of Bucharest throughout July and August. The greatest risk of physical harm they faced was from the stray Allied bombs that landed near the camp during raids on the nearby Bucharest marshalling yards. First Lt. Marshall Samms described their first air raid as follows. "The anti-aircraft guns opened up and the noise was terrific. We could see the black puffs of flak bursting around the bombers, and hear the crash of the bombs as they hit the ground. All was calm for a few minutes, and then another group of bombers came. This group was making its bomb run directly overhead, so we all hit the floor and crawled under the bunks. Again [there was] the flak and the deafening drone of engines. Then a terrific explosion [made] the ground tremble ... in the next wave ... bombs dropped near us. The ground shook and one of the windows crashed to the floor, narrowly missing Cox, who scurried back under one of the bunks. Then all was quiet for ten or fifteen minutes before the all-clear siren sounded. It was decided then and there that it was better to be up in the air with the flak, than down on the ground with the bombs." Similar air raids occurred for the next two months as the Allies tightened the noose on Romania.[71]

Depression was another factor with which the prisoners had to cope. Second Lt. William R. Cubbins, a pilot in the 450th BG, was in the same POW camp with Robinson and Olney. In his post-war memoirs he described the feelings as follows. "The deep depression that had plagued me during my initial hours of captivity returned with a vengeance. I didn't want to talk to anyone or even go to the dining room for meals. One of the most curious aspects of captivity is the very deep sense of isolation that seizes one even in the midst of a crowd. It was as though the other prisoners didn't exist."[72] Each man had to deal with these feelings at some point during the ordeal. Each came to realize how important freedom was.

By early August 1944, the Allies were pressing into southern France. Meanwhile, the Russians continued their advance in Romania. Their advance, combined with the 15th AAF's hammer blows on Ploesti and other key targets in the country, had weakened German resistance. On August 23, Romania's King Michael ordered his armed forces to cease fire against the Allied forces, and he dismissed Mashal Antonescu, the pro–Axis premier. Two days later Paris was liberated. Initially, there was a great celebration in Bucharest. Unfortunately, Olney, Robinson, and the other prisoners were still in harm's way. Although the Romanians freed their captives, the Germans still controlled the airfields and all the roads leading out of city. The Americans were uncertain what to do. Because the Germans still controlled the area, they could not leave. This confusion intensified over the next few days when the Germans bombed the city in an attempt to regain control. The Germans wanted to recapture the American prisoners, but if that was not possible they would try to kill them. The former POWs sought refuge in their former prisons, in nearby basements, in individual homes, and in other shelters.[73]

Lt. Col. James A. Gunn, commander of the 454th BG and the current senior acting officer at the prison, solved their dilemma. The Romanian government was not well organized, a fact that was further highlighted in the days after its capitulation. Lack of phone and water service became major issues. Gunn could not simply call the 15th AAF HQ in Italy to request help. Something dramatic and daring had to be done. Gunn orchestrated a plan, which was called "Operation Gunn." First, he had to get word to Twining of the situation in Bucharest. There were nearly 1,100 American prisoners in the city at the time of the capitulation, and there was no feasible way to get them quickly out of danger. By a good stroke of luck, Gunn was able to liberate a Romanian plane and pilot. The plan was to fly to Italy to meet with Maj. Gen. Twining and advise him of the situation. After a minor setback, which took him to Popesti, Gunn did make it to Italy. Twining was not at headquarters, but Gunn briefed Brig. Gen. Charles Born, the 15th AAF's chief operations officer, of the situation. Plans were then prepared to rescue the prisoners. After some debate, it was decided that thirty-six B-17s from the 2nd and 97th Bomb Groups would fly to Bucharest and bring the prisoners home in waves. The B-17s were modified with plywood floors, and each could hold up to twenty prisoners.[74]

On August 28, Samms and the other liberated prisoners saw "three B-17s circle the city and land" at the airport. Word soon spread that they would be evacuated on August 31. The three B-17s were just the first of several groups to arrive. Operation Gunn was a success. Olney, Robinson, and nearly 1,100 other prisoners returned safely to Italy. Upon arrival, each man was deloused with DDT and given new clothes. Their ordeal was over.[75]

The 450th BG continued to fly combat missions from Manduria for another ten months. It completed its 265th and final mission on April 26, 1945. As a member of the ground crew, Samuel Stein did not rotate home, as did the men on combat aircrews. As were most of the ground crew, he was in Manduria all eighteen months that the 450th BG was there, and he was among the last to leave in May 1945. Sam recalls that there was quite a celebration on base once they learned that they would be going home. They had ice cream from Manduria. Unfortunately, it made

Left to right: unknown, Robinson, Olney and Shackleford after their return from POW camp in Bucharest. (Marshall Samms)

most of the men violently ill. Until the cause could be determined, the base was placed under a brief quarantine. Once it was verified that the ice cream was the culprit, the 450th BG packed up and prepared to ship out.[76]

On May 16, 1945, eight days after the Germans surrendered, Sam and the remaining members of the 450th BG took trucks to Taranto. A ship was waiting to take them back to the United States. Each man clambered on board up a rope ladder, carrying his duffle bag. After boarding, Sam learned that the ship was the USS *Wakefield*. The news gave him goose bumps. Prior to entering the service, he had worked on the USS *Wakefield* in the Boston Navy Yard as an electrician's helper. It had been in for repairs after a fire. Unlike most returning soldiers, Sam had the good fortune that his ship returned to his hometown, Boston. The *Wakefield* arrived at the South Boston Navy Yard, where his father worked as an electrician. After a quick doughnut and glass of milk provided by the Red Cross, the soldiers headed to the train station. There, Pullman cars took them to Camp Myles Standish in Taunton, Massachusetts, for processing. On the train ride, Sam passed within two blocks of his home.[77]

Sam took a taxi home from Taunton for his 30-day furlough. He spent every moment he could with his parents, brother, and three sisters. After his furlough, Sam was stationed in Clovis, New Mexico. This time he was being further trained to use his radio and radar expertise on B-29s. After training, Sam was headed for the Pacific theater. Those plans changed on August 6, when the *Enola Gay* dropped the first of two atomic bombs on Japan. On August 14, 1945, Japan surrendered unconditionally, and brought the war to an end. On September 27, 1945, Sam was honorably discharged at Camp Chaffee at Fort Smith in Arkansas. As did the other surviving members of the 450th BG, he headed home to start the next chapter in his life.[78]

Epilogue: Legacy

According to statistics after the war, more than 103,000 AAF airmen were listed as killed or missing in action in all theaters from December 1941 to August 1945. Astonishingly, the 450th BG losses accounted for over one percent of this figure. A total of 1,505 Cottontail airmen were listed as killed or missing in action during the group's sixteen months of active combat duty. A plaque at the Air Force Memorial Park at Wright-Patterson AFB in Ohio commemorates not only the lives of these brave men, but also the group's two Distinguished Unit Citations.[1]

As for the crew of *Shadow*, all but Robert Stricklin survived the war and returned home. They were truly a statistical anomaly. Each returned to the obscurity of his everyday life. Those who had not started families did so. Except for a few isolated incidents, most of the crew lost touch with each other. Constant movement by some of them made it nearly impossible to find one another. Each started new chapters in his life. They put their war experiences "on the shelf." It was each man's duty to serve, and he did it. Then they came home. In their minds, the most rewarding and exciting periods of their lives were just beginning. They were right.

After his discharge in September 1945, Maurice Gilliam returned home to Rockingham County, North Carolina. Two months later, Stella gave birth to the couple's second child, a son they named Larry Maurice Gilliam. Maurice got a job as a mechanic in Reidsville, and the family lived in a rented house on Highway 87 about five miles outside of town. Maurice liked his job. He loved to tinker with cars and motors (and still does), but he felt compelled to answer a higher calling.[2]

Maurice first felt the call to ministry in the spring of 1943, while stationed at Keesler during basic training. He answered the call six years later in the spring of 1949. In order to be eligible to attend the seminary at Wake Forest College, Maurice

The 450th Bomb Group's memorial plaque. (Neil H. Raiford)

enrolled at Campbell College to take preparatory courses and to earn a two-year degree. In preparation, Maurice borrowed some money for tuition. He worked part-time as a clerk in a Western Auto store; he also sold cookware door-to-door. While a student at Campbell and Wake Forest, he served as a pastor for several small country churches.[3]

On Friday, January 25, 1957, Maurice graduated from the Southeastern Baptist Theological Seminary in Wake Forest, N.C. He then began a rewarding life as a minister in various churches throughout the state. He "officially" retired in 1984 after four decades in the pulpit. But his popularity, engaging personality, and local reputation have only allowed him very few months of retirement. For almost twenty years he has served as an interim pastor at various churches in the county. Every new church begs him to stay on permanently, but retirement calls, and he always makes way for a new, younger pastor—at least until he is asked to pastor for a new church. Turning eighty has not slowed him down. When not tending to the needs of his congregation, he can be found working in his garden or in the yard.[4]

After the war, Grant Caywood returned to Sacramento. Because he loved to fly, he decided to become a pilot for United. This did not last long, however, because he did not like being away from Beo and his family. After some thought, he decided to go back to architecture. "To obtain an architect's license, I had to work two years under an architect in the state, have responsible charge of five million dollars worth of construction, make application to the Board of Architectural Examiners, submit recommendations, and take a four day test.... If I passed the test and successfully met the Board for an oral interview, I could call myself an *Architect*, but not until," wrote Caywood in his memoir. While Grant was working as a draftsman during this interim period, Beo gave birth to a lovely daughter, Lindi, in April 1946.[5]

By 1950, Grant had obtained his architect's license and opened his own office. He remained in the Air Force Reserve and became the wing commander of his reserve unit. Fate would play a hand in Caywood's life as the conflict in Korea heated up. The 12th Air Force was charged with building five new air bases in Germany and three in France. General Strother commanded the 12th Air Force in Wiesbaden, Germany. He needed a unique individual to head up the construction of the new bases. Strother needed an architect or structural engineer who was also a field grade officer, rated as a pilot, and had combat and command experience. The personnel files (on punch cards) were run through the IBM machine. Three names met his requirements. One of them was Grant Dodd Caywood.[6]

General Strother had met Caywood in 1943 at San Marcos. Strother was the major that Grant pulled from the burning twin-engine Lockheed trainer dubbed the "Burbank Bonfire." The general never forgot the act of heroism. He made Caywood the chief of design and planning for the 12th Air Force. In that role, Grant was the architect for and oversaw the construction of five major air bases in Germany and France. He also interacted with General Eisenhower, who took an immediate liking to him. In late 1952, Caywood returned home to Sacramento after two years in Germany.[7]

Grant re-started his architecture business. He began small. "Beo was the secretary and bookkeeper... Bookshelves were concrete blocks and boards. The drafting tables were sawhorses and plywood.... We bought a second-hand manual typewriter and a manual calculator. A hand cranked mimeograph was our printing machine." At first, he handled houses and remodels. It was a constant struggle to get contracts, but the business grew over the years. Grant made a name for himself in Sacramento and California. He added partners to the firm. When he retired in 1986, his company had completed over a billion dollars worth of construction. They built schools, government buildings, and office complexes. Grant won countless awards for his work.[8]

In September 1989, Grant lost the love of his life. Beo passed away after a battle with pancreatic cancer. "No one ever faced death with such calmness and good nature," wrote Grant in his memoir. "One day before her death, Beo was reading her bible—'I'm cramming for my finals,' she said." Grant was devastated, but kept his tears in private.[9]

A few years later, the widow of a dear friend asked him to escort her to her 55th high school reunion. "You can never trust a lonely female," he jokes. "She began getting her hooks into me immediately." Ruth was a soul mate for Grant, just as Beo had been. After a few months of courting, they were married in a private ceremony. As a shrewd businessman, Grant did not stumble into the new relationship lightly. "We have a pre-nuptial agreement," he reflects. "What's hers is hers and what's mine is hers." Grant and Ruth know that "to luck out twice in the same lifetime is rare indeed." Ruth still lets Grant think he is the head of the house, but really he now spends his time working in the garden and taking orders from the "boss." He loves every minute of it.[10]

Maurice Erickson remained in the Air Force after the war. He was a wonderful pilot and officer, but he was an even better instructor. He taught cadets in Waco, Texas, and Great Falls, Montana. During the Korean War, Maurice commanded the 2nd Air Rescue Squadron at Okinawa. He then served as base commander at a series of posts, which included Travis AFB, Wake Island, and Hickam AFB. During the Vietnam War, Maurice commanded the 4th Airlift Squadron stationed at McChord AFB, south of Tacoma, Washington. His group provided the airlift service in and out of Vietnam. He retired in 1966 a full (bird) colonel. He continued to work as a civilian in the airlift training section at McChord for another 18 years. His hobbies now include golf and spending time with his wife, grandchildren and great grandchildren.[11]

After the war, Ted Morris returned home to St. Louis. He tried his hand at many jobs, but none seemed to suit him. In the early 1950s, Ted got a job with Modern American Mortgage Company as a mortgage lender. He enjoyed the work, especially when he could help fellow servicemen buy their first houses. Ted married Jeanetta Bechtel in 1952. Over the next few years, he and Jeanetta had two children: a son, Terry, and a daughter, Donna. Ted was good about keeping in touch with the members of the crew he could find. He visited Manny in New Orleans, and went to see Woody in New York and Grant in California. He also kept in touch with Stan via phone. Ted's injuries are a constant reminder of *Shadow*'s crash and the war. He makes frequent trips to VA hospitals in St. Louis. But his spirit has never been broken. He had a job to do, and he did it without complaint or regret.[12]

After Stan Butynski was discharged in October 1945, he and Margie made immediate plans to get married. They were wed in a beautiful ceremony on May 25, 1946. Stan got a job as a machine operator in a factory that made Craftsman power tools. After taking some classes at Eastern Michigan University, he worked as an engineer for Argus Camera. He later worked as a plant operator for the Town of Ypsilanti and then as the county's chief of operations and maintenance. Stan counts trout fishing among his many hobbies. He has fished the same "secret spot" for five decades. Despite a stroke a few years ago, Stan still cuts his own grass.[13]

Manny Esquivel was discharged a month before his first son, James (called Jimmy) was born. He and Rita moved into a house on Desire Street in the Ninth Ward of New Orleans. It was a "double shotgun" house (duplex); Rita's parents lived in the other half. Manny put his radio and mechanical know-how to use. He repaired pinball machines. He later fixed televisions for Bart's Appliances. Manny eventually opened his own business, AC-DC Television Repair Service. Rita and Manny had three other sons, Rick, Barry, and Wayne. In 1954, the family moved to Arabi, a suburb of New Orleans. Manny's sons remember him as always being "content." He was fun-loving and had a wonderful sense of humor. The Esquivels had lots of friends and were very social.[14]

Unfortunately, Manny began to experience headaches and memory loss. He was hospitalized in 1972 for what was thought to be a brain tumor. A series of tests ruled out the brain tumor and Manny was sent to a psychiatrist, "who thought he possibly had a mental block from when he was a child." In late 1976 he was finally diagnosed with Alzheimer's disease. He slowly withdrew from social circles and passed away quietly in a nursing home on September 6, 1980. It was sad end for such an intelligent and fun-loving man. As a final tribute to a remarkable man, nearly five hundred mourners attended his funeral.[15]

After his return home, Richard Jacobson pursued his dream of becoming a major league baseball player. His uncle, the restaurant owner, arranged a tryout for him with the Lynn Red Sox, a minor league team. But Dick had been in the military for three years, and he was now married and had his first child. In his heart he knew that he no longer had the ambition or skills to chase the dream; so he jumped at the first opportunity to do something else. Through a chance meeting at a returning veterans' event, Dick met Jack Sandler, the president of Sandler of Boston, a local shoe company. Sandler took a liking to Dick at the event and asked how he was doing with the ball team. "I told him that I had been to bat eleven times and had gotten on base once. But it was when I was hit by a pitch," Jacobson recalls. Sandler laughed and asked, "How would you like to work for me?" Dick took the job.[16]

Despite several moves with the shoe company, Dick was a loving and active parent. A son, William (Bill) was born on June 3, 1947; this completed the Jacobson family. Baseball was still in Dick's blood, and he instilled the love for the game in Bill. In 1956, Dick formed the Garden City (New York) Athletic Association and helped build other youth programs in the community. His daughter, Joanne, was musically talented, and Dick attended all of her recitals. Upon graduation from high school, she received a music scholarship to college.[17]

Dick was also successful in business. His drive to succeed was noticed by everyone. In the thirty-plus years he worked for Sandler (which later merged with Bostonian shoes), Jacobson worked his way up from a stock boy to become the company's executive vice president. Dick left in 1974 to become the EVP of Nina Footwear. He is recognized as a pioneer in the shoe industry for being one of the first American executives to develop Italian-branded shoes to sell in America. Dick jokingly reflects that he had no idea that he would be going back to Italy so much after the war. Dick was the founder, president, and CEO of the Fashion Footwear Association of New York. After he lost Phyllis to breast cancer, Jake orchestrated major fund-raising events. The most famous is the annual "Shoes on Sale" on QVC (shopping channel) to benefit breast cancer research and education. It has raised over $12,000,000. Dick has been inducted into the Footwear Industry Hall of Fame, and in 1997 he was presented a lifetime achievement award for his fifty years of service in the shoe industry. Dick is now happily remarried and is finally enjoying retirement. When not traveling, he can be found on the golf course.[18]

After his discharge, Norman Woodward returned to his home in New York. There he started a family and a construction business. Woody prefers not to discuss the war, because he lost so many good friends. There is no doubt that his mind often drifts to the day in April 1944 when he traded positions with Ted in the ball turret on *Shadow*.

Epilogue: Legacy

After his discharge, Herb Gouldon returned home Jackson Heights with Fay. There he decided to finish college at New York University under the G.I. Bill. Herb was able to complete a bachelor of science degree in foreign marketing. He put his studies to quick use with Kohorn, a company that specialized in rayon fiber. Herb also remained in the Air Force Reserves and became the "department manager of the V.I.P. motor pool."[19]

After several years, Herb joined a process engineering company that built refineries. He was first sent to Japan to manage the company's Far East operations in Osaka. During his five years there, his three young children (two boys and a girl) became fluent in Japanese. From Japan, Herb was sent to London to manage the company's European operations. Other assignments with the company took him and his family to Germany and Hong Kong. Herb finally retired in 1996. He now enjoys playing golf and spending time with his family.[20]

Dick and Phyllis Jacobson after competing in a 1967 golf tournament. After Dick lost Phyllis to breast cancer, he organized "Shoes on Sale" with the QVC shopping channel. To date it has raised nearly $12 million for breast cancer research and education. (Richard M. Jacobson)

Vincent Olney returned to Stamford, Nebraska. He first got a job with the local co-op filling station and delivered fuel to area farmers. Vince lost the sight in his right eye during a hunting accident in December 1945. In 1946 he decided to start farming with his dad; it was a partnership that lasted until his dad died in 1965. While farming, Vince also began buying feeder calves. Alice worked as a nurse for the doctor in Oxford. She passed away in 1964 after a battle with cancer. Losing Alice and his father so close to the same time devastated Vince. But as with Caywood, love would come again. In 1970, he met a local widow, Marilyn Kay Jenkins, who taught school in Oxford. They married after a year and a half of courtship. The same year Vince bought the Oxford Livestock Commission, which he owned and managed until his death in 1978. Vince will always be remembered as the life of the party. He was a practical joker, and brought a smile to everyone's face. But his second wife, Marilyn, recalls that above all else, "he was a gentleman."[21]

Like Maurice Erickson, Floyd Robinson remained in the Air Force after the war. Robbie served in Germany and Spain. He later served at various Air Force bases in Texas, Georgia, and Louisiana. He ended up in the Pentagon. Floyd retired in 1968, after over 29 years of military service. He now enjoys playing golf and fishing. He still volunteers at Bolling Air Force Base in Washington, D.C. He is active in the 450th BG Association and attends various military reunions whenever possible.[22]

Shadow's legacy is her crew. The extraordinary men who flew her share an unconditional bond. It is an unconscious loyalty to one another that is hard to articulate. It was created by the intensity of their experience. They do not boast or brag of their military service; rarely do they even discuss it. But, in private, they all think of their time together in the skies above Europe. On most of Ted Morris' many visits to VA hospitals, he gets a new doctor, either in training or just out of residency. Each time they go through his medical history they inquire about the April 24, 1944, mission to Ploesti. Invariably, the new doctor asks him, "Mr. Morris, do you still think about the war?" Tears well up each time he gets the question. His quiet answer, which is always the same, echoes the sentiments of the crew. "Every day."[23]

Appendix A: Organization of the 15th Army Air Force, May 1944

Wing	Group	Squadrons	Base	Aircraft
	2nd	20th, 49th, 96th, 429th	Amendola, Italy	B-17
5th	97th	340th, 341st, 342nd, 414th	Amendola, Italy	B-17
Bomb	99th	346th, 347th, 348th, 416th	Tortorella, Italy	B-17
Wing	301st	32nd, 352nd, 353rd, 419th	Lucera, Italy	B-17
	463rd	772nd, 773rd, 774th, 775th	Celone, Italy	B-17
	483rd	815th, 816th, 817th, 819th	Sterparone, Italy	B-17
47th	98th	343rd, 344th, 345th, 346th	Lecce, Italy	B-24
Bomb	376th	512th, 513th, 514th, 515th	San Pancrazio, Italy	B-24
Wing	449th	716th, 717th, 718th, 719th	Grottaglie, Italy	B-24
	450th	720th, 721st, 722nd, 723rd	Manduria, Italy	B-24
49th	451st	724th, 725th, 726th, 727th	Castellucio, Italy	B-24
Bomb	461st	764th, 765th, 766th, 767th	Torretto, Italy	B-24
Wing	484th	824th, 825th, 826th, 827th	Torretto, Italy	B-24
55th	460th	760th, 761st, 762nd, 763rd	Spinazzola, Italy	B-24
Bomb	464th	776th, 777th, 778th, 779th	Pantanella, Italy	B-24
Wing	465th	780th, 781st, 782nd, 783rd	Pantanella, Italy	B-24
	485th	828th, 829th, 830th, 831st	Venosa, Italy	B-24
304th	454th	736th, 737th, 738th, 739th	San Giovanni, Italy	B-24
Bomb	455th	740th, 741st, 722nd, 743rd	San Giovanni, Italy	B-24
Wing	456th	744th, 745th, 746th, 747th	Stornara, Italy	B-24

	459th	756th, 757th, 758th, 759th	Giulia, Italy	B-24
	1st	27th, 71st, 94th	Salsola, Italy	P-38
	14th	37th, 48th, 49th	Triolo, Italy	P-38
306th	31st	307th, 308th, 309th	San Severo, Italy	P-51
Fighter	52nd	2nd, 4th, 5th	Madna, Italy	P-51
Wing	82nd	95th, 96th, 97th	Vinenzo, Italy	P-38
	325th	317th, 318th, 319th	Lesina, Italy	P-38
	332nd	99th, 100th, 301st, 302nd	Ramitelli, Italy	P-51

Appendix B: Combat Missions

This appendix provides the verifiable information on the combat missions of three men covered in this book: Maurice Gilliam, Richard Jacobson, and Grant Caywood. Information is not available for the missions flown by the other men. In fact, crew-level mission information is usually very difficult to come by. Since it does not exist in any archive, it can be drawn only from combat diaries (often incomplete and hard to verify) or scattered government memos. I feel fortunate to have successfully compiled information on the three men listed here, whose accomplishments are certainly worth preserving for posterity, even as other men's records await discovery.

—NHR

S/Sgt. Maurice Holt Gilliam

Date	Target	Mission Credits	Mission Total
March 11, 1944	Toulon, France	1	1
March 17, 1944	Schwechat, Austria	2	3
March 18, 1944	Lavariano, Italy	1	4
March 19, 1944	Graz, Austria	2	6
March 24, 1944	Rimini, Italy	1	7
March 28, 1944	Mestre, Italy	1	8
March 29, 1944	Balzano, Italy	2	10
March 30, 1944	Sofia, Bulgaria	1	11
April 2, 1944	Steyr, Austria	2	13
April 3, 1944	Budapest, Hungary	2	15
April 4, 1944	Bucharest, Romania	2	17
April 7, 1944	Mestre, Italy	1	18
April 12, 1944	Wiener-Neustadt, Austria	2	20
April 13, 1944	Budapest, Hungary	2	22
April 15, 1944	Bucharest, Romania	2	24
April 17, 1944	Sofia, Bulgaria	1	25
April 20, 1944	Treviso, Italy	1	26
April 24, 1944	Ploesti, Romania	2	28

Date	Target	Mission Credits	Mission Total
April 28, 1944	Orbetello, Italy	1	29
April 30, 1944	Allessandia, Italy	1	30
May 5, 1944	Ploesti, Romania	2	32
May 6, 1944	Brasov, Romania	2	34
May 12, 1944	San Stephano, Italy	1	35
May 22, 1944	Latisano, Italy	1	36
May 25, 1944	Porto Marghera, Italy	1	37
May 26, 1944	Nice, France	1	38
May 27, 1944	Marseille, France	1	39
May 31, 1944	Ploesti, Romania	2	41
June 2, 1944	Simeria, Romania	2	43
June 4, 1944	Genoa, Italy	1	44
June 6, 1944	Ploesti, Romania	2	46
June 9, 1944	Munich, Germany	2	48
June 11, 1944	Constanto, Romania	2	50

S/Sgt. Richard Morton Jacobson

Date	Target	Mission Credits	Mission Total
March 17, 1944	Schwechat, Austria	2	2
March 18, 1944	Lavariano, Italy	1	3
March 19, 1944	Graz, Austria	2	5
March 24, 1944	Rimini, Italy	1	6
March 28, 1944	Mestre, Italy	1	7
March 29, 1944	Balzano, Italy	2	9
March 30, 1944	Sofia, Bulgaria	1	10
April 2, 1944	Steyr, Austria	2	12
April 3, 1944	Budapest, Hungary	2	14
April 4, 1944	Bucharest, Romania	2	16
April 7, 1944	Mestre, Italy	1	17
April 12, 1944	Weiner-Neustadt, Austria	2	19
April 13, 9144	Budapest, Hungary	2	21
April 15, 1944	Bucharest, Romania	2	23
April 17, 1944	Sofia, Bulgaria	1	24
April 20, 1944	Treviso, Italy	1	25
April 24, 1944	Ploesti, Romania	2	27
April 28, 1944	Orbetello, Italy	1	28
April 30, 1944	Allessandia, Italy	1	29
May 5, 1944	Ploesti, Romania	2	31
May 6, 1944	Brasov, Romania	2	33
May 12, 1944	San Stephano, Italy	1	34
May 22, 1944	Latisano, Italy	1	35
May 25, 1944	Porto Marghera, Italy	1	36
May 26, 1944	Nice, France	1	37
May 27, 1944	Marseille, France	1	38
May 31, 1944	Ploesti, Romania	2	40
June 2, 1944	Simeria, Romania	2	42
June 4, 1944	Genoa, Italy	1	43
June 6, 1944	Ploesti, Romania	2	45
June 9, 1944	Munich, Germany	2	47

Date	Target	Mission Credits	Mission Total
June 11, 1944	Constanto, Romania	2	49
June 14, 1944	Osijck, Yugoslavia	1	50

Capt. Grant Dodd Caywood

Date	Target	Mission Credits	Mission Total
March 11, 1944	Toulon, France	1	1
March 17, 1944	Schwechat, Austria	2	3
March 18, 1944	Lavariano, Italy	1	4
March 19, 1944	Graz, Austria	2	6
March 24, 1944	Rimini, Italy	1	7
March 29, 1944	Balzano, Italy	2	9
March 30, 1944	Sofia, Bulgaria	1	10
April 2, 1944	Steyr, Austria	2	12
April 3, 1944	Budapest, Hungary	2	14
April 12, 1944	Weiner-Neustadt, Austria	2	16
April 17, 1944	Sofia, Bulgaria	1	17
April 20, 1944	Treviso, Italy	1	18
April 28, 1944	Orbetello, Italy	1	19
May 5, 1944	Ploesti, Romania	2	21
May 12, 1944	San Stefano, Italy	1	22
May 17, 1944	Porto San Stefano, Italy	1	23
May 22, 1944	Latisano, Italy	1	24
May 25, 1944	Porte Marghera, Italy	1	25
May 30, 1944	Weiner-Neustadt, Austria	2	27
June 4, 1944	Genoa, Italy	1	28
June 9, 1944	Munich, Germany	2	30
June 13, 1944	Munich, Germany	2	32
June 22, 1944	Ferrara, Italy	1	33
June 26, 1944	Schwechat, Austria	2	35
June 27, 1944	Brod, Yugoslavia	1	36
July 4, 1944	Pitesti, Romania	2	38
July 20, 1944	Fredrickshaven, Germany	2	40
July 23, 1944	Berat, Albania	1	41
July 31, 1944	Targoviste, Romania	1	42
August 9, 1944	Budapest, Hungary	1	43
August 23, 1944	Vosendorf, Austria	2	45
August 29, 1944	Ferrara, Italy	1	46
September 4, 1944	Trento, Italy	1	47
September 6, 1944	Lefkovac, Yugoslavia	1	48
September 13, 1944	Ora, Italy	1	49
September 15, 1944	Larrissa, Greece	1	50

Chapter Notes

1. Dutiful Sons

1. Maurice Gilliam Papers; Interviews with Maurice Gilliam, August 2000 and September 2000; Reidsville has always been listed as his hometown because the family's mailing address was at Route 1, Reidsville.
2. Interviews with Maurice Gilliam, October 2000 and September 1, 2002; Interview with Sally McKinney, March 2001.
3. Interviews with Maurice Gilliam, September 2000 and October 2000.
4. Interviews with Maurice Gilliam, September 2000 and October 2000; Interview with Sally McKinney, March 2001.
5. Interview with Maurice Gilliam, October 2000; Interview with Sally McKinney, March 2001.
6. Interviews with Maurice Gilliam, August 2000, September 2000, and September 1, 2002; Interview with Sally McKinney, March 2001; Interview with Gayle Sutton, May 11, 2001.
7. Interview with Maurice Gilliam, September 2000.
8. Interviews with Maurice Gilliam, August 2000, September 2000, and September 1, 2002.
9. Interviews with Maurice Gilliam August 2000 and September 1, 2002.
10. Interviews with Maurice Gilliam, August 2000, September 2000, and September 1, 2002.
11. Maurice Gilliam Papers; Interviews with Maurice Gilliam, August 2000 and September 1, 2002.
12. Interview with Maurice Gilliam, September 1, 2002.
13. Interviews with Maurice Gilliam, August 2000 and October 2000.
14. Interview with Maurice Gilliam, August 2000.
15. Interviews with Maurice Gilliam, August 2000, September 2000, and September 1, 2002.
16. Caywood memoir, *I Remember*, Section 1; Interviews with Grant Caywood, April 8, 2002, and August 26, 2002.
17. Caywood memoir, *I Remember*, Section 1; Interview with Grant Caywood, August 26, 2002.
18. Interview with Grant Caywood, August 26, 2002.
19. Interview with Grant Caywood, August 26, 2002.
20. Caywood memoir, *I Remember*, Section 1; Interviews with Grant Caywood, April 8, 2002, and August 26, 2002.
21. Caywood memoir, *I Remember*, Section 1.
22. Caywood memoir, *I Remember*, Section 1.
23. Caywood memoir, *I Remember*, Section 1; Interview with Grant Caywood, August 26, 2002.
24. Caywood memoir, *I Remember*, Section 1.

25. Caywood memoir, *I Remember,* Section 1.
26. Interview with Grant Caywood, July 6, 2001.
27. Caywood memoir, *I Remember,* Section 1; Interview with Grant Caywood, September 11, 2002.
28. Caywood memoir, *I Remember,* Section 1; Grant Caywood letter to author, August 26, 2002.
29. Caywood memoir, *I Remember,* Section 1; Interview with Grant Caywood, September 11, 2002.
30. Caywood memoir, *I Remember,* Section 1.
31. Caywood memoir, *I Remember,* Section 1.
32. Caywood memoir, *I Remember,* Section 1; Interview with Grant Caywood, September 11, 2002.
33. Caywood memoir, *I Remember,* Section 1; Grant Caywood Papers.
34. Interview with Grant Caywood, July 6, 2001.
35. Caywood memoir, *I Remember,* Section 1; Interview with Grant Caywood, September 11, 2002.
36. Interview with Grant Caywood, July 6, 2001.
37. Interviews with Maurice Erickson, January 2002 and November 21, 2002.
38. Interviews with Maurice Erickson, January 2002 and November 21, 2002.
39. Interview with Maurice Erickson, January 2002.
40. Interviews with Maurice Erickson, January 2002 and November 21, 2002.
41. Theodore Morris Papers; Interviews with Ted Morris, July 26, 2001, November 22, 2002, and December 10, 2002.
42. Interviews with Ted Morris, July 26, 2001, and November 22, 2002.
43. Theodore Morris Papers; Interviews with Ted Morris, July 26, 2001, and November 22, 2002.
44. Theodore Morris Papers; Interviews with Ted Morris, July 26, 2001, and November 22, 2002.
45. Interviews with Stan Butynski, August 26, 2001, and November 15, 2002.
46. Interviews with Stan Butynski, August 26, 2001, and November 15, 2002.
47. Interviews with Stan Butynski, August 26, 2001, and November 15, 2002.
48. Interviews with Stan Butynski, August 26, 2001, and November 15, 2002.
49. Interview with Rick Esquivel, April 24, 2002; Interview with Jim Esquivel, April 14, 2002; Interview with Raul Esquivel, October 2, 2001.
50. Interview with Rick Esquivel, April 24, 2002; Interview with Jim Esquivel, April 14, 2002; Interview with Raul Esquivel, October 2, 2001.
51. Interview with Rick Esquivel, April 24, 2002; Interview with Jim Esquivel, April 14, 2002.
52. Rita Esquivel Memoir, copy in possession of author, 1. Hereafter referred to as Esquivel Memoir.
53. Interviews with Richard Jacobson, September 23, 2002, and November 25, 2002.
54. Interview with Richard Jacobson, September 23, 2002.
55. Interview with Richard Jacobson, November 25, 2002.
56. Interview with Richard Jacobson, September 23, 2002.
57. Interviews with Richard Jacobson, September 23, 2002, and November 25, 2002.
58. Interview with Richard Jacobson, September 23, 2002.
59. Interviews with Richard Jacobson, September 23, 2002, and November 25, 2002.
60. Interviews with Richard Jacobson, September 23, 2002, and December 19, 2002.
61. Interview with Richard Jacobson, September 23, 2002.
62. Interview with Richard Jacobson, September 23, 2002.
63. Interview with Richard Jacobson, September 23, 2002.
64. Interview with Richard Jacobson, September 23, 2002.
65. Interview with Norman Woodward, October 4, 2002.
66. Interview with Herb Gouldon, June 18, 2003.
67. Interview with Herb Gouldon, June 18, 2003.
68. Interview with Herb Gouldon, June 18, 2003.
69. Interview with Herb Gouldon, June 18, 2003.
70. Interview with Herb Gouldon, June 18, 2003; NARA Form 13164 for Herb Gouldon.
71. Interview with Irene S. Frazier, December 6, 2002; Robert Bryant Stricklin Birth Certificate, Texas Department of Health, Bureau of Vital Statistics.
72. Interview with Irene S. Frazier, December 6, 2002.
73. 1920 U.S. Census (Dallas, Texas); Interview with Irene S. Frazier, December 6, 2002.

74. Sammie T. Lee (Dallas Public Library) letter to author, September 23, 2002.
75. Interview with Irene S. Frazier, December 6, 2002; Robert Stricklin Papers. Stricklin's military identification card dated Aug. 26, 1943, states that he was 5 foot 9 inches tall, had hazel eyes, brown hair, and weighed 140 pounds. The ID's photo reveals that he is at least 5 foot 10 inches tall, which is consistent with the family's memory of him.
76. Interview with Irene S. Frazier, December 6, 2002; Dava Ladymon (Dallas Genealogical Society) letter to author, September 24, 2002.
77. Interview with Irene S. Frazier, December 6, 2002; NARA Form 13164 for Robert B. Stricklin.
78. Interview with Marilyn Siebels, September 1, 2002; Interview with Susan Rhynalds, January 15, 2003.
79. Interview with Susan Rhynalds, January 15, 2003.
80. Interview with Marilyn Siebels, September 1, 2002; Interview with Susan Rhynalds, January 15, 2003.
81. Interview with Marilyn Siebels, September 1, 2002; Interview with Susan Rhynalds, January 15, 2003.
82. Interview with Susan Rhynalds, January 15, 2003.
83. Interview with Susan Rhynalds, January 15, 2003.
84. Interview with Susan Rhynalds, January 15, 2003.
85. Interview with Susan Rhynalds, January 15, 2003.
86. Interview with Susan Rhynalds, January 15, 2003.
87. Interview with Marilyn Siebels, September 1, 2002; Vincent Olney Papers; Interview with Susan Rhynalds, January 15, 2003.
88. Interview with Marilyn Siebels, September 1, 2002; Interview with Susan Rhynalds, January 15, 2003.
89. Interview with Floyd Robinson, December 11, 2002.
90. Interview with Floyd Robinson, December 11, 2002.
91. Interview with Floyd Robinson, January 3, 2003.
92. Interviews with Floyd Robinson, December 11, 2002, and January 3, 2003.

2. Training

1. *The Official Guide to the Army Air Forces: A Directory, Almanac and Chronicle of Achievement*, New York, June 1944, p. 103-104. Hereafter referred to as *AAF Guide*.
2. *AAF Guide*, p. 104.
3. Maurice Gilliam Papers; Interviews with Maurice Gilliam, August 2000 and September 2000.
4. Interview with Maurice Gilliam, August 2000.
5. Interview with Maurice Gilliam, April 2002.
6. Interviews with Maurice Gilliam, August 2000 and April 2002.
7. Interviews with Maurice Gilliam, August 2000 and April 2002.
8. Grant Caywood Papers; Interview with Maurice Gilliam, August 2000.
9. *AAF Guide*, 104. Bowman, *USAAF Handbook*, 82.
10. Bowman, *USAAF Handbook*, 83.
11. Bowman, *USAAF Handbook*, 83.
12. Bowman, *USAAF Handbook*, 82.
13. Caywood, *I Remember*, Volume 1.
14. Caywood, *I Remember*, Volume 1.
15. *AAF Guide*, 104.
16. Caywood, *I Remember*, Volume 1.
17. *AAF Guide*, 104.
18. Caywood, *I Remember*, Volume 1.
19. Caywood, *I Remember*, Volume 1.
20. Caywood, *I Remember*, Volume 1.
21. Caywood, *I Remember*, Volume 1.
22. Caywood, *I Remember*, Volume 1; Shadow's Log, Grant Caywood Papers.
23. Grant Caywood letters to author, July 26, 2001 and July 27, 2001.
24. Caywood, *I Remember*, Volume 1.
25. Caywood, *I Remember*, Volume 1.
26. Caywood, *I Remember*, Volume 1.
27. Caywood, *I Remember*, Volume 1.
28. *AAF Guide*, 105.
29. Grant Caywood Papers.
30. *AAF Guide*, 104; Interview with Maurice Erickson, January 2002; Bowman, *USAAF Handbook*, 82.
31. Interviews with Maurice Erickson, January 2002 and November 21, 2002; Grant Caywood Papers; Lou Thole, *Forgotten Fields of America: World War II Bases and Training Then and Now, Volume 2*, Montana, 1999, 164.
32. Interview with Ted Morris, February 14, 2002.
33. Interview with Ted Morris, February 14, 2002.
34. Interview with Ted Morris, February 14, 2002.
35. Interviews with Stan Butynski, August 26, 2001 and November 15, 2002.

36. Interviews with Stan Butynski, August 26, 2001 and November 15, 2002.
37. Esquivel Memoir, 1.
38. Esquivel Memoir, 1.
39. Esquivel Memoir, 2.
40. Esquivel Memoir, 2.
41. Esquivel Memoir, 2-3.
42. NARA Form 13161 "Richard M. Jacobson"
43. Interview with Richard Jacobson, September 2002. Copy of program from the 14th Station Complement "Madman's Minstrel Menagerie" December 22-23, 1942 from the Richard Jacobson Papers.
44. Richard Jacobson Papers; Interviews with Richard Jacobson, September 23, 2002 and November 25, 2002.
45. Interviews with Richard Jacobson, September 23, 2002 and November 25, 2002.
46. NARA Form 13164 for Norman L. Woodward.
47. Interview with Herb Gouldon, June 18, 2003; NARA Form 13164 for Herb Gouldon.
48. Interview with Herb Gouldon, June 18, 2003; NARA Form 13164 for Herb Gouldon; *AAF Guide*, 105.
49. Interview with Herb Gouldon, June 18, 2003; NARA Form 13164 for Herb Gouldon; *AAF Guide*, 106.
50. Interview with Herb Gouldon, June 18, 2003; NARA Form 13164 for Herb Gouldon.
51. Interview with Irene S. Frazier, December 6, 2002.
52. Interview with Irene S. Frazier, December 6, 2002; Thole, *Forgotten Fields of America, Volume 2*, 167.
53. *AAF Guide*, 106.
54. Interview with Susan Rhynalds, January 15, 2003; Susan C. Rhynalds letter to author, November 12, 2002.
55. Susan C. Rhynalds letter to author, November 12, 2002; *The Perculator of Class '43-G: Class Book Published by The Aviation Cadets of Class 43-G, Coffeyville Army Air Field, Coffeyville, Kansas*, copy from the Vincent Olney Papers.
56. *Pampa Army Air Field Calling*, WWII cadet souvenir brochure.
57. Aircraft Accident Report (AAR) #44-7-5-60.
58. *The Times-Tribune* (Beaver City, NE), Thursday, July 13, 1944; Interview with Susan Rhynalds, January 15, 2003; Susan C. Rhynalds letter to author, November 12, 2002.
59. Interviews with Floyd Robinson, December 11, 2002 and January 3, 2003.
60. Interviews with Floyd Robinson, December 11, 2002 and January 3, 2003

3. A Liberator Crew

1. Grant Caywood Papers.
2. Grant Caywood Papers.
3. AAF Guide, 258–266; Stewart Wilson, *Aircraft of WWII*, 28, 116, 139.
4. Perret, *Winged Victory*, 99; Wilson, *Aircraft of WWII*, 27; Dan Patterson, Paul Perkins and Michelle Crean. *The Soldier: Consolidated B-24 Liberator*, Charlottesville, VA, 1994, 10; Frederick A. Johnsen, *B-24 Liberator*, Osceola, WI, 1993, 11.
5. Patterson, *The Soldier*, 10; Steve Birdsall, *Log of the Liberators*, New York, 1973, 41.
6. Perret, *Winged Victory*, 92; Patterson, *The Soldier*, 10–12; Birdsall, *Log of the Liberators*, 38–40.
7. Martin Bowman, *The B-24 Liberator 1939–1945*, New York, 1980, 8.
8. Robert F. Dorr, *B-24 Liberator Units of the Fifteen Air Force*, Oxford, England, 2000, 14; Maurice Erickson letter to author, December 12, 2001.
9. *These statistics are for "true air speed," which is corrected for altitude, temperature, humidity, etc. The actual adjusted average air speed was closer to 200 miles per hour.
10. Wilson, *Aircraft of WWII*, 41–42; Birdsall, *Log of the Liberators*, 57.
11. Wilson, *Aircraft of WWII*, 41–42; *AAF Guide*, 148.
12. *AAF Guide*, 123; Michael O'Leary, *Consolidated B-24 Liberator*, Oxford, England, 2002, 139.
13. O'Leary, *Consolidated B-24*, 139; Bowman, *B-24 Liberator*, 8; Perret, *Winged Victory*, 101.
14. Steinbeck, *Bombs Away*, 69.
15. *AAF Guide*, 109.
16. *AAF Guide*, 110.
17. *AAF Guide*, 110.
18. Interview with Maurice Gilliam, April 2002.
19. Grant Caywood Papers.
20. Interview with Gayle Sutton, May 11, 2001.
21. Maurice Gilliam letter to author, January 21, 2003; Interview with Maurice Gilliam, February 4, 2003.
22. Esquivel Memoir, 3.
23. Grant Caywood letter to author, December 10, 2002.
24. Interview with Maurice Erickson, November 21, 2002.
25. Interview with Maurice Gilliam, November 28, 2002.
26. *AAF Guide*, 79; Maurice Gilliam letter to author, January 21, 2003.

27. Interview with Maurice Gilliam, November 28, 2002.
28. Interview with Maurice Gilliam, August 2000; Interview with Irene S. Frazier, December 6, 2002; Interview with Herb Gouldon, June 18, 2003.
29. Grant Caywood Papers.
30. Interview with Maurice Gilliam, April 2002.
31. Interview with Maurice Gilliam, October 2000.
32. Interview with Maurice Gilliam, February 4, 2003.
33. Interview with Maurice Gilliam, July 22, 2002; Interview with Maurice Erickson, January 2002.
34. C.G. Sweeting, *Combat Flying Clothing*, Washington, 1984, 32–38, 77, 85, 93, 101–102; C.G. Sweeting, *Combat Flying Equipment*, Washington, 1989, 137; Jon A. Maguire, *Gear Up! Flight Clothing & Equipment of USAAF Airmen World War II*, Atglen, PA, 1995, 124; Interview with Richard Jacobson, November 25, 2002.
35. Grant Caywood memoir, *The Air Battle of Ploesti*, 8.
36. Interview with Richard Jacobson, November 25, 2002; Interview with Maurice Gilliam, August 2000; Grant Caywood memoir, *The Air Battle of Ploesti*, 8.
37. Grant Caywood Papers; *AAF Guide*, 128; Interview with Ted Morris, December 2, 2002; Birdsall, *Log of the Liberators*, 313.
38. Grant Caywood Papers.
39. Interview with Richard Jacobson, September 23, 2002.
40. Interview with Maurice Gilliam, September 2, 2001.
41. Interview with Richard Jacobson, September 23, 2002.
42. Grant Caywood Papers.
43. Interview with Maurice Gilliam, September 2, 2001; Interview with Richard Jacobson, September 23, 2002.
44. Interview with Maurice Gilliam August 2000 and September 2, 2001; Interview with Richard Jacobson, September 23, 2002; Interview with Ted Morris, February 14, 2002; Interview with Stan Butynski, August 26, 2001.
45. Interview with Richard Jacobson, September 23, 2002; Interview with Herb Gouldon, June 18, 2003.
46. Interviews with Richard Jacobson, September 23, 2002 and November 25, 2002; William R. Cubbins, *The War of the Cottontails: Memoirs of a WWII Bomber Pilot*, Chapel Hill, NC, 1989, 7; Grant Caywood letter to author, January 16, 2003.
47. Photo, dated March 4, 1944, Maurice Gilliam Papers; Interview with Richard Jacobson, September 23, 2002; Grant Caywood Papers

4. "Cottontails" in the Heel of the Boot

1. Edward Bunting, senior editor, *World War II Day by Day*, London, 2001, 429, 440, 442–443.
2. Kenn C. Rust, *Fifteenth Air Force Story*, Temple City, CA, 1976, 5.
3. Rust, *Fifteenth Air Force*, 5; John C. McManus, *Deadly Sky: The American Combat Airman in World War II*, Novato, CA, 2000, 152; *AAF Guide*, 256.
4. Rust, *Fifteenth Air Force*, 5; John C. McManus, *Deadly Sky: The American Combat Airman in World War II*, Novato, CA, 2000, 152; Maurer, Maurer, editor, *Air Force Combat units of World War II*, Edison, NJ, 1994, 467–468, 470.
5. Maurer, Air Force Combat Units, 377, 391–393, 397–398, 416–418, 470; Rust, *Fifteenth Air Force*, 4; *AAF Guide*, 21.
6. Rust, *Fifteenth Air Force*, 6–7.
7. Robert A. Davis, *450th Bomb Group (H): The "Cottontails" of WWII*, Paducah, KY, 1996, 8 (hereafter referred to as Davis, *Cottontails*); Robert A. Davis, editor, *History of the 450th Bombardment Group*. Privately published, November 1989, 1–20 (hereafter referred to as Davis, *History of 450th BG*); Interview with Floyd Robinson, December 11, 2002.
8. Davis, *History of the 450th BG*, 31, 65; Davis, *Cottontails*, 11; Thole, Volume II, 164.
9. Davis, *History of the 450th BG*, 31–76.
10. Davis, *History of the 450th BG*, 65; William R. Cubbins, *The War of the Cottontails*, Chapel Hill, NC, 1989, 9 (Hereafter referred to as Cubbins, *Cottontails*).
11. Undated 1944 newspaper clipping from *The Bomb Blast* titled "Italy—An Historical Treasure," in the Maurice Gilliam Papers.
12. Undated 1944 newspaper clipping from *The Bomb Blast* titled "Italy—An Historical Treasure," in the Maurice Gilliam Papers.
13. Davis, *History of the 450th BG*, 65–75; Davis, *Cottontails*, 16; Interview with Sam Stein, December 30, 2002; Sam Stein Diary, January 4, 1944.
14. Davis, *History of the 450th BG*, 72–80; Davis, *Cottontails*, 16–17.
15. Davis, *Cottontails*, 17–18.

16. Geoffrey Perret, *Winged Victory*, 287–289; *AAF Guide*, 61, 63; Davis, *History of the 450th BG*, iv; Davis, *Cottontails*, 18.
17. Davis, *Cottontails*, 8; Dale P. Harper, "Axis Sally," *World War II Magazine*, November 1985.
18. Davis, *Cottontails*, 8; Harper, "Axis Sally."
19. Gilliam, *Diary of My Missions*, Maurice Gilliam Papers; Jacobson, *Diary of Combat Missions*, Richard Jacobson Papers; Interview with Maurice Erickson, January 2002.
20. Interview with Grant Caywood, July 6, 2001; Interviews with Maurice Erickson, January 2002 and November 21, 2002; Interview with Ted Morris, June 21, 2001; Interview with Stan Butynski, August 26, 2001; Interviews with Maurice Gilliam, August 2000 and September 2000; Maurice Gilliam Papers.
21. Interview with Floyd Robinson, December 11, 2002; Interview with Grant Caywood, July 6, 2001.
22. Interview with Grant Caywood, July 6, 2001; Interview with Maurice Erickson, November 11, 2002.
23. Interview with Floyd Robinson, December 11, 2002; Interview with Grant Caywood, July 6, 2001; Interview with Maurice Erickson, November 11, 2002.
24. Interview with Maurice Gilliam, August 2000; Interview with Maurice Erickson, January 2002; Interview with Stan Butynski, August 26, 2001; *AAF Guide*, 220–221; Interview with Sam Stein, December 30, 2002.
25. Interview with Stan Butynski, August 26, 2001; Interview with Maurice Erickson, November 21, 2002; Interview with Grant Caywood, April 8, 2002; Interview with Sam Stein, December 30, 2002; Interview with Ted Morris, June 21, 2001

5. A Typical Mission

1. Interview with Maurice Gilliam, August 2000; Interview with Maurice Erickson, January 2002; Interview with Ted Morris, December 2, 2002; Grant Caywood memoir, *The Air Battle of Ploesti*, 6–8; Interview with Grant Caywood, April 8, 2002; Grant Caywood letter to author, January 23, 2003; *AAF Guide*, 44–45.
2. Interview with Sam Stein, December 30, 2002.
3. Interview with Grant Caywood, April 8, 2002; Interview with Maurice Erickson, January 2002; Robert A. Davis letter to author, November 4, 2002; Interview with Maurice Gilliam, August 2000.
4. Interviews with Maurice Erickson, January 2002 and November 21, 2002; Caywood memoir, *The Air Battle of Ploesti*, 21.
5. Interview with Maurice Erickson, January 2002; Interview with Stan Butynski, August 26, 2001; Interviews with Grant Caywood, July 6, 2001 and April 8, 2002; Interview with Floyd Robinson, December 11, 2002; Caywood memoir, *The Air Battle of Ploesti*, 9; Grant Caywood letters to author, November 17, 2002 and January 23, 2003.
6. Interview with Maurice Erickson, January 2002; Interview with Grant Caywood, April 8, 2002; Interview with Maurice Gilliam, August 2000; Interview with Stan Butynski, August 26, 2001.
7. Interview with Ted Morris, July 26, 2001; Interview with Stan Butynski, August 26, 2001; Grant Caywood letter to author, February 8, 2003; Richard Jacobson letter to author, February 9, 2003.
8. Grant Caywood memoir, *The Air Battle of Ploesti*, 9–10.
9. There are some variations to this formation, but this was the most common and the one flown by Caywood's crew on most missions.
10. Interviews with Maurice Erickson, January 2002 and November 21, 2002; Interview with Grant Caywood, April 8, 2002; Caywood memoir, *The Air Battle of Ploesti*, 10, 20; Perret, *Winged Victory*, 255; Richard Jacobson, letter to author January 28, 2003; *AAF Guide*, 259.
11. Interview with Richard Jacobson, November 25, 2002; Interview with Grant Caywood, July 6, 2001; Robert A. Davis letter to author, November 4, 2002; Interview with Maurice Gilliam, August 2000.
12. Interview with Grant Caywood, July 6, 2001.
13. Interview with Grant Caywood, July 6, 2001; Interviews with Maurice Gilliam, August and September 2000; Interview with Ted Morris, May 29, 2003.
14. Interview with Grant Caywood, July 6, 2001; Dorr, *B-24 Liberator Units of the Fifteenth Air Force*, 16.
15. *AAF Guide*, 43, 69.
16. Patterson, *The Soldier*, 18; Headquarters Army Air Forces, *Pilots' Information File (PIF)*, Washington, DC, 1945, 1–4.
17. Grant Caywood letter to author, February 6, 2003.
18. *AAF Guide*, 43; Patterson, *The Soldier*, 20; Grant Caywood letter to author, February 17, 2003; Thomas A. Dickinson, *The Aeronautical Dictionary*, New York, 1945, 248–249.

19. *AAF Guide*, 43; Patterson, *The Soldier*, 19; Grant Caywood memoir, *The Air Battle of Ploesti*, 13–14.
20. *AAF Guide*, 43; Interview with Richard Jacobson, February 5, 2003; Patterson, *The Soldier*, 19, 37.
21. *AAF Guide*, 43; Patterson, *The Soldier*, 19; Grant Caywood letter to author, April 8, 2003; Interview with Maurice Gilliam, August 2000.
22. *AAF Guide*, 44; Patterson, *The Soldier*, 20, 47, 49.
23. Walter J. Boyne, *Clash of Wings, WWII in the Air*, 317.
24. Grant Caywood memoir, *The Air Battle of Ploesti*, 13; Boyne, *Clash of Wings*, 317–318.
25. Interview with Ted Morris, July 6, 2001; Patterson, *The Soldier*, 20.
26. Interview with Ted Morris, July 6, 2001.
27. Interview with Maurice Gilliam, August 2000.
28. Interview with Richard Jacobson, November 25, 2002; Interviews with Grant Caywood, July 6, 2001 and April 8, 2002; Interview with Maurice Gilliam, August 2000; Wilson, *Aircraft of WWII*, 70–72, 96–98, 117–121.
29. Interview with Maurice Erickson, November 21, 2002; Interview with Richard Jacobson, November 25, 2002; Interviews with Grant Caywood, July 6, 2001 and April 8, 2002; Interview with Maurice Gilliam, August 2000; Grant Caywood letter to author, January 23, 2003.
30. Grant Caywood memoir, *The Air Battle of Ploesti*, 17, 21; Interview with Herb Gouldon, June 18, 2003; Interview with Richard Jacobson, December 19, 2002; Interview with Grant Caywood, July 6, 2001.
31. Interview with Richard Jacobson, December 19, 2002; Interview with Maurice Gilliam, September 2000; Grant Caywood memoir, *The Air Battle of Ploesti*, 13; Perret, *Winged Victory*, 248; Grant Caywood letter to author January 23, 2003.
32. Interview with Richard Jacobson, December 19, 2002; Interview with Maurice Gilliam, September 2000; Grant Caywood memoir, *The Air Battle of Ploesti*, 13, 21.
33. Shepherd, *Of Men and Wings*, 213.
34. Grant Caywood memoir, *The Air Battle of Ploesti*, 14.
35. Interview with Maurice Erickson, November 21, 2002; Interview with Richard Jacobson, November 25, 2002; Grant Caywood memoir, *The Air Battle of Ploesti*, 14.
36. Interview with Richard Jacobson, November 25, 2002; Grant Caywood memoir, *The Air Battle of Ploesti*, 14; Interview with Maurice Gilliam, August 2000; Perret, *Winged Victory*, 255.
37. Interview with Maurice Erickson, November 21, 2002; Interview with Maurice Gilliam, April 2002;
38. Interview with Maurice Gilliam, April 2002; Interview with Richard Jacobson, November 25, 2002; Interview with Grant Caywood, April 8, 2002; Grant Caywood letter to author, January 23, 2003.
39. Grant Caywood letter to author, September 19, 2002; Robert A. Davis letter to author, November 4, 2002

6. March 1944

1. Interview with Maurice Gilliam, August 2000; Interview with Stan Butynski, August 26, 2001; Interview with Richard Jacobson, November 25, 2002; Interview with Grant Caywood, July 6, 2001.
2. Davis, *History of the 450th BG*, 92; Davis, *Cottontails*, 19; Gilliam *Diary*, 1.
3. Gilliam *Diary*, 1; Interview with Harold McCraw, March 12, 2003; Reaford McCraw's *Distinguished Flying Cross* Citation (copy in possession of author).
4. Grant Caywood Papers.
5. Davis, *Cottontails*, 19; Gilliam *Diary*, 1.
6. Perret, *Winged Victory*, 247.
7. 450th Bombardment Group, Special Narrative Report No. 34, Mission of March 11, 1944, 450th Bombardment Group Records, Air Force Historical Research Agency, Maxwell Air Force Base, Alabama. (Hereafter, all Special Narrative Reports will be referenced as 450th S-2 Report No., followed by the date of the mission); Wesley Frank Craven and James Lea Cate, editors, *The Army Air Forces in World War II, Volume III Europe: Argument to V-E Day January 1944 to May 1945*, Chicago, 1951, 358 (Hereafter referred to as Craven and Cate, *AAF WWII*, Vol. III).
8. Gilliam *Diary*, 1.
9. 450th S-2 Report No. 34, March 11, 1944; Gilliam *Diary*, 1.
10. Robinson *Diary*, March 12 and 13, 1944 entries; Interview with Richard Jacobson, November 25, 2002.
11. 450th S-2 Report No. 35, March 17, 1944; Gilliam *Diary*, 1; Jacobson *Diary*, March 17, 1944 entry; Craven and Cate, *AAF WWII*, Vol. III, 283.
12. 450th S-2 Report No. 35, March 17, 1944;

Interview with Ted Morris, July 6, 2001; Gilliam *Diary*, 1.

13. 450th S-2 Report No. 35, March 17, 1944; Gilliam *Diary*, 1; Jacobson *Diary*, March 17, 1944 entry.

14. Interview with Carol Ritter, April 21, 2003; John Barnacle Diary, March 17, 1944 entry; Interview with Harold McCraw, June 3, 2003. McCraw's mother wanted to bring his body home, but the family decided that "it would just be more grief." Therefore, after the war his remains were moved to the Rome-Sicily Cemetery near Anzio.

15. 450th S-2 Report No. 36, March 18, 1944; Gilliam *Diary*, 1; Jacobson *Diary*, March 18, 1944 entry; Craven and Cate, *AAF WWII*, Vol. III, 351.

16. 450th S-2 Report No. 36, March 18, 1944; Gilliam *Diary*, 1; Jacobson *Diary*, March 18, 1944 entry.

17. 450th S-2 Report No. 37, March 19, 1944; Gilliam *Diary*, 1–2; Jacobson *Diary*, March 19, 1944 entry; Craven and Cate, *AAF WWII*, Vol. III, 38; Shepherd, *Of Men and Wings*, 80–81.

18. 450th S-2 Report No. 37, March 19, 1944; Gilliam *Diary*, 1–2; Jacobson *Diary*, March 19, 1944 entry.

19. 450th S-2 Report No. 37, March 19, 1944.

20. Richard Jacobson letter to author, March 6, 2003.

21. 450th S-2 Report No. 38, March 24, 1944; Gilliam *Diary*, 2; Jacobson *Diary*, March 24, 1944 entry.

22. Gilliam *Diary*, 2; Grant Caywood Papers.

23. 450th S-2 Report No. 39, March 28, 1944; Gilliam *Diary*, 2.

24. 450th S-2 Report No. 39, March 28, 1944; Gilliam *Diary*, 2; Jacobson *Diary*, March 28, 1944 entry.

25. 450th S-2 Report No. 40, March 29, 1944; Gilliam *Diary*, 2; Jacobson *Diary*, March 29, 1944 entry.

26. 450th S-2 Report No. 40, March 29, 1944; Gilliam *Diary*, 2; Jacobson *Diary*, March 29, 1944 entry.

27. 450th S-2 Report No. 40, March 29, 1944.

28. 450th S-2 Report No. 41, March 30, 1944; Shepherd, *Of Men and Wings*, 108.

29. 450th S-2 Report No. 41, March 30, 1944; Robinson *Diary*, March 30, 1944 entry; Gilliam *Diary*, 2; Jacobson *Diary*, March 30, 1944 entry.

30. Due to his early start, Maurice Gilliam had 11 credited missions at the end of March 1944.

7. April 1944

1. Romania was spelled Rumania during WWII and appears as such on most period documents. The modern-day spelling is used throughout the text to avoid any confusion

2. Davis, *History of the 450th BG*, 101; Shepherd, *Of Men and Wings*, 79–80; Patrick Macdonald, *Through Darkness to Light*, Worcestershire, England, 1994.

3. 450th S-2 Report No. 42, April 2, 1944; Shepherd, *Of Men and Wings*, 80–81.

4. 450th S-2 Report No. 42, April 2, 1944; Shepherd, *Of Men and Wings*, 81.

5. 450th S-2 Report No. 42, April 2, 1944; Gilliam *Diary*, 3; Jacobson *Diary*, April 2, 1944 entry.

6. 450th S-2 Report No. 42, April 2, 1944; Gilliam *Diary*, 3; Jacobson *Diary*, April 2, 1944 entry.

7. Shepherd, *Of Men and Wings*, 83.

8. 450th S-2 Report No. 42, April 2, 1944; Gilliam *Diary*, 3; Jacobson *Diary*, April 2, 1944 entry.

9. 450th S-2 Report No. 43, April 3, 1944; Craven and Cate, *AAF WWII*, Vol. III, 281, 290; Shepherd, *Of Men and Wings*, 84.

10. Grant Caywood Papers; 450th S-2 Report No. 43, April 3, 1944; Shepherd, *Of Men and Wings*, 84

11. 450th S-2 Report No. 43, April 3, 1944; Gilliam *Diary*, 3; Jacobson *Diary*, April 3, 1944 entry.

12. Grant Caywood Papers; Gilliam *Diary*, 3; Jacobson *Diary*, April 4, 1944 entry; Craven and Cate, *AAF WWII*, Vol. III, 283, 290.

13. 450th S-2 Report No. 44, April 4, 1944; Shepherd, *Of Men and Wings*, 86.

14. 450th S-2 Report No. 44, April 4, 1944; Shepherd, *Of Men and Wings*, 86–90.

15. Gilliam *Diary*, 3; Jacobson *Diary*, April 4, 1944 entry; Shepherd, *Of Men and Wings*, 85, 90.

16. Craven and Cate, *AAF WWII*, Vol. III, 172–173; Davis, *Cottontails*, 20.

17. Craven and Cate, *AAF WWII*, Vol. III, 172–173, 177.

18. Grant Caywood memoir, *The Air Battle of Ploesti*, 2; 450th S-2 Report No. 45, April 5, 1944.

19. Davis, *History of the 450th BG*, 102; Richard Jacobson letter to author, March 13, 2003; Shepherd, *Of Men and Wings*, 94.

20. Grant Caywood Papers; Interview with Grant Caywood, April 8, 2002.

21. 450th S-2 Report No. 46, April 7, 1944; Shepherd, *Of Men and Wings*, 95.

22. 450th S-2 Report No. 46, April 7, 1944; Craven and Cate, *AAF WWII*, Vol. III, 380; Shepherd, *Of Men and Wings*, 95–96.
23. 450th S-2 Report No. 46, April 7, 1944; Gilliam *Diary*, 3–4; Jacobson *Diary*, April 7, 1944 entry; 720th Squadron War Diary, April 7, 1944 entry.
24. Robinson *Diary*, April 9, 1944 entry; 720th Squadron War Diary, April 9, 1944 entry.
25. Shepherd, *Of Men and Wings*, 98–99; Robinson *Diary*, April 11, 1944 entry.
26. Davis, *Cottontails*, 21–22; Gilliam *Diary*, 4; Jacobson *Diary*, April 12, 1944 entry; Shepherd, *Of Men and Wings*, 99; Perret, *Winged Victory*, 264.
27. 450th S-2 Report No. 47, April 12, 1944; Gilliam *Diary*, 4; Jacobson *Diary*, April 12, 1944 entry.
28. Interviews with Ted Morris, July 6, 2001 and December 10, 2002; *St. Louis Star-Times*, May 2, 1944, 7.
29. Interviews with Ted Morris, July 6, 2001 and December 10, 2002.
30. Interviews with Ted Morris, July 6, 2001 and December 10, 2002; *St. Louis Star-Times*, May 2, 1944, 7; *St. Louis Post-Dispatch*, June 22, 1944.
31. Interviews with Ted Morris, July 6, 2001 and December 10, 2002.
32. 450th S-2 Report No. 47, April 12, 1944.
33. 450th S-2 Report No. 47, April 12, 1944; Shepherd, *Of Men and Wings*, 100–101; *AAF Guide*, 230.
34. 450th S-2 Report No. 48, April 13, 1944; Shepherd, *Of Men and Wings*, 101–102.
35. 450th S-2 Report No. 48, April 13, 1944; Jacobson *Diary*, April 13, 1944 entry; Shepherd, *Of Men and Wings*, 103.
36. 450th S-2 Report No. 49, April 15, 1944; Shepherd, *Of Men and Wings*, 103; Jacobson *Diary*, April 15, 1944 entry; Gilliam *Diary*, 4.
37. Bowman, *B-24 Liberator*, 56.
38. Bowman, *B-24 Liberator*, 56.
39. Boyne, *Clash of Wings*, 296.
40. Bowman, *B-24 Liberator*, 57.
41. Craven and Cate, *AAF WWII*, Vol. III, 14; Undated, clipped advertisement for "Mickey" Radar Bombsight by Philco, from the Sam Stein Papers.
42. Bowman, *B-24 Liberator*, 56; Undated, clipped advertisement for "Mickey" Radar Bombsight by Philco, from the Sam Stein Papers; Undated, clipped advertisement for War Bonds featuring "Mickey" Radar Bombsight, from the Sam Stein Papers.
43. Bowman, *B-24 Liberator*, 56; Shepherd, *Of Men and Wings*, 104; Interview with Ted Morris, July 6, 2001.
44. Interview with Grant Caywood, June 28, 2001.
45. 450th S-2 Report No. 49, April 15, 1944; Gilliam *Diary*, 4; Jacobson *Diary*, April 15, 1944 entry; Robinson *Diary*, April 15, 1944 entry.
46. 450th S-2 Report No. 49, April 15, 1944; 720th Squadron War Diary, April 15, 1944 entry; Gilliam *Diary*, 4; Jacobson *Diary*, April 15, 1944 entry.
47. 450th S-2 Report No. 49, April 15, 1944; Gilliam *Diary*, 4; Jacobson *Diary*, April 15, 1944 entry; Davis, *Cottontails*, 22; Robinson *Diary*, April 16, 1944 entry.
48. Davis, *Cottontails*, 22.
49. Shepherd, *Of Men and Wings*, 105.
50. Gilliam *Diary*, 4–5; Jacobson *Diary*, April 17, 1944 entry; Robinson *Diary*, April 17, 1944 entry; 720th Squadron War Diary, April 16, 1944 entry.
51. Robinson *Diary*, April 17, 1944 entry; 720th Squadron War Diary, April 17, 1944 entry; Shepherd, *Of Men and Wings*, 108.
52. 450th S-2 Report No. 51, April 17, 1944; Robinson *Diary*, April 17, 1944 entry; Grant Caywood Papers.
53. Robinson *Diary*, April 17, 1944 entry; Gilliam *Diary*, 4–5; Jacobson *Diary*, April 17, 1944 entry; 450th S-2 Report No. 51, April 17, 1944.
54. 450th S-2 Report No. 51, April 17, 1944.
55. 720th Squadron War Diary, April 17, 1944 entry; Gilliam *Diary*, 5; Robert Stricklin to Sister, Letter of April 19, 1944, copy in possession of author, courtesy of Irene Stricklin Frazier; Robinson *Diary*, April 19, 1944 entry.
56. 450th S-2 Report No. 52, April 20, 1944.
57. 450th S-2 Report No. 52, April 20, 1944; Gilliam *Diary*, 5; Robinson *Diary*, April 20, 1944 entry; Jacobson *Diary*, April 20, 1944 entry; Shepherd, *Of Men and Wings*, 109–110.
58. Jacobson *Diary*, April 20, 1944 entry; Gilliam *Diary*, 5. For Maurice Gilliam the April 20, 1944 mission was his twenty-sixth one.
59. *Cottontails*, 22; Robinson *Diary*, April 21, 1944 entry; 720th Squadron War Diary, April 22, 1944 entry.
60. Interview with Ted Morris, July 6, 2001; Interview with Maurice Erickson, January 2002.
61. Perret, *Winged Victory*, 232; *AAF Guide*, 62; Davis, *Cottontails*, 21–22; Gilliam *Diary*, 5.
62. 450th S-2 Report No. 55, April 24, 1944; Interviews with Ted Morris, July 6, 2001 and December 2, 2002; Interview with Maurice Erickson, January 2002.
63. Interviews with Ted Morris, July 6, 2001 and December 2, 2002; Interview with Maurice Erickson, January 2002; Interview with Richard Jacobson, December 19, 2002.

64. Interview with Ted Morris, July 6, 2001; Gilliam *Diary*, 5; Jacobson *Diary*, April 24, 1944 entry.

65. Interviews with Ted Morris, July 6, 2001, December 2, 2002 and April 3, 2003; Interviews with Maurice Gilliam, August 2000 and June 27, 2001; Interview with Stan Butynski, August 26, 2001.

66. Interviews with Ted Morris, July 6, 2001 and December 2, 2002; Interview with Richard Jacobson, December 19, 2002; Interview with Maurice Erickson, January 2002; Interview with Maurice Gilliam, August 2000.

67. Interview with Maurice Erickson, January 2002.

68. Richard Jacobson letter to author, April 12, 2003. When Jake returned to base, he took the parachute to be inspected. It had been packed wrong. A detailed inspection also revealed that the chute had a large hole. They gave Jake a portion of the parachute as a souvenir. Ironically, it bore the number 13.

69. Interviews with Ted Morris, July 6, 2001 and December 2, 2002; Interview with Richard Jacobson, December 19, 2002; Interview with Maurice Erickson, January 2002; Interview with Maurice Gilliam, August 2000; Robinson *Diary*, April 24, 1944 entry.

70. Interview with Ted Morris, July 6, 2002; Interview with Maurice Gilliam, June 27, 2001.

71. Interview with Maurice Gilliam, June 27, 2001.

72. Interview with Maurice Gilliam, June 27, 2001.

73. Interview with Ted Morris, July 6, 2001.

74. Interview with Richard Jacobson, December 19, 2002; Interview with Maurice Erickson, January 2002.

75. Interview with Maurice Gilliam, August 2002; Interview with Maurice Erickson, January 2002; Interview with Richard Jacobson, December 19, 2002.

76. Interview with Ted Morris, July 6, 2001.

77. Interview with Richard Jacobson, December 19, 2002; Gilliam *Diary*, 5. An accident report for Shadow's crash of April 24, 1944 does not exist. For various reasons, this is the case for nearly 40% of WWII air crashes.

78. Interview with Ted Morris, July 6, 2002; Mae Mills Link and Hubert A. Coleman, *Medical Support: Army Air Forces in World War II*, 469, 471; Robinson *Diary*, April 25, 1944 entry; Jacobson *Diary*, May 31, 1944 entry.

79. Interview with Richard Jacobson, December 19, 2002; Interview with Maurice Gilliam, August 2000; Interview with Maurice Erickson, January 2002.

80. Robinson *Diary*, April 26, 1944 entry; 450th S-2 Report No. 57, April 28, 1944; Shepherd, *Of Men and Wings*, 116; Jacobson *Diary*, April 28, 1944 entry; 720th Squadron War Diary, April 28, 1944 entry.

81. 450th S-2 Report No. 57, April 28, 1944; Jacobson *Diary*, April 28, 1944 entry; Gilliam *Diary*, 6; Robinson *Diary*, April 28, 1944 entry.

82. 450th S-2 Report No. 59, April 30, 1944; Jacobson *Diary*, April 30, 1944 entry; Gilliam *Diary*, 6; Shepherd, *Of Men and Wings*, 119.

83. 450th S-2 Report No. 59, April 30, 1944; Jacobson *Diary*, April 30, 1944 entry; Gilliam *Diary*, 6; Shepherd, *Of Men and Wings*, 120

8. May 1944

1. 720th Squadron War Diary, May 1, 1944 entry; Davis, *History of the 450th BG*, 109.

2. Davis, *History of the 450th BG*, 109; 720th Squadron War Diary, May 2, 1944 entry; Interview with Richard Jacobson, December 19, 2002.

3. 720th Squadron War Diary, May 3, 1944 entry; Gilliam Diary, 6.

4. Evans E. Kerrigan, *American War Medals and Decorations*, New York, 1964, 36.

5. Perret, *Winged Victory*, 415.

6. Perret, *Winged Victory*, 415; Kerrigan, *American War Medals and Decorations*, 36.

7. Grant Caywood memoir, *The Air Battle of Ploesti*, 7–9.

8. Grant Caywood memoir, *The Air Battle of Ploesti*, 8.

9. 450th S-2 Report No. 60, May 5, 1944; Shepherd, *Of Men and Wings*, 123; Gilliam *Diary*, 6; Jacobson *Diary*, May 5, 1944 entry; 720th Squadron War Diary, May 5, 1944 entry.

10. 450th S-2 Report No. 60, May 5, 1944.

11. 450th S-2 Report No. 60, May 5, 1944; Shepherd, *Of Men and Wings*, 127.

12. 450th S-2 Report No. 60, May 5, 1944; Shepherd, *Of Men and Wings*, 127.

13. Gilliam *Diary*, 6; Jacobson *Diary*, May 5, 1944 entry.

14. Shepherd, *Of Men and Wings*, 128; Carter and Mueller, *AAF Combat Chronology 1941–1945*, 335.

15. 450th S-2 Report No. 61, May 6, 1944; 720th Squadron War Diary, May 6, 1944 entry.

16. 450th S-2 Report No. 61, May 6, 1944; Gilliam *Diary*, 6.

17. 450th S-2 Report No. 61, May 6, 1944.

18. 720th Squadron War Diary, May 6, 1944 entry; Grant Caywood letter to author, April 8, 2003.

19. Davis, *Cottontails*, 23; Shepherd, *Of Men and Wings*, 128; 720th Squadron War Diary, May 7, 1944 entry.
20. 720th Squadron War Diary, May 8, 1944 entry; Shepherd, *Of Men and Wings*, 129.
21. Davis, *Cottontails*, 23; Interview with Richard Jacobson, September 23, 2002; 720th Squadron War Diary, May 9 and 10, 1944 entries.
22. Gilliam *Diary*, 7; Jacobson *Diary*, May 12, 1944 entry; 720th Squadron War Diary, May 12, 1944 entry.
23. 450th S-2 Report No. 64, May 12, 1944; Gilliam *Diary*, 7; Jacobson *Diary*, May 12, 1944 entry.
24. 720th Squadron War Diary, May 12, 1944 entry.
25. Interview with Richard Jacobson, December 19, 2002; Interview with Maurice Gilliam, April 2002; McManus, *Deadly Sky*, 235–238; Perret, *Winged Victory*, 412.
26. Interview with Richard Jacobson, December 19, 2002.
27. Interview with Richard Jacobson, December 19, 2002.
28. Davis, *Cottontails*, 23; Gilliam *Diary*, 7; Jacobson *Diary*, May 22, 1944 entry.
29. 450th S-2 Report No. 70, May 22, 1944; 720th Squadron War Diary, May 22, 1944 entry; Shepherd, *Of Men and Wings*, 138.
30. 450th S-2 Report No. 70, May 22, 1944; Gilliam *Diary*, 7; Jacobson *Diary*, May 22, 1944 entry.
31. 720th Squadron War Diary, May 22, 1944 entry; Interview with Maurice Gilliam, June 27, 2001; Interview with Sam Stein, December 30, 2002.
32. Davis, *Cottontails*, 24; 720th Squadron War Diary, May 23 and 24, 1944 entries.
33. 450th S-2 Report No. 73, May 25, 1944; Jacobson *Diary*, May 25, 1944 entry; Shepherd, *Of Men and Wings*, 141; Davis, *History of the 450th BG*, 114; Robinson *Diary*, May 25, 1944 entry.
34. Gilliam *Diary*, 7; Jacobson *Diary*, May 26, 1944 entry; Shepherd, *Of Men and Wings*, 142.
35. 450th S-2 Report No. 74, May 26, 1944; Gilliam *Diary*, 7; Jacobson *Diary*, May 26, 1944 entry; Shepherd, *Of Men and Wings*, 142.
36. 450th S-2 Report No. 74, May 26, 1944.
37. Robert Stricklin to "Dearest Merle," Letter of May 26, 1944, Robert Stricklin Papers.
38. Gilliam *Diary*, 7–8; 450th S-2 Report No. 75, May 27, 1944.
39. 450th S-2 Report No. 75, May 27, 1944; Gilliam *Diary*, 7–8; Jacobson *Diary*, May 27, 1944 entry; Shepherd, *Of Men and Wings*, 143.
40. 450th S-2 Report No. 75, May 27, 1944; Gilliam *Diary*, 7–8; Jacobson *Diary*, May 27, 1944 entry; Shepherd, *Of Men and Wings*, 143.
41. 720th Squadron War Diary, May 27, 1944 entry; Gilliam *Diary*, 7–8; Robinson *Diary*, May 28, 1944 entry; Davis, *History of the 450th BG*, 115.
42. Davis, *Cottontails*, 24; Gilliam *Diary*, 8; Jacobson *Diary*, May 31, 1944 entry.
43. Gilliam *Diary*, 8; Jacobson *Diary*, May 31, 1944 entry.
44. Gilliam *Diary*, 8; Jacobson *Diary*, May 31, 1944 entry; Shepherd, *Of Men and Wings*, 146.
45. 450th S-2 Report No. 78, May 31, 1944.
46. 450th S-2 Report No. 78, May 31, 1944; Jacobson *Diary*, May 31, 1944 entr

9. June 1944

1. 720th Squadron War Diary, June 1, 1944 entry.
2. 450th S-2 Report No. 79, June 2, 1944; Gilliam *Diary*, 8; Carter and Mueller, *AAF Combat Chronology 1941–1945*, 359, 695.
3. 450th S-2 Report No. 79, June 2, 1944.
4. 720th Squadron War Diary, June 3, 1944 entry; Carter and Mueller, *AAF Combat Chronology 1941–1945*, 360; Caywood, *I Remember*, Volume 1.
5. Davis, *History of the 450th BG*, 119; Gilliam *Diary*, 8; Shepherd, *Of Men and Wings*, 148.
6. 450th S-2 Report No. 80, June 4, 1944; Shepherd, *Of Men and Wings*, 149–150.
7. 450th S-2 Report No. 80, June 4, 1944.
8. 720th Squadron War Diary, June 5, 1944 entry; Interview with Irene Frazier, December 6, 2002; Robert Stricklin to "Dearest Merle and Carolyn," Letter of June 5, 1944, Robert Stricklin Papers; Gilliam *Diary*, 8; Bunting, *World War II Day by Day*, 521.
9. Robert Stricklin to "Dearest Merle and Carolyn," Letters of June 5, 1944, Robert Stricklin Papers.
10. 450th S-2 Report No. 82, June 6, 1944; Shepherd, *Of Men and Wings*, 151.
11. 450th S-2 Report No. 82, June 6, 1944.
12. 450th S-2 Report No. 82, June 6, 1944
13. 450th S-2 Report No. 82, June 6, 1944; Interview with Floyd Robinson, December 11, 2002.
14. 720th Squadron War Diary, June 6, 1944 entry; Gilliam *Diary*.
15. Davis, *Cottontails*, 24; 720th Squadron

War Diary, June 8 and 9, 1944 entries; Jacobson *Diary*, June 9, 1944 entry.

16. 720th Squadron War Diary, June 9, 1944 entry; Davis, *Cottontails*, 34–35; Grant Caywood letter to author, June 4, 2003.

17. Shepherd, *Of Men and Wings*, 153; 450th S-2 Report No. 83, June 9, 1944.

18. Gilliam *Diary*, 9; Jacobson *Diary*, June 9, 1944 entry; 450th S-2 Report No. 83, June 9, 1944.

19. Shepherd, *Of Men and Wings*, 153–154.

20. 450th S-2 Report No. 83, June 9, 1944; 720th Squadron Summary Report for June 1944, 450th Bombardment Group Records, Air Force Historical Research Agency, Maxwell Air Force Base, Alabama.

21. 450th S-2 Report No. 83, June 9, 1944; Interview with Stan Butynski, August 26, 2001; Gilliam *Diary*; Jacobson *Diary*; James Strickland letter to author, July 15, 2003.

22. 720th Squadron War Diary, June 10, 1944 entry.

23. Grant Caywood letter to author, June 4, 2003; Shepherd, *Of Men and Wings*, 156.

24. Carter and Mueller, *AAF Combat Chronology 1941–1945*, 368; Shepherd, *Of Men and Wings*, 156; 720th Squadron War Diary, June 11, 1944 entry.

25. 450th S-2 Report No. 85, June 11, 1944.

26. 450th S-2 Report No. 85, June 11, 1944; 720th Squadron War Diary, June 11, 1944 entry.

27. 450th S-2 Report No. 85, June 11, 1944; 720th Squadron War Diary, June 11, 1944 entry; Gilliam *Diary*; Jacobson *Diary*, June 14, 1944 entry.

28. Shepherd, *Of Men and Wings*, 159.

29. Carter and Mueller, *AAF Combat Chronology 1941–1945*, 371.

30. Shepherd, *Of Men and Wings*, 159.

31. 450th S-2 Report No. 87, June 14, 1944; Jacobson *Diary*, June 14, 1944 entry.

32. Interview with Maurice Erickson, January 2002.

33. Grant Caywood Papers; Caywood, *I Remember*, Volume 1; Interviews with Maurice Erickson, January 2002 and November 21, 2002; Interview with Floyd Robinson, December 11, 2002; Robinson *Diary*; Interview with Irene Frazier, December 6, 2002; Interview with Maurice Gilliam, July 22, 2003.

34. Robinson *Diary*, June 24, 1944 entry; Robinson *POW Diary*, June 24, 1944 entry; Marshall Samms, "I Was Shot Down Over Romania." *Sir! A Magazine for Males*. Vol. 2, No. 12 (September 1945), 12–14, 46–47.

35. 450th S-2 Report No. 90, June 24, 1944; Shepherd, *Of Men and Wings*, 163; Samms, "Romania," 12.

36. 450th S-2 Report No. 90, June 24, 1944; Samms article, 12.

37. 450th S-2 Report No. 90, June 24, 1944.

38. Samms, "Romania," 12; 450th S-2 Report No. 90, June 24, 1944.

39. Samms, "Romania," 12.

40. Samms, "Romania," 12–14.

41. Samms, "Romania," 12–14; Interview with Marshall Samms, June 3, 2003.

42. Interview with Susan Rhynalds, January 15, 2003.

43. Robinson *POW Diary*, June 24, 1944 entry.

44. Robinson *POW Diary*; Samms, "Romania," 46; Interview with Susan Rhynalds, January 15, 2003.

45. Davis, *Cottontails*, 34; 450th S-2 Report No. 105, July 15, 1944; Missing Air Crew Report (MACR) #6995, Record Group 92, Records of the Quartermaster General, National Archives and Records Administration, College Park, Maryland.

46. 450th S-2 Report No. 105, July 15, 1944; Davis, *Cottontails*, 34; Interview with Richard Jacobson, November 25, 2002.

47. Davis, *Cottontails*, 26–27; Shepherd, *Of Men and Wings*, 193–194.

48. 450th S-2 Report No. 105, July 15, 1944; Shepherd, *Of Men and Wings*, 194.

49. MACR #6995.

50. 450th S-2 Report No. 105, July 15, 1944.

51. MACR #6995.

52. Cubbins, *War of the Cottontails*, 178–179.

53. MACR #6995; Robinson *POW Diary*, July 19, 1944 entry.

54. 450th S-2 Report No. 105, July 15, 1944.

55. Interview with Maurice Gilliam, August 2000.

56. Interview with Maurice Gilliam, August 2000; Maurice Gilliam Papers.

57. Interview with Grant Caywood, July 6, 2001; Grant Caywood Papers; Caywood memoir, *I Remember, Section 2*; NARA Form 13038 for Grant D. Caywood.

58. Interview with Maurice Erickson, January 2002.

59. Interview with Ted Morris, July 26, 2001; Ted Morris letter to mother, April 30, 1944 (copy in possession of author).

60. Interviews with Ted Morris, July 26, 2001 and February 14, 2002.

61. Interviews with Ted Morris, July 26, 2001 and February 14, 2002.

62. Interview with Stan Butynski, August 26, 2001.

63. Esquivel Memoir, 4–5.

64. Esquivel Memoir, 5–6; Manuel F. Esquivel, Jr. Papers.

65. Interviews with Richard Jacobson, September 23, 2002, January 23, 2003 and February 5, 2003.

66. Interviews with Richard Jacobson, September 23, 2002 and February 5, 2003.

67. Jacobson *Diary*, June 14, 1944 entry; National Personnel Records Center letter to author, March 13, 2003.

68. Interview with Herb Gouldon, June 18, 2003.

69. Interview with Herb Gouldon, June 18, 2003.

70. Interview with Herb Gouldon, June 18, 2003; NARA Form 13164 for Herbert Gouldon.

71. Interview with Irene Frazier, December 6, 2002; NARA Form 13164 for Robert B. Stricklin; Individual Deceased Personnel File (IDPF) for Robert B. Stricklin, Department of the Army, US Total Army Personnel Command, Alexandria, Virginia. Stricklin was originally buried in the US Military Cemetery in Nueville en Condroz, Belgium as Unknown Soldier X-8213. After careful review of his remains, dental records, and his personnel effects, the Graves Registration Department was able to identify the remains as Robert B. Stricklin. His mother was notified. Once identified, his remains were moved to the Ardennes American Cemetery in Neupre, Belgium.

72. Samms, "Romania," 46; Robinson *POW Diary*.

73. Cubbins, *War of the Cottontails*, 194.

74. Bunting, *World War II Day by Day*, 550–555; Cubbins, *War of the Cottontails*, 238.

75. Cubbins, *War of the Cottontails*, 244–254.

76. Samms, "Romania," 47; Interview with Marshall Samms, June 3, 2003.

77. Davis, *Cottontails*, 35; Interview with Sam Stein, December 30, 2002.

78. Interview with Sam Stein, December 30, 2002.

79. Interview with Sam Stein, December 30, 2002.

Epilogue

1. Bowman, *USAAF Handbook*, 236; Sam Stein Papers.

2. Interviews with Maurice Gilliam, August 2000 and September 2000.

3. Interview with Maurice Gilliam, September 2000.

4. Interview with Maurice Gilliam, September 2000.

5. Caywood, *I Remember*, Volume 2.

6. Caywood, *I Remember*, Volume 2.

7. Caywood, *I Remember*, Volume 2.

8. Caywood, *I Remember*, Volume 2.

9. Caywood, *I Remember*, Volume 2.

10. Caywood, *I Remember*, Volume 2.

11. Interviews with Maurice Erickson, January 2002 and November 21, 2002.

12. Interviews with Ted Morris, December 2, 2002, December 10, 2002 and May 29, 2003.

13. Interviews with Stan Butynski, August 26, 2001 and November 15, 2002.

14. Interview with Jim Esquivel, April 14, 2002; Interview with Rick Esquivel, April 24, 2002; Esquivel Memoir, 6–7.

15. Interview with Jim Esquivel, April 14, 2002; Interview with Rick Esquivel, April 24, 2002; Esquivel Memoir, 6–7.

16. Interviews with Richard Jacobson, September 23, 2002 and April 16, 2003.

17. Interview with Richard Jacobson, September 23, 2002.

18. Interviews with Richard Jacobson, September 23, 2002 and April 16, 2003; Richard Jacobson Papers.

19. Interview with Herb Gouldon, June 18, 2003.

20. Interview with Herb Gouldon, June 18, 2003.

21. Interview with Susan Rhynalds, January 15, 2003; Interview with Marilyn Siebels, September 1, 2002.

22. Interviews with Floyd Robinson, December 11, 2002 and January 3, 2003.

23. Interview with Ted Morris, December 10, 2002.

Bibliography

Interviews

(All conducted by the author; notes are in the possession of the author)

Butynski, Stanley Samuel. Nose Gunner, *Shadow*. Interviews, August 26, 2001, and November 15, 2002.
Caywood, Grant Dodd. Pilot, *Shadow*. Interviews, June 28, 2001, July 6, 2001, April 8, 2002, August 26, 2002 and September 11, 2002.
Erickson, Maurice A. Co-pilot, *Shadow*. Interviews, January 2002 and November 21, 2002
Esquivel, Jim. Son of Manuel Esquivel, Radio Operator, *Shadow*. Interview April 14, 2002.
Esquivel, Rick. Son of Manuel Esquivel, Radio Operator, *Shadow*. Interview April 24, 2002.
Frazier, Irene Stricklin. Sister of Robert B. Stricklin, Bombardier, *Shadow*. Interview December 6, 2002.
Gilliam, Maurice Holt. Tail Gunner, *Shadow*. Interviews of August 2000, September 2000, October 2000, June 27, 2001, September 2, 2001, April 2002, July 22, 2002, September 1, 2002, November 28, 2002, February 4, 2003 and July 22, 2003.
Gouldon, Herb. Navigator, *Shadow*. Interview of June 18, 2003.
Jacobson, Richard Morton. Engineer & Top Turret Gunner, *Shadow*. Interviews of September 23, 2002, November 25, 2002, December 19, 2002, January 23, 2003, February 5, 2003 and April 16, 2003.
McCraw, Harold. Brother of Reaford McCraw, Pilot, *True Love*. Interviews of March 12, 2003 and June 3, 2003.
McKinney, Sallie Gilliam. Sister of Maurice Gilliam, Tail Gunner, *Shadow*. Interview of March 2001.
Morris, Theodore H. Ball Turret Gunner, *Shadow*. Interviews of July 26, 2001, February 14, 2002, June 22, 2002, November 22, 2002, December 2, 2002, December 10, 2002, April 3, 2003 and May 29, 2003.
Rhynalds, Susan C. Sister of Vincent Olney, Replacement Pilot, *Shadow*. Interview of January 15, 2003.
Ritter, Carol. Daughter of John Barnacle, Ball Turret Gunner, *True Love*. Interview of April 21, 2003.

Robinson, Floyd Irvin. Replacement Pilot, *Shadow*. Interview of December 11, 2002.
Samms, Marshall. Navigator, *Shoo Shoo Baby*. Interviews of May 20, 2003 and June 3, 2003.
Siebels, Marilyn. Wife of Vincent Olney, Replacement Pilot, *Shadow*. Interview of September 1, 2002.
Stein, Samuel. Ground Crew, 721st Squadron, 450th Bomb Group. Interview of December 30, 2002.
Sutton, Gayle Gilliam. Sister of Maurice Gilliam, Tail Gunner, *Shadow*. Interview of May 11, 2001.
Woodward, Norman L. Waist Gunner, *Shadow*. Interview of October 4, 2002.

Private Manuscript Sources

(Copies are in the possession of the author)

John Barnacle, *Mission Diary*
Stanley Samuel Butynski Papers
Grant Caywood memoir, *I Remember* (in 2 volumes)
Grant Caywood memoir, *The Air Battle of Ploesti*
Grant Caywood Papers
Manuel F. Esquivel, Jr. Papers
Rita Esquivel memoir (courtesy of Rick Esquivel)
Maurice Holt Gilliam, *Diary of My Missions*
Maurice Holt Gilliam Papers
Richard Morton Jacobson, *Diary of Combat Missions*
Richard Morton Jacobson Papers
Reaford McCraw Papers (courtesy of Harold McCraw)
Theodore H. Morris Papers
Vincent Henry Olney Papers (courtesy of Marilyn Siebels)
Floyd Irvin Robinson, *Diary*
Floyd Irvin Robinson, *POW Diary*
Marshall Samms Papers
Samuel Stein Diary (excerpts)
Samuel Stein Papers
Robert B. Stricklin Papers (courtesy of Irene Stricklin Frazier)

Miscellaneous Correspondence

(With the author)

Grant Dodd Caywood
Robert Davis
Rick Esquivel
Maurice Holt Gilliam
Richard Morton Jacobson
Dava Ladymon (Dallas Genealogical Society)
Suzanne Snaith Levy
Theodore H. Morris
Susan C. Rhynalds
Floyd I. Robinson
Marilyn Siebels
Samuel Stein
James Strickland

Official Documents

Air Force Historical Research Agency, Maxwell Air Force Base, Alabama
Aircraft Accident Report (AAR) #44-7-5-60
450th Bombardment Group Records: microfilm reel 1774
450th Bombardment Group Records: microfilm reel 1775
450th Bombardment Group Records: microfilm reel 1776
Department of the Army, US Total Army Personnel Command, Alexandria, Virginia
Individual Deceased Personnel File (IDPF) for Robert B. Stricklin
National Archives and Records Administration, College Park, Maryland
Missing Aircrew Report (MACR) #6995, Records of the Quartermaster General (Record Group 92)

Training Manuals & Catalogs

Headquarters Army Air Forces, Washington, DC
Bombardiers' Information File (BIF), 1945
Navigators' Information File (NIF), 1945
Gunners' Information File: Flexible Gunnery (GIF), May 1944
Pilots' Information File (PIF), 1945
Pilot Training Manual for the Liberator B-24, 1945
Radio Operator's Information File (ROIF), 1945

Newspapers

Boston Evening Globe, 1945
Cotton Tales, 1945
Cotton Tales Continued, 1997–2003
Hood County News (Granbury, TX), 1998
Molto Buono (450th Bomb Group), 1944–1945
Northwest Arkansas Times (Fayetteville), 1943
Oxford Standard (NE), 1978
Sacramento Bee, 1989
St. Louis Post-Dispatch, 1944
St. Louis Star-Times, 1944
Sortie (15th Air Force), 1944–1945
Stars and Stripes, 1944–1945
The Bomb Blast (47th Wing), 1944–1945
The News-Reporter (Whiteville, NC), 2001
The Times-Tribune (Beaver City, NE), 1944
Yank: The Army Weekly, 1944

Articles

Hansen, Chuck. "Flying Guns: Shooting Up the Stratosphere...The First Quarter Century!" *Wings*, Volume 10, Number 4 (August 1980).
Harper, Dale P. "Axis Sally." *World War II*, November 1985.
Mizrahi, Joe. "Sky Guns." *Wings*, Volume 30, Number 3 (June 2000).

Samms, Marshall. "I Was Shot Down Over Romania." *Sir! A Magazine for Males*, Volume 2, Number 12 (September 1945), 12-14, 46-47.

Books

Ambrose, Stephen E. *The Wild Blue: The Men and Boys Who Flew the B-24s Over Germany*. New York: Simon & Schuster, 2001.
Ardery, Philip. *Bomber Pilot: A Memoir of World War II*. Lexington: University of Kentucky Press, 1978.
Bailey, Ronald H. *The Air War in Europe*. Alexandria, VA: Time-Life Books, 1981.
Birdsall, Steve. *Log of the Liberators: An Illustrated History of the B-24*. New York: Doubleday, 1973.
Bowman, Martin. *The B-24 Liberator 1939-1945*. Chicago: Rand McNally, 1979.
Bowman, Martin W. *USAAF Handbook 1939-1945*. Mechanicsburg, PA: Stackpole, 1997.
Boyne, Walter J. *Clash of Wings: World War II in the Air*. New York: Touchstone (Simon & Schuster), 1997.
Breast, John, editor. *Missions Remembered: Recollections of the World War II Air War*. New York: McGraw-Hill, 1998.
Bunting, Edward, senior editor. *World War II Day by Day*. London: Dorling Kindersley, 2001.
Campbell, John M., and Donna Campbell. *Consolidated B-24 Liberator*. Atglen, PA: Schiffer Publishing, 1993.
Carigan, William. *AD LIB: Flying the B-24 Liberator in World War II*. Manhattan, KS: Sunflower University Press, 1988.
Carter, Kit C., and Robert Mueller, editors. *The Army Air Forces in World War II: Combat Chronology, 1941-1945*. Washington, DC: U. S. Government Printing Office, 1973.
Childers, Thomas. *Wings of Morning: The Story of the Last American Bomber Shot Down Over Germany in World War II*. Reading, MA: Perseus Books, 1995.
Comer, John. *Combat Crew: A True Story of Flying and Fighting in World War II*. New York: William Morrow, 1988.
Craven, Wesley Frank, and James Lea Cate, editors. *The Army Air Forces in World War II, Volume III Europe: Argument to V-E Day January 1944 to May 1945*. Chicago: University of Chicago Press, 1951.
Cubbins, William R. (Lt. Col., USAF ret.) *The War of the Cottontails: A Bomber Pilot with the Fifteenth Air Force Against Nazi Germany*. Chapel Hill, NC: Algonquin Books, 1989.
Currier, Donald R. *50 Mission Crush*. Shippensburg, PA: Burd Street Press, 1992.
Davis, Larry. *B-24 Liberator in Action*. Carrollton, TX: Squadron/Signal Publications, 1987.
Davis, Robert A. *450th Bomb Group (H): The "Cottontails" of World War II*. Paducah, KY: Turner, 1996.
_____, editor. *History of the 450th Bombardment Group*. Privately published, November 1989.
Dickinson, Thomas A. *The Aeronautical Dictionary*. New York, Thomas Y. Crowell, 1945
Dorr, Robert F. *B-24 Liberator Units of the Fifteenth Air Force*. London: Osprey, 2000.
Ethell, Jeffrey L. *Bomber Command*. Osceola, WI: Motorbooks International, 1994.
_____. *Bombers of World War II*. Ann Arbor, MI: Lowe & B. Publishers, 2001.
Fagan, Vincent F. *Liberator Pilot: The Cottontails' Battle for Oil*. Carlsbad, CA: California Aero Press, 1991.
Fili, William J. *Passage to Valhalla: The Human Side of Aerial Combat Over Nazi Occupied Europe*. Media, PA: Filcon Pulishers, 1991.
Frankland, Noble. *Bomber Offensive: The Devastation of Europe*. New York: Ballantine, 1970.
Freeman, Roger A. *Experiences of War: The American Airman in Europe*. Osceola, WI: Motorbooks International, 1991.
Hammel, Eric. *Air War Europa: America's Air War Against Germany in Europe and North America 1942-1945, Chronology*. Pacifica, CA: Pacifica Press, 1994.
Hastings, Max. *Bomber Command*. New York: Touchstone, 1989.

Hemphill, William Edwin, editor. *Aerial Gunner from Virginia: The Letters of Don Moody to His Family during 1944.* Richmond: Virginia State Library, 1950.
Hess, William N., Frederick A. Johnsen and Chester Marshall. *Big Bombers of World War II.* Ann Arbor, MI: Lowe & B. Publishers, 1998.
Gatewood, Betty Jean Belkham, and Vernon L. Gatewood. *Kriegie 7956: A World War II Bombardier's Pursuit of Freedom.* Shippensburg, PA: Burd Street Press, 2001.
Johnsen, Frederick A. *B-24 Liberator.* Osceola, WI: Motorbooks International, 1993.
Kaplan, Philip. *Bombers: The Aircrew Experience.* London: Aurum Press, 2000.
Kerrigan, Evans B. *American War Medals and Decorations.* New York: Viking Press, 1964.
Lake, Jon. *The Great Book of Bombers.* San Diego: Thunder Bay Press, 2002.
Link, Mae Mills, and Hubert A. Coleman. *Medical Support of the Army Air Forces in World War II.* Washington, DC: Office of the Surgeon General, USAF, 1955.
Macdonald, Patrick. *Through Darkness to Light* (205 Group RAF). Worcestershire, England: Images Publishing, 1994.
Maguire, Jon A. *Gear Up! Flight Clothing & Equipment of USAAF Airmen in World War II.* Atglen, PA: Schiffer Publishing, 1995.
_____. *More Silver Wings, Pinks & Greens: An Expanded Study of USAS, USAAC, & USAAF Uniforms, Wings & Insignia 1913-1945, including Civilian Auxiliaries.* Atglen, PA: Schiffer Publishing, 1996.
McCutcheon, Marc. *The Writer's Guide to Everyday Life from Prohibition through World War II.* Cincinnati: Writer's Digest Books, 1995.
McGuire, Melvin W. and Robert Hadley. *Bloody Skies, A 15th AAF B-17 Combat Crew: How They Lived and Died.* Las Cruces, NM: Yucca Tree Press, 1993 (June 2000 reprint).
McGuire, William C., II. *After the Liberators: A Father's Last Mission, a Son's Lifelong Journey.* Boone, NC: Parkway Publishers, 1999.
McManus, John C. *Deadly Sky: The American Combat Airman in World War II.* Novato, CA: Presidio Press, 2000.
Maurer, Maurer, editor. *Air Force Combat Units of World War II.* Edison, NJ: Chartwell Books, 1994 (reprint of 1961 edition).
Morgan, Col. Robert with Ron Powers. *The Man Who Flew the Memphis Belle: Memoir of a World War II Bomber Pilot.* New York: Dutton, 2001.
Muller, Werner. *German Flak in World War II.* Atglen, PA: Schiffer Publishing, 1998.
Nalty, Bernard C., John F. Shiner and George M. Watson. *With Courage: The U.S. Army Air Forces in World War II.* Washington, DC: U.S. Government Printing Office, 1994.
Newby, Leroy W. *Into the Guns of Ploesti.* Osceola, WI: Motorbooks International, 1991.
_____. *Target Ploesti: View from a Bombsight.* Novato, CA: Presidio, 1983.
Nijboer, Donald, and Dan Patterson. *Gunner: An Illustrated History of World War II Aircraft Turrets and Gun Positions.* Ontario: Boston Mills Press, 2001.
Norris, John. *88mm Flak 18/36/73/41 & PaK 43: 1936-1945.* Oxford, England: Osprey, 2002.
Novey, Jack. *The Cold Blue Sky: A B-17 Gunner in World War Two.* Charlottesville, VA: Howell Press, 1997.
The Official Guide to the Army Air Forces: A Directory, Almanac and Chronicle of Achievement. New York: Pocket Books, June 1944.
O'Leary, Michael. *Production Line to Frontline (4): Consolidated B-24 Liberator.* Oxford, England: Osprey, 2002.
O'Neill, Brian D. *Half a Wing, Three Engines and a Prayer: B-17s Over Germany.* New York: McGraw-Hill, 1999.
Overy, Richard. *Bomber Command 1939-1945.* London: Harper Collins, 1997.
Patterson, Dan, Paul Perkins and Michelle Crean. *The Soldier: Consolidated B-24 Liberator.* Charlottesville, VA: Howell Press, 1994.
Perret, Geoffrey. *Winged Victory: The Army Air Forces in World War II.* New York: Random House, 1993.
Rochlin, Fred. *Old Man in a Baseball Cap: A Memoir of World War II.* New York: HarperCollins, 1999.

Bibliography

Rottman, Gordon and Francis Chin. *US Army Air Force: 1.* London: Osprey, 1993.

_____ and _____. *US Army Air Force: 2.* London: Reed International, 1994.

Rust, Kenn C. *Fifteenth Air Force Story.* Temple City, CA: Historical Aviation Album, 1976.

Shepherd, D. William. *Of Men and Wings: The First 100 Missions of the 449th Bombardment Group (January 1944–July 1944) Fifteenth Air Force World War II.* Panama City, FL: Norfield, 1996.

Steinbeck, John. *Bombs Away: The Story of a Bomber Team.* New York: Viking Press, 1942.

Stewart, John L. *The Forbidden Diary: A B-24 Navigator Remembers.* New York: McGraw-Hill, 1998.

Sweeting, C. G. *Combat Flying Clothing: Army Air Force Clothing through World War II.* Washington, DC: Smithsonian Institution Press, 1984.

_____. *Combat Flying Equipment: U.S. Army Aviators' Personal Equipment, 1917–1945.* Washington, DC: Smithsonian Institution Press, 1989.

Swift, Michael, and Michael Sharpe. *Historical Maps of World War II Europe.* London: PRC Publishing Ltd., 2000.

Thole, Lou. *Forgotten Fields of America: World War II Bases and Training Then and Now, Volume 1.* Missoula, MT: Pictorial Histories Publishing Co., 1996.

_____. _____. *Volume 2.* Missoula, MT: Pictorial Histories Publishing Co., 1999.

Verrier, Anthony. *The Bomber Offensive: The Exciting Saga of the American and British Strategic Bomber Offensive Against Germany from 1939 to 1945.* London: B. T. Batsford, 1968.

Watry, Charles A., and Duane L. Hall. *Aerial Gunners: The Unknown Aces of World War II.* Carlsbad, CA: California Aero Press, 1986.

Wilson, Stewart. *Aircraft of World War II.* Fyshwick, ACT 2609, Australia: Aerospace Publications, 1998.

Index

*Numbers in **boldface** indicate photographs.*

ADF (automatic direction finder) 99
Adriatic Sea 72, 101, 120, 123, 133, 165, 167
Aero Engine Works 78
Air Force Historical Research Agency 6
Air Force Memorial Park 198
Air Medal 123, 157, 158, 159, 184, 192
Alamogordo, NM 58, 73
Albuquerque, NM 58
Alderson, WV 79
Alexandria, LA 45
Algiers, Algeria 68
Allen, T/Sgt. Woodrow 188
Alton, Lt. T. 51
Amarilllo, TX 29
Ames, IA 18
Amster, Louis 183, 185, 186
Anderson, Maj. Gen. Frederick L. 78
Andes, 2nd Lt. Otis K. 188, 189
Ann Arbor, MI 44
Ansin, Lalessia 14
Antonescu, Marshal 196
Anzio, Italy 168
Arabi, LA 201
Arcadia, FL 43
Archidamo (King of Sparta) 74
Ardennes American Cemetery (Neupre, Belgium) 195
Argus Camera 201
Arlen, Richard 41
Army Air Corps (AAC) 20, 21, 22, 23, 27, 28, 33, 34, 48, 49, 50, 52, 55, 56

Army Air Force (AAF) 35, 36, 37, 38, 44, 45, 53, 56, 58, 66, 72, 75, 83, 129, 139, 163, 164, 165, 189, 195
Army Air Forces: 2nd Army Air Force 73; 8th Army Air Force 2, 71, 78, 139, 157; 9th Army Air Force 157; 12th Army Air Force 72, 157, 200; 15th Army Air Force 2, 67, 70, 71, 72, 73, 78, 104, 125, 126, 129, 130, 131, 132, 133, 139, 142, 153, 157, 161, 170, 171, 173, 176, 177, 181, 187, 189, 196
Arnold, Henry H. "Hap" 55, 96
Arsenal Technical School 34
AT-7 41
AT-9 40
AT-10 40
AT-17 40
AT-24 40
Atlantic City, NJ 47
ATO (fraternity) 20
Austria 73, 107, 122, 180
Axis Sally 79, 107; *see also* Gillars, Mildred
Axton, VA 9
Ayr, MA 184

B-17 (Flying Fortress) 43, 55, 56, 101, 139, 161, 177, 178, 180, 196
B-24 (Liberator) 43, 44, 49, 53, 55, 56, 57, 58, 60, 65, 77, 79, 80, **81**, **85**, 91, 93, 95, 96, 98, 99, 101, **105**, **106**, **107**, **111**, 112, 114, 115, 116, 117, **118**, 120, 123, 126, 127, 128, 129, 131, 132, 134, **135**, 137, 139, 140, **141**, 142, 143, 149, 153, 156, 161,

162, 163, 164, 166, 167, 169, 170, 172, 173, 174, 175, 176, 177, 178, 179, 180, 181, 190, 191, 193
B-25 (Mitchell) 43, 49
B-26 (Marauder) 55
B-29 55
Back River, VA 60
Baird, Mary Fay 194
Balkans 73
Baltimore, MD 194
Banash, Bernice 22
Bari, Italy 52, 75, 131, 170, 192
Barnacle, Sgt. John 112, **120**
Battle of San Jacinto 29
Bechtel, Jeanetta 201
Belem, Brazil 68
Ben Blewett High School (St. Louis, MO) 22
Benjamin, S/Sgt. Sidney D. 179
Berlin, Germany 79, 115, 130, 158
Berlin Bitch 79; *see also* Axis Sally
Berlitz School of Languages 79
Bethel Evangelical Church 31
Big Week (Feb. 1944) 77
Biggs Field, TX 52
Biloxi, MS 36, 44, 45
Blumenthal, Morty 26
Boca Raton, FL 194
Boca Raton Army Air Field, FL 194
Boeing 55, 56
Boise, ID 73
Bolling Air Force Base 204
Bologna, Italy 132, 176
Bolonzo, Italy 122
Bomb Groups: 2nd Bomb Group 196; 97th Bomb Group 196; 98th Bomb Group 114, 118, 121, 124, 128, 129, 131, 132, 135, 137, 143, 153, 161, 168, 170, 171, 175, 179, 180, 181, 183, 187; 205th Bomb Group (RAF) 125; 376th Bomb Group 114, 115, 122, 126, 127, 128, 129, 131, 133, 135, 137, 143, 153, 161, 169, 170, 171, 174, 175, 179, 180, 181, 183, 187; 449th Bomb Group 122, 128, 129, 131, 133, 135, 137, 140, 141, 142, 143, 153, 159, 161, 163, 164, 167, 168, 169, 170, 171, 174, 175, 179, 181, 182, 183, 187; 450th Bomb Group 2, 4, 5, 6, 7, 52, 70, 71, 72, 73, **75**, 77, 78, **79**, 80, 81, **82**, **83**, **84**, 87, 88, 89, **90**, 93, 95, **104**, **105**, 112, **114**, 116, 118, 119, 120, 121, 122, 124, 125, 126, 127, 128, 129, 131, 132, 133, 135, 137, 138, 139, 140, 142, 143, 153, 156, 159, 160, 161, 162, 163, 164, 166, 167, 168, 169, 170, 171, 172, 174, 175, 176, 177, 178, 179, 180, 181, 182, 183, 187, 188, 189, 195, 196, 197, 198, 199, 204; 451st Bomb Group 114, 115, 117, 122, 128, 131; 454th Bomb Group 196; 482nd Pathfinder Group 139
Bomb Wings: 5th Bomb Wing 72, 126, 127, 132, 171, 176, 178, 180, 188; 47th Bomb Wing 70, 72, 81, 89, 123, 124, 126, 128, 129, 131, 132, 133, 135, 137, 138, 139, 143, 153, 159, 161, 163, 168, 171, 173, 175, 176, 178, 180, 181, 187; 49th Bomb Wing 72, 131, 132, 138, 171, 176, 178, 180, 181; 55th Bomb Wing 72, 132, 138, 171, 176, 178; 304th Bomb Wing 72, 126, 127, 132, 138, 171, 176, 178, 180
Book of Life 16
Bor, Yugoslavia 163
Born, Brig. Gen. Charles 196
Boston, MA 25, 27, 64, 193, 197
Boston Latin School 27
Boston Navy Yard 197
Boston Technical Institute 27
Boston University 27
Bostonian Shoes 202
Boulder Dam 19
Brandisi, Italy 88
Brasov, Romania 140, 161, 162, 173, 176
Braves Field (Boston, MA) 26
Brenner Pass 73
Bridgeport, OH 188
Briell, Ethel 21
Brindisi, Italy 131
Britton, S/Sgt. William H. **120**
Brokaw, Tom 4
Brooklyn, NY 2, 27, 66
Brooks Field, TX 52
Broome County, NY 27
Brownwood, TX 29
Bucharest, Romania 104, 129, 130, 138, 139, 140, 163, 183, 186, 189, 195, 196, 197
Buckingham Field, FL 46
Buckley Field, CO 36
Budapest, Hungary 128, 137, 140, 181
Buffalo, NY 21, 43, 191
Burbank Bonfires 42, 200
Burtcheall, Rita 23
Burton, Lindsay 13
Bush, Stella 22
Butynski, Bernice 22
Butynski, Marge 1, **2**, 193
Butynski, Samuel 22
Butynski, Stan 1, **2**, 5, 6, 7, 22–23, 44, 53, 58, 61, **62**, **63**, 67, 83, **85**, 93, 111, **123**, 145, 148, **154**, 157, **159**, **160**, 165, 177, 179, 192, 193, 201

Camp Chaffee, AR 197
Camp Croft, SC 36
Camp Gordon, GA 189
Camp Myles Standish, MA 197
Camp Patrick Henry, VA 73
Camp Shelby, MS 193
Camp Wolters, TX 30
Campbell, Dwight 17
Campbell College 198
Campino, Romania 161
Cannes, France 170
Carlstrom Field, FL 43
Carmel, convent of 75
Casey Jones School of Aeronautics, NJ 47
Casper, WY 193

Casper Army Air Field, WY 193
Cassalnuovo 74
Castellano, Gen. Giuseppe 71
Cathedral of St. Gregory Magnum (Manduria, Italy) 75
Caywood, Gladys "Bud" 16–18
Caywood, Grant Cecil "Pat" 16–20
Caywood, Grant Dodd 2, 5, 16–20, 37–44, 53, **54**, 55, 58, 59, 60, 61, **62**, 63, 65, **67**, 68, 69, 71, 72, 80, 81, 89, 93, 94, **95**, **97**, 99, 103, 104, 105, 110, 111, 112, **113**, 114, 115, 116, 117, 119, 120, **121**, 122, **123**, 124, 126, 128, 131, **132**, 133, 134, 135, 139, 140, 141, 149, 157, 158, 159, 161, 162, 163, 164, 174, 178, 182, 190, 192, 199, 200, 203
Caywood, Grant Nicolaus 42, 190
Caywood, Jeanne "Beo" 41, 42, 53, 190, 199, 200
Caywood, Lindi 200
Caywood, Ruth 200, 201
Cedono, P. F. C. Marquis 140
Centenary Christian Church (Indianapolis, IN) 34
chaff *see* window
Chanute Field, IL 194
Charleston, SC 189
Charleston Army Air Base, SC 189
Charlotte, NC 15, 16, 36
Cheasapeake Bay, VA 60
Chicago, IL 6, 33, 44, 188
Chrysler Corp. 23
Churchill, Sir Winston 138
Civilian Pilot Examining Board 40
Clark, Ed 18
Clark, T/Sgt. Julian C. 140
Clearwater, FL 44
cloud coverage (definition) 106
Clovis, NM 3, 37, 43, 44, 47, 48, 49, 50, 53, 55, 58, 73, 132, 143, 197
Cobb, Bethel Mae 33
Coffeyville, KS 50, 51
Coffeyville Army Air Field, KS 50, **51**
Cohen, Mel 27
Colley, Capt. Gordon T. 162
combat box (element) 94, **95**
Combined Bomber Offensive (CBO) 71, 72, 73
Concordia Vega (oil refinery) 163
Connors, 2nd Lt. Ernest D. **120**
Consolidated Aircraft Corporation 55, 57
Constanta, Romania 180
Convair 57
Copernicus Junior High (Hamtramck, MI) 23
Coral Gables, FL 48, 49
Corsicanna, TX 51
Cotton Club 81, 111
Cottontail Club 111, **114**, 133, 140
Cottontail Theater 168, 171, 177
Cottontails 71, 79, 80, 81, **107**, 115, 119, 126, 129, 131, 134, 140, 141, 142, 153, 167, 170, 178, 182, 187, 189
Courtland, AL 193

Cox, James 183, 184
Craiovi, Romania 161
C-ration 174
Crawford, S/Sgt. Penn W. 188
Crevita, Harold 115, 117
Crosby Metal Stamping Co. 21
Cubbins, 2nd. Lt. William R. 195
Cugine, S/Sgt. Lawrence H. 179
Curtis Wright 22, 44

Daimler-Benz 103
Dakar, Africa 49, 68
Dallas, TX 2, 7, 28, 29, 49, 57, 188
Dallas (TX) Genealogical Society 7
Dallas (TX) Public Library 7
Daly, Capt. 38
Davis, David R. 55
Davis, Robert 6
Davis Wing 55
Davis-Monthan Field, AZ 52
DC-3 20
DDT 196
Deaconess Hospital (Buffalo, NY) 21
Denver, CO 36
Des Moines, IA 16, 18
Detroit, MI 27, 44
Distinguished Flying Cross 112, 192, 195
Distinguished Unit Citation 198
Dobbs, George 183, **184**, 185
Dodd, Gladys Venus 16
Donaldson, William C. 53, 55
Doolittle, James 72
Douglas Company 57
Dundee School 16

Eagle Scout 17
East Carolina University (Brody School of Medicine) 3
East Kane, PA 21
East Kane Grade School 21
Eastern Michigan University 201
Ebriechsdorf, Austria 171
88mm antiaircraft gun 103–104
El Paso, TX 52
element *see* combat box
11th Infantry, Indiana National Guard 34
Elias, Phyllis Harriet 26, 64, 193
Embry-Riddle Company 43
Emmanuel, King Victor III 71
England 71, 72
Enola Gay 197
Erchie, Italy 149, 191
Erickson, Eva 21
Erickson, Gerry 21
Erickson, Lillian 191
Erickson, Maurice 21
Erickson, Maurice A. 2, 7, 20–21, 43–44, **54**, 55, 58, 60, **62**, **67**, 68, 80, 82, 83, 93, 95, **97**, 99, 107, **113**, 121, 122, **123**, 126, 131, 132, 133,

139, 143, 144, 145,147, 148, 153, 155, 157, 159, 162, 163, 164, 165, 168, 170, 171, 172, 173, 174, 177, 179, 181, 182, 190, 191, 201, 204
Esquivel, Barry 201
Esquivel, Carlos 23
Esquivel, James 201
Esquivel, Manuel F., Jr. 3, 5, 23, 45–47, 53, 58, 59–60, 61, **62**, 63, **65**, **67**, **100**, **101**, 107, **109**, 111, **121**, 143, 145, **154**, **159**, **160**, 171, 182, 193, 201, 202
Esquivel, Manuel F., Sr. 23
Esquivel, Raul 23
Esquivel, Renan 23
Esquivel, Rick 201
Esquivel, Rita 23, 45, 46, 59–60, 100, 193, 201
Esquivel, Wayne 201
Evans, S/Sgt. Edward W. 188

Falmouth, MA 43
Fashion Footwear Association of New York 202
Fayetteville, NC 189
Ferdinand, King 74
Ferrara, Italy 132
Fighter Group: 31st 131; 52nd 131
Fighter Wing: 306th 72, 131
First Baptist Church (Omaha, NE) 16
Fisk, Greenleaf 29
Flak (flugzeug abfall kanon) 3, 103–104, **105**, **106**, 107
Flanagan, Sgt. Charles 112, **120**
Flannery, 2nd Lt. John F. 179
Fleet, Dorothy 56
Fleet, Reuben 55
Focke-Wulf FW-190 **97**, 103, 112, 118, 120, 124, 128, 172, 183
Footwear Industry Hall of Fame 202
Ford, Henry 44, 58
Ford Motor Company 57, 58, 66
Forest Avenue High School (Dallas, TX) 30, 195
Fort Beauregard, LA 45
Fort Benjamin Harrison, IN 34
Fort Bragg, NC 189
Fort Devans, MA 194
Fort Dix, NJ 191
Fort George Meade, MD 194
Fort Jackson, SC 36
Ft. Lauderdale, FL 195
Fort Myers, FL 46
Fort Sheridan, IL 44
Fort Smith, AR 197
Fort Worth, TX 43, 57
471st Combat Crew Training School 44
Franklin Park Zoo (Roxbury, MA) 25
FRANTIC 173
Frazier, Irene Stricklin 7
Fresno, CA 45, 46
Fritz, 2nd Lt. George H. 188
Fuggia, Italy 72

Fulks, 2nd Lt. John S. **120**
Furnas County, NE 30
Future Farmers of America 14

Gable, Clark 41, 48
Gaines, MI 5
Galveston, TX 193
Galveston Army Air Field, TX 193
Garden City (NY) Athletic Association 202
Garrison, Whitt 13
"Gee" 138; *see also* Pathfinder
Genoa, Italy 153, 168, 175
George Field, IL 43
German Air Force (GAF) 73, 115, 130, 133
German Army 129
Germany 71, 173, 181
Ghost o' the Omar 179
Gideon, Col. Robert 171, 181
Gillars, Mildred 79–80
Gilliam, David 10
Gilliam, David Walter 14
Gilliam, Donald 13
Gilliam, Gayle 11, 12
Gilliam, Henshaw 10
Gilliam, John 10
Gilliam, Julia Virginia 12
Gilliam, Julian 13
Gilliam, Larry Maurice 198
Gilliam, Lawrence Holt 9–12, 64
Gilliam, Maurice Holt 1, 2, **3**, 4, 5, 6, 7, 9–12, **13**, **14**, 15–16, 35–37, 44, 46, 47, 48, 53, 58, 59, 60, 61, **62**, 63, 64, **67**, 68, 69, **70**, 80, 81, 89, 96, 101, 104, 105, 110, 111, **112**, 114, 119, 120, **123**, 126, 128, 135, 141, 142, 143, 144, 145, 146, 147, 148, **149**, **154**, 156, 157, **159**, 161, 162, 164, 165, 166, 167, 168, 170, 171, 178, 179, 180, **181**, 182, 189, 198, 199
Gilliam, Sallie 11, 12
Gilliam, Sandra Kay 189
Gilliam, Stella Hicks 10–12
Gilliam, Stella McKinney 1, **3**, **37**, 59, 61, 189, 198
Gilliam, Vera 14, 15
Gilliam, Volney Hicks 12
Giulianova, Italy 167
Glen Allen, VA 5
Goldvarg, Capt. Jerome R. 188
Goodfellow Field, TX 49
Goodman, Benny 27
Goths 74
Gouldon, Alfred 27, 28
Gouldon, Fay 195, 203
Gouldon, Hazel 27
Gouldon, Herbert 2, 27–28, 48–49, 53, **54**, 59, **62**, **67**, 68, **98**, 103, **115**, 121, 122, **123**, 131, 146, 157, **158**, 168, 194, 195, 203
Gouldon, Hilda 27
Gouldon, Ruth 27
Gouldon, Stephen 27
Gowan Field, ID 73, 156

Grable, Betty 168
The Grand Ole Opry 13
Grataferrata, Italy 168
Graz, Austria 118, 119, 127
Great Falls, MT 201
The Greatest Generation 4
Griener Field, NH 195
Grottaglie Field, Italy 174
Guilford County, NC 10
Gundlach Elementary (St. Louis, MO) 22
Gunn, Lt. Col. James A. 196
Gunter Field, AL 43

H2S 38, 139; *see also* Pathfinder
H2X 139; *see also* Pathfinder
Hackney, Richard 183, **184**
Hampton, VA 52, 60, 61, 73
Hamtramck, MI 5, 22
Hamtramck (MI) High School 23
Hannibal 74
Hansen, Alice Lucinda 51
Harlingen, TX 44, 45
Harlingen Army Air Field, TX 44, **45**
Haw River (NC) 10, 13
Hawkins, Coleman 26
Hemphill, TX 188
Hempstead, NY 63
Henschel and Sohn Factory 137
Herington, KS 73
Herington Army Air Field, KS 73
Heyman, Etta 25
Heyman, Fred 26
Heyman, George 26
Heyman, Harry 25
Heyman, Paul 26
Hickman AFB 201
Hicks, Helen 16
Hicks, R. W. 15, 16
Hicks, Sallie Lou 9
Hicks, Stella Boyd 9
Hicks, Thomas C. 9
Highwood, IL 44
Hill, Charlotte More 52
Hitler, Adolf 2, 14, 71, 118, 123, 128, 130, 158, 161, 177
Holbrook Elementary School (Hamtramck, MI) 23
Hollinger, NE 30
Holy Family Catholic Church (Stamford, NE) 31
Hondo, TX 191, 193
Hope, Bob 174
Hotel Miramar (Bari, Italy) 131
Houlle, Ethel 192
Houlle, Louis 192
Houston, TX 193
Hughes, Col. Richard D'Oyly 77, 78
Hungary 107, 132, 180, 181
Hutton, Betty 174

Indianapolis, IN 33
Initial Point (IP) 91, 105, 129, 133, 135, 140, 144, 171, 178, 180, 188
International Aerobatic Championship 19
Iowa State College 18, 20
Iowa University 20
Isle of Capri 114
Italy 71, 72, **76**, 77, 122, 142, 167

Jackson Heights, NY 27, 28
Jacksonville, FL 49
Jacobson, Etta **24**, 25
Jacobson, Joanne 194
Jacobson, Phyllis 194, 202, **203**
Jacobson, Richard 3, 5, 6, 23, **24**, 25–27, 47, 53, 58, 59, 61, **62**, 63, **64**, **65**, **67**, 68, 69, **70**, 80, 95, 98, 99, 106, 107, 111, **112**, 114, 115, 117, 118, 120, **123**, 127, 128, 135, 137, 144, 145, 146, 147, 148, **154**, 156, 157, **158**, 163, 165, 166, 167, 171, 172, 181, 182, **183**, 193, 202, **203**
Jacobson, Zismund 25
Jefferson Barracks, MO 22, 44
Jenkins, Marilyn Kay 203
John Henry Brown Elementary School (Dallas, TX) 29
Johnson, S/Sgt. Andrew N., Jr. 188
JU-88 (Junker) 103, 120, 128, 172, 183
Juneau, T/Sgt. Dominique **120**
Jung, Justine 51
Jung family 50

Kalispell, MT 188
Kane, PA 2
Kane (PA) General Hospital 20
Kane (PA) High School 21
Keesler Field, MS 36, 44, 45, 198
Kelly Field, TX 50
K-rations 84, 110

Lackland Field, TX 49
La Guardia Field, NY 47, 190
Lake Orbetello, Italy 153
Lake Success, Long Island 66
Langley Field, VA 59, 60, **61**, 194
La Spezia, Italy 153
Latisano, Italy 166
Lavariano Airdrome 117
Lawrenceville, IL 43
Lecce, Italy 131
Leshner, Marty 25, 27
Let's Face It 174
Ley, Ed 149
L'Heureaux, Armand J. 183, **184**, 185, 186
Liberator *see* B-24
Link trainer 51
Lisbon, Portugal 71
Lisle, NY 3, 27
Litke, Hilda Rejan 27
Lockheed Hudson 42

236 Index

Log Cabin Restaurant (Boston, MA) 26
Longobards 74
Lowes Methodist Church (Rockingham Co., NC) 15
Lowry Field, CO 36, 50
Lubbock, TX 58
Lucky City Motors (Reidsville, NC) 15
Luftwaffe 78, 79, 80, 130
Lycoming R670 39
Lynn Red Sox 202

MacDuff, Dick 18
Macedonia 124
Macy's Department Store 28
Madison, WI 46
Mae West life vest 65, 185
Manchester, NH 195
Manduria, Italy 2, 4, 27, 52, 68, 70, 72, 73, 74, 75, 77, **78**, **79**, 80, **82**, **83**, **84**, **85**, **86**, **87**, **88**, **90**, **91**, 93, 110, **111**, 112, 114, 115, 116, 117, 120, 121, 123, 124, 125, 127, 129, 133, 135, **136**, 138, 139, 140, 142, 146, 153, 154, 155, 156, 159, 161, 162, 163, 164, 165, 166, 167, 170, 172, 174, 176, 177, 178, 180, 182, 187, 189, 193, 196
Manhattan, NY 27
March Army Air Field, CA 190
Marion County, IN 34
Marrakech, French Morocco 68
Marseilles, France 168, 170
Marston mats 83
Marzano, Italy 164
Mason, S/Sgt. John 179
Mason, Red 115, **117**
Massachusetts Homeopathic Hospital (Boston, MA) 25
Massachusetts Institute of Technology (M. I. T.) 139
Massachusetts Institute of Technology Radiation Laboratory 139
Mather Field, CA 40, 41
Maxwell Field, AL 28, 43, 48
McChord Air Force Base, WA 201
McClure, 1st. Lt. Barney H. 179
McCollum's Market (Reidsville, NC) 15
McCraw, 1st Lt. Reaford 111, 112, 114, **116**, 117, 120, 134
McKinney, Stella Leath 14, 15, 36, 38
McNulty, 2nd Lt. Irving B. 179
ME-109 (Messerschmitt Bf-109) 103, 112, 115, 118, 120, 122, 123, 124, 126, 128, 133, 156, 160, 161, 170, 172, 183, 184, 188
ME-110 (Messerschmitt Bf-110) 103, 172, 183
Medical College of Virginia (VCU-MCV) 5
Mediterranean Sea 72, 110, 173
Memphis, TN 188
Memphis Belle 2
Merida, British Honduras (Belize) 23
Messapians 74
Messerschmitt 78, 134

Mestre, Italy 122, 123, 132, 134
Miami, FL 193, 194
Miami University 48
Michael, King (Romania) 196
Mickey see Pathfinder
milk run 89, 182
Miller, Glenn 26
Mills, Col. John Stuart 73, 156, 157
Milwaukee Brewers 26
Mineola, NY 47
Mineral Wells, TX 30
Mitchell Field, NY 63, 64, 66
Model 31 "flying boat" 55
Moffett Field, CA 39, 40
Monroe, LA 48
Montesilvano, Italy 167
Montfalcone, Italy 142
Montgomery, AL 28, 43, 48
Morris, Arthur Holden 21–22
Morris, Donna 201
Morris, Ethel 21
Morris, Ethel Briell 21, 192
Morris, Jeanetta 201
Morris, Ralph 21
Morris, Terry 201
Morris, Theodore H. 3, 5, 21–22, 44, 53, 58, 59, **62**, 63, **67**, 69, **70**, 81, **87**, 88, 96, 101, 111, 116, 128, 135, 137, **138**, 139, 140, 141, 143, 144, 145, **146**, **147**, 149, **150**, 154, 170, 172, 191, **192**, 201, 202, 204
Morrison Field, FL 66, 73
Morse Code 46
Mostar, Yugoslavia 77, 137
Mount Vesuvius 121, **122**, 192
Mountain Home, ID 190
Mountain Home Army Air Field, ID 190
Munich, Germany 27, 104, 178, 179
Muroc, CA 190
Mussolina, Benito 71

Nantasket Beach, MA 25–26
Nanticoke, NY 27
Naples, Italy 52, **122**, 182, 189, 191, 192, 193
Nashville, TN 13, 43
Natal, Brazil 68
National Archives and Records Administration (NARA), College Park, MD 7
National Athletic Honor Society 18
National Personnel Records Center (St. Louis, MO) 6
Netherton, S/Sgt. Thomas W. **120**
Neupert, Eva May 21
Neupre, Belgium 195
New Orleans, LA 3, 23, 45, 47, 193, 201
New York, NY 63, 191
New York University 28, 203
Newport News, VA 59, 192, 193
Newton High School (Brooklyn, NY) 28
Nice, France 168, 169, 170

Nicolaus, Jeanne 40, 41
Nina Footwear 202
1939 World's Fair (NY) 28
Norfolk, VA 189
Normandy, France 176
North American 57
North American AT-6 (Army Trainer) 37, 40, 48
North Great Falls, MT 188

Oboe 138; *see also* Pathfinder
Ocala, FL 48
Ohio Weslyan 80
O'Key Marge 44
Oklahoma University 111
Olney, Alice 51, 203
Olney, Cornelia Susan 30, 31, 32
Olney, Henry Weed 30, 31, 32, 33
Olney, Leonard 30, 31, 33
Olney, Marilyn 204
Olney, Sophia 30
Olney, Vincent 7, 30–32, **33**, 50, **51**, **123**, 129, 132, 133, **135**, 149, **158**, 171, 172, 178, 182, 183, 185, 186, 187, 189, 195, 196, **197**, 203
Olson, Charles J. 51
Omaha, NE 2, 16, 17, 33, 50, 183
Omaha (NE) Central High School 18
Omaha Municipal Airport 17, 18
Operation Gunn 196
Orange Julius (Charlotte, NC) **15**, 16
Orbetello, Italy 153
Oria, Italy 142, 163
Orr, John E. 51
Osborne, 2nd Lt. Lloyd 179
Osijek, Yugoslavia 181
Ostuni, Italy 122, 123
Otis Field, MA 43
OVERLORD 130, 176, 177
Oxford, NE 203, 204
Oxford (NE) Livestock Commission 204
Oxford (NE) Standard 7

P-38 (Lightning) 103, 104, 120, 123, 133, 137, 142, 153, 159, 161, 171, 175, 176, 179, 190
P-47 (Thunderbolt) 137, 142, 159
P-51 (Mustang) 103, 131, 141, 142, 159, 161, 171
Padova (Padua), Italy 123
Palace Dragonetti (Manduria, Italy) 75
Palace Gatti (Manduria, Italy) 75
Palace Giannuzzi (Manduria, Italy) 75
Palace Gigli (Manduria, Italy) 75
Palace Imperiali (Manduria, Italy) 75
Palm Beach, FL 191
Pampa, TX 50
Pampa Air Field, TX 50, 51
Pan American 48, 49
Panama City, FL 36, 48
Partridge, "Rose" Jane 27
Pathfinder 106, 138, 139, 140, 141, 171, 178, 182, 187, 188

PBY-1 55
Pearl Harbor, HI (bombing of) 28, 33, 40, 50
Perkins, Floyd 4
Perret, Geoffrey 157
Pescaro, Italy 167
Petitjean, George 30, 32
Petitjean, Sophia Marie 30
Phenis, Robert H. 51
Piacenzo, Italy 166
Pierce, Ray E. 51
Pierre, SD 17
Piggly Wiggly (Dallas, TX) 29
Piper Cub 18
Pitesti, Romania 161
Ploesti, Romania 2, 7, 104, 129, 130, 131, 133, 140, 143, 144, 146, 147, **148**, 156, 157, 158, 159, 161, 162, 163, 166, 170, 171, 172, 173, 176, 177, 180, 181, 182, 183, 184, 187, 188, 189, 196, 204
POINTBLANK 73, 130
Portland, ME 79
Porto Marghera, Italy 132, 168, **169**, 179
Postal Telegraph (Western Union) 23
Pratt & Whitney 39, 40, 42, 56
Primrose, 2nd Lt. Clyde O. 188
Pritchett family 13
PT-17 Stearman 39
Pueblo, CO 44, 53, 193
Punic War 74
Purple Heart 192, 195

QVC 202, 203

Radio Berlin 79
RAF Bomber Command 78
Raiford, Karen Gilliam 3, 4
Raiford, Neil Hunter 5
Randolph Field, TX 51, 191
Rankin, John G. "Tex" 19, 38
Rankin Aeronautical Academy 20, 37, 38, 39
Rankin Air Circus 19
Red Cross 60, 107–**108**, 165, 197
Regensburg, Germany 78, 79, 111, 134, 178
Reid, Sgt. John R. 188
Reidsville, NC 10, 11, 15, 189, 198
Reidsville (NC) High School 13, 15
Reserve Officers Training Corps (ROTC) 19
Reveille with Beverly 163
Rhynalds, Susan 7, 50, 186, 187
Rimini, Italy 120, 153
River Edge, NJ 188
Riverside, CA 190
Riverside Elementary (Indianapolis, IN) 33
Robertson, Paul 13
Robinson, Alva Mason 33
Robinson, Bethel Mae 33
Robinson, Floyd 7, 33–34, 51, 114, 124, 133, 134, 135, 139, 140, 142, 143, 144, 145, 148, 149, 163, 164, 168, 171, 177, 182, 183, 184, 185, 186, 189, 190, 192, 195, 196, **197**, 204

Rockingham County, NC 10, 61, 198
Rolfe, Lillian Geraldine 21, 43
Romania 107, 125, 129, 132, 161, 173, 174, 189, 196
Romanian National Guard 186
Romano Americana refinery (Ploesti, Romania) 182, 187
Romans 74
Rome, Italy 71, 90, 121
Rome Air Depot, NY 47
Roosevelt Field, NY 47, 48
Roswell Army Air Field, NM 51
Roxbury, MA 3, 25
Roxbury (MA) Memorial High School 26, 27
Royal Air Force (RAF) 71, 125
Rush, Brig. Gen. Hugo P. 72
Russian Army 125
Rustad, 2nd Lt. Warren N. 137

S-2 Narrative (intelligence report) 109, 126, 137, 161, 168, 173
Sacramento, CA 5, 40, 199, 200
St. Louis, MO 3, 16, 19, 21, 22, 44, 201
St. Petersburg, FL 44
Salerno, Italy 71, 72
Saline River, Italy 167
Salt Lake City, UT 37, 41, 44, 46, 53
Samms, Marshall 183, **184**, 186, 195, 196
San Angelo, TX 49
San Antonio, TX 43, 49, 50–52, 191
San Diego, CA 56, 57
San Marcos, TX 41, 43, 200
San Pancrazio, Italy 126, 140, 174, 176, 183
San Stephano, Italy 163, **164**, 166
San Vito Di Normanni(e), Italy 124, 126, 143, 153
Sandler of Boston 202
Santa Ana, CA 43, 192
Santa Cesario, Italy 165, **166**, 167
Santa Maria 193
Santa Monica, CA 190
Saracens 74
Schwab, Edward 183, 185
Schweinfurt, Germany 78
Selman Field, LA 48
Senator Hotel (Sacramento Hotel) 40
Septika, Bill 22
Shackleford, Lewis 183, **184**, **197**
Shadow (B-24) 1, 3, 4, 5, 6, 7, 48, 49, 63, 64, 66, **67**, 68, **69**, 80, 83, **85**, 88, 93, 95, 96, 97, 98, 99, **100**, 102, 107, 108, 109, 110, 111, 116, **118**, 119, 120, **121**, 122, 123, 124, 125, 126, **127**, 128, 129, 132, 133, 135, 137, 140, 142, 143, 145, 146, 147, 148, **151**, **152**, 157, 163, 164, 170, 172, 182, 187, 194, 198, 201, 202, 204
Shadow (Caywood's cocker spaniel) 41, **42**, 43, 53, 55, 62, 66, 190
Shane, Billy 25
Shaw, Artie 26
Shepherd, Dr. William 167, 176
"Shoes on Sale" (QVC) 202

Shoo Shoo Baby (B-24) 182, 183, 184, 185, 187, 189, 195
Sicily 71
Siebels, Marilyn 7
Silver Star 157
Simeria, Romania 173
Sisak, Yugoslavia 181
Sisk, Mildred Elizabeth 79–80
Skopje, Yugoslavia 124
Sleepy Time Gal (B-24) 149, 153, 154, **155**, 157, 159, **160**, 163, 165, 166, 168, 170, 171, 173, 174, 175, 176, 177, 179, 180
Smederevo, Romania 180
Smith, Gen. Bedell 71
Smith, S/Sgt. Lloyd T. 179
Smith, S/Sgt. Philip A. 179
Snaith, William G. 7, 73, **74**, 171, 187, **188**, 189
Sofia, Bulgaria 124, 140, 141
Southern Baptist Theological Seminary 199
Spaatz, Lt. Gen. Carl 78, 130
Specification C-212 55, 56
Sperry bombsite 177
Sperry Gyroscope 66
Spezia, Italy 166
Springfield, MO 192
Squadrons 2nd Air Rescue Squadron 201
Squadrons 4th Airlift Squadron 201
Squadrons 15th Combat Mapping Squadron 72
Squadrons 37th Photo Reconnaissance Squadron 72
Squadrons 720th Squadron 70, 73, **81**, 82, 91, **94**, 111, 131, 132, 133, **134**, 139, 140, 142, **154**, 156, 162, 163, 168, 172, 178, 180, 190
Squadrons 721st Squadron 7, 73, 75, 80, 82, 90
Squadrons 885th Bomb Squadron 72
Stamford, NE 30, 31, 203
Stamford (NE) High School 32
Stanfield, Louise 14
Statue of Liberty 66
Stein, Samuel 75, **80**, 84, 88, 90, 196, 197
Stephenson, Bob 41
Stevens, Chaplain Paul 134
Stewart, Jimmy 41
Steyr, Austria 78, 118, 120, 126, 127, 128
strategic bombing 72
Stricklin, Bessie Merle 29, 176
Stricklin, Charles Fisk 29
Stricklin, Irene 7, 29, 30, 195
Stricklin, Irene Gertrude 29
Stricklin, Mattie Bell 29
Stricklin, Robert Bryant 2, 5, 6, 7, 28–30, 49, **50**, 53, **54**, **62**, 63, **66**, **67**, 96, **115**, 116, **119**, 129, 131, 135, 137, 139, 140, 142, 145, 156, 157, 159, 168, 170, 176, 177, 187, 188, 192, 195, 198
Stricklin, William Edward 29
Stricklin, Wilson Edward 29
Stricklin's Food Store (Dallas, TX) 30
Strother, Maj. (later Gen.) 42, 200
Sunnyvale, CA 39

Index

Surry County, VA 10
Sweet Rosie O'Grady 168
Swisher County, TX 29
Switzerland 122

Tacoma, WA 201
tactical bombing 72
Tagliamento River, Italy 166
"tail end Charlie" 126
Tanem, Vernon 183
Taranto, Italy 73, 88, 110, 197
Targoviste, Romania 159
Taunton, MA 197
Tautfest, 1st Lt. Earl W. 188
Taylor, Corp. Carl L. 188, 189
Taylor, 2nd Lt. William R. **120**
Taylor Field, FL 48
Ten Fighting Cocks (B-24) 179
Theodore Roosevelt Junior High (Roxbury, MA) 26
Third Reich 2, 123, 128, 130, 134
35th Field Hospital (Erchie, Italy) 149, **150**, 191, **192**
Thompson, John W. 56
Thompsonville, NC 10, 11, 12, 14
341st Field Artillery (U.S. Army Reserves) 20
Time Square (NY) 63
Toni Gayle (B-24) 57, **104**
Toulon, France 113, 114, 153
Travelers Health Insurance 16
Travis Air Force Base 201
Treviso, Italy 125, 132, 142
Trieste, Italy 120, 180
Trinity tests 58
Truax Field, WI 46
True Love (B-24) 111, 112, 116, 117, **120**
Tucson, AZ 52
Tucumcari, NM 58
tufa block(s) 81, **109**
Tulare, CA 20, 37
Tulsa, OK 57
Tunis, Tunisia 68
Turner Publishing 7
Twain, Mark 49
Twining, Maj. Gen. Nathan F. 72, 125, 131, 178, 196
Tyndall Field, FL 36, 37, 47, 48

UC-78B 51
Udine, Italy 117
Umberto of Savoia (King of Italy) 74
Unirea Sperantza refinery (Ploesti, Romania) 182, 187
United Air Lines 20, 199
U.S. Military Academy (West Point) 18, 34, 38, 51, 52
U.S. Naval Academy 28
U.S. Navy 55
U.S.O. 44, 61, 163
USS *A. P. Hill* 52

USS *Benjamin S. Milam* 73
USS *Henry Baldwin* 73
USS *Wakefield* 197

Var River 169
Venice, Italy 125, 132
Vicenza, Italy 166
Vichy fleet 114
Victoria, KS 190
Vienna, Austria 2, 115, 117, 130, 134, 143, 158
Villagio Mancuso, Italy **190**, **191**
Villetta, Italy 164
Violet, S/Sgt. Harold J. **120**
Vultee BT-13 39

Waco, TX 201
Wagner, Capt. Al 156, 174, 175
Wake Forest, NC 199
Wake Forest College 198, 199
Wake Island 201
Walker Army Air Field, KS 190
Waller Field, Trinadad 68
Ward's Fine Cakes 33
Warner, Capt. Gerald W. 169
"washed out" 38
Washington, DC 204
Watkins, S/Sgt. Eugene L. 179
Wearth, Marion 18, 19
Wearth Airport 18
Wendover, UT 44
West, Jack 41
West Monroe, LA 188
West Palm Beach, FL 66, 73
West Point Preparatory School (WPPS) 34
White Sands Missile Range 58
Whiteville, NC 1, 3
Wiener-Neustadt, Austria 133, 134, 135, 153, 163, 168, 171
Wilhelm, Tom 22
Williamsburg Township, NC 10, 13
Willow Run, MI 44, 57, 58, 66
Wilmington, NC 61
Wilson, Irene 29
window (chaff—electronic countermeasure) 100, 177
Wojcik, S/Sgt. Chester 179
Wollersdorf Airdrome 168, 171
Woodward, Charles Clark 27
Woodward, Norman L. 3, 27, 48, 55, 58, **62**, 63, **65**, 67, 111, **123**, 143, 144, 145, 148, 149, 165, 179, 182, **194**, 202
Wright-Patterson Air Force Base, OH 198

XB-24 55

YMCA (Roxbury, MA) 26
York, SC 37
Ypsilanti, MI 44
Yugoslavia 77, 116, 130, 134, 140, 142, 167, 180, 181

www.ingramcontent.com/pod-product-compliance
Ingram Content Group UK Ltd.
Pitfield, Milton Keynes, MK11 3LW, UK
UKHW050533150426
5217IPUK00026B/1923